Functionalism Historicized

Functionalism Historicized

ESSAYS ON BRITISH SOCIAL ANTHROPOLOGY

Edited by

George W. Stocking, Jr.

HISTORY OF ANTHROPOLOGY
Volume 2

THE UNIVERSITY OF WISCONSIN PRESS

Published 1984

The University of Wisconsin Press
114 North Murray Street
Madison, Wisconsin 53715

The University of Wisconsin Press, Ltd.
1 Gower Street
London WC1E 6HA, England

First printing

Printed in the United States of America

For LC CIP information see the colophon

ISBN 0-299-09900-8

Contents

CONTENTS

MISCELLANEOUS STUDIES

Functionalism Historicized

FUNCTIONALISM HISTORICIZED

To what extent one may appropriately speak of differing "national traditions" in such a problematically "scientific" discipline as anthropology is a moot matter. Although the often-argued cultural variability of systems of belief and knowledge pulls in a quite opposite direction, the discipline's name bespeaks a unity of scientific discourse, and its historiographers characteristically write as if this were the case. But if the logic of logos discourages the addition of nationalizing adjectives, one suspects that the chapter headings and the index entries of works in German and in English on the history of anthropology would suggest quite substantial differences in national perspective (cf. Mühlmann 1968; Harris 1968), and several symposia on "national traditions in anthropology" have indicated a considerable heterogeneity of historical development (Diamond, ed. 1980; Gerholm & Hannerz, eds. 1982). True, the editor of one of them spoke of a single "international anthropology" as a "diffused technic" now being exported "in various permutations and combinations" to academic centers all over the world (Diamond, ed. 1980:11); but if that comment perhaps suggests something about historically emergent relationships of knowledge and power, it does not do justice to the historical diversity of the discipline.

Indeed, the unity of anthropology as a discipline is itself historically problematic. Our most widely held models of the structure of knowledge and the emergence of disciplines are those of a tree or a segmentary lineage: disciplines emerge by branching or fission. From this perspective, one might perhaps think of anthropology not as one branch of the human sciences but as the end growth of the trunk itself. And indeed it may enrich our understanding to think of anthropology circa 1900 in such terms—as the residuary disciplinary legatee of an holistic approach to man, invoked in a discourse of the discarded. With the development of specialized disciplines devoted primarily to the study of the various manifestations of "civilized" human nature —the psychology of rational consciousness, the economy of money, the social organization of European societies, the politics of the state, the history of written sources—anthropology was left to study analogous and often oppositionally conceived manifestations of human nature in the life of dark-skinned "savages." Certainly, some practitioners thought of the discipline in terms that might be so construed—although in this context the unity of anthropology could still be seen as historically contingent and likely to fragment (cf. Boas 1904).

On the other hand, it may be that the model of discipline fission does not adequately represent the historical emergence of anthropology. Perhaps anthropology may better be thought of in terms of a model of fusion: the coming together of a number of historically and conceptually distinguishable modes of scientific and other scholarly inquiry—comparative anatomy, comparative psychology, comparative philology, archeology, folklore, among others —in relation to a specific subject matter, which historically has been for the most part that encompassed by the nineteenth-century image of the "dark-skinned savage." If the history of this fusion is obscured by the umbrella-usage adopted around 1870 in the Anglo-American traditions, it was then still evident in the full titles of German anthropological societies, which were devoted to *anthropologie, ethnologie, und urgeschichte,* and in the still current usage of "anthropology" on the European continent to refer to the physical study of man. In France, where "ethnology" and "anthropology" have had quite distinct histories, the establishment of an inclusive national "anthropological" society is in fact an event of the last several years (Condominas et al., eds. 1979). Variable nationally, this fusion has been imperfect even in the Anglo-American context, where the departmental cohabitation of social and biological anthropologists has often been tension-ridden, and in at least one instance has ended in divorce—and where the formal national organizational unity of the discipline has recently become somewhat problematic, as some component subdisciplinary groups contemplate nonparticipation in a restructured American Anthropological Association (A.A.A. 1983).

Another way of looking at the matter is to suggest that the general tradition we call retrospectively "anthropological" embodies a number of antinomies logically inherent or historically embedded in the Western intellectual tradition: an ontological opposition between materialism and idealism, an epistemological opposition between empiricism and apriorism, a substantive opposition between the biological and the cultural, a methodological opposition between the nomothetic and the idiographic, an attitudinal opposition between the racialist and the egalitarian, an evaluational opposition between the progressivist and the primitivist—among others. Although such oppositions do not form mutually exclusive antithetical groupings, it is possible to view the study of human unity-in-diversity historically in terms of their varying manifestations in differing traditional orientations (or perduring paradigms) —the historical/ethnological, the developmental/evolutionary, the polygenetic/ physical anthropological, the functional/synchronic, and perhaps others—as well as within different subdisciplines, in different national traditions, and in different historical periods—as we hope will be by implication manifest in the Miscellaneous Study included in the present volume (cf. Stocking 1981).

Yet another factor contributing to the diversity of national anthropological traditions has been their differing histories of national and colonial development, and their consequently differing confrontations with the Other. "Otherness" is surely a multidimensional phenomenon, which may be envisioned in terms of the crossing of various sorts of boundaries, including those of language, body type, class, and time (as well as others such as gender). National anthropological traditions differ as to whether their primary experience of otherness has been "internal" or "external"—whether the anthropologically significant "other" is a class (e.g., the peasantry) within the territory of the national society, or a geographically and culturally marginal ethnic group (e.g., the "Celtic fringe" of Great Britain), or an historically significant ancestral population (e.g., the Saxon), or an expropriated racial group within an internal empire (e.g., the American Indian), or the distant populations to whom the "White Man's Burden" of imperial exploitation was carried overseas. In these terms we may contrast anthropologies of nation-building and empire-building, and within the former we may distinguish between those continental European traditions where strong traditions of *Volkskunde* focussed on the internal peasant others who composed the nation, or the potential nations within an imperial state, and those postcolonial nation-building anthropologies of the Third World, whose relation to internal otherness in some cases approximates that of an internal colonialism.

And finally, we may perhaps distinguish between metropolitan and peripheral anthropologies, or between anthropologies along some scale of knowledge/power: the hegemonic anthropologies of the United States, Great Britain, France, and perhaps the Soviet Union; the postimperial anthropology of the German tradition; the secondary metropolitan anthropologies of Scandinavia and central Europe; the "white settler" anthropologies of Canada and Brazil; and the various "postcolonial" anthropologies struggling to define their own peculiar national identities or to adapt the "diffused technic" of "international anthropology" to the problems of national development (cf. Stocking 1982).

The major European anthropological traditions—the British, the French, and the German—doubtless exemplify the respective national manifestations of the "scientific spirit" described many years ago by J. T. Merz in his magisterial history of science in the nineteenth century (1904:I). And while they can scarcely be disposed in these terms, one can see them also in relation to the characteristic national preoccupations Michel Foucault noted in his discussion of the emergence of the human sciences: life, language, and labor (1970: 250). France was the home of comparative anatomy, and this was reflected in the predominance of physical anthropology until the early decades of the twentieth century. Germany was the home of comparative philology, and, while the German tradition in anthropology was heavily influenced also by physical anthropology, it is there that we look for the roots of linguistic anthropology. So also, Britain was the home of political economy, and, while we can scarcely characterize the British anthropological tradition as a direct offshoot, it can easily be regarded as the antiscience of political economy, insofar as it attempted to bring the apparently irrational behavior of uncivilized man within the framework of utilitarian explanation.

There were in fact significant Germanic influences on the British anthropological tradition in the nineteenth century, especially during the early "ethnological" period dominated by James Cowles Prichard (Stocking 1973), as well as in the thought of such figures as Henry Maine and William Robertson Smith (see Jones in this volume). Nevertheless, the contrast between the British and the German traditions is quite striking, as the relative neglect of linguistic anthropology in the modern British tradition attests (Henson 1974). From this perspective one notes also the irreducible residue of intellectual miscommunication when Friedrich Max Müller, the Kantian ambassador of comparative philology to the British empiricists, tried to accommodate an ultimately idealistic and apriorist position to Tylorian and Darwinian evolutionism (Schrempp 1983; cf. Leopold 1980). On the whole, the contrast between the British and the Germanic traditions remains quite striking.

In seeking the roots of British anthropology, it has been customary, both for retrospectively minded practitioners (Radcliffe-Brown 1958; Evans-Pritchard 1964) and disciplinary historians (Burrow 1966) to look to the eighteenth-century Scottish "conjectural historians," who—much influenced by Montesquieu—were quite sociological in outlook, and made some use of available ethnographic information to discuss the manifestations of natural human capacity in the behavior of "rude" or "savage" man (Bryson 1945). But in the light of the deeper philosophically rooted contrast between British and German anthropology, it seems appropriate to return to the thought of John Locke, the philosopher most quintessentially identified with the British intellectual tradition in so many of its aspects—epistemological, psychological, political, economic, etc. Although the ethnographic documentation for his suggestion that "in the beginning, all the world was America" consisted of little more than a reference to Acosta's *Natural and Moral History of the Indies*, Locke's thought conditioned later British anthropology in a variety of ways that have only begun to be explored (see Zengotita in this volume). If other currents of intellectual influence and historical experience flowed into the later British functional tradition, Locke seems an appropriate place to begin placing that tradition in historical context.

To jump from Locke to two second-generation evolutionary writers, skipping over eighteenth-century Scottish developmentalists, pre-Darwinian ethnologists, and the great figures of classical evolutionary anthropology—as well as all that surrounded them and lay between—is to leave untouched vast areas of the British anthropological tradition. Even limiting our focus to the functionalist tradition, there is much more to be said than can be encompassed in a volume of this size. We have dealt only incidentally with its colonial context (cf. Asad, ed. 1973; Loizos 1977), and much more could be said to place it in the context of other currents within British anthropology (cf. Trigger 1980). In undertaking to give a posteriori thematic unity to a varied group of contributions, we have emphasized certain aspects of the immediate intellectual and cultural context in which the modern British social anthropological tradition emerged—the fundamental intellectual tensions in two immediately precursory evolutionary writers (Jones); the ideological context of traditional British "folk models" of the polity (Kuklick); the ethnographic manifestation of the general anthropological orientation from which social anthropology sought to distinguish itself (Urry); the most important single foreign intellectual influence (Stocking, ed.); the immediate contexts of intellectual opposition in which the dehistoricization and refinement of functionalist anthropology took place (Stocking); and the persistence of historical interests within the functionalist tradition (Kuper).

As early as 1950, historical interests were in fact strongly reasserted by one of the leading figures in the "structural-functionalist" school, when Evans-Pritchard argued in his Marett Lecture that social anthropology was one of the humanities rather than a "natural science of society." Echoing from the very precincts in which Radcliffe-Brownian social anthropology had first established itself, his insistence that "social anthropology, for all its present disregard of history," was "itself a kind of historiography" (Evans-Pritchard 1962: 145, 148; cf. 1970), reminds us how historically problematic the notion of "dehistoricization" must be. Certainly many of those who today are calling it into question look back to Evans-Pritchard for historical validation (Lewis 1984).

It may yet be premature to suggest that anthropology is finally reaching the moment, foreseen by the historian F. W. Maitland back at the turn of the century, when it "will have the choice between being history and being nothing" (Bock 1956:18). Facing today the same sort of demographic and institutional problems that confront other hegemonic anthropologies in their postclassical, postcolonial period (cf. Rivière n.d.), British anthropology seems now in a state of considerable intellectual indeterminacy. What will emerge lies beyond the reach of this volume. But perhaps *Functionalism Historicized*—in the context of any other recent historical contributions—may contribute to the outcome.

Acknowledgments

Aside from the editor, the editorial board, the contributors, and the staff of the University of Wisconsin Press, several other individuals and organizations facilitated the preparation of this volume. The Wenner-Gren Foundation for Anthropological Research, Inc., provided a grant to underwrite editorial expenses. The staffs of the University of Chicago Department of Anthropology (especially Kathryn Barnes), the Morris Fishbein Center for the Study of the History of Science and Medicine (Elizabeth Bitoy), and the Social Science Division Duplicating Service provided necessary support. David Koester served as editorial assistant, and Bernard Cohn, John Comaroff, Raymond Fogelson, Samuel Sandler, and Howard Stein offered editorial advice. Our thanks to them all.

References Cited

A.A.A. (American Anthropological Association). 1983. *Anthropology Newsletter* 24(6/8).

Asad, T., ed., 1973. *Anthropology and the colonial encounter*. London.

Boas, F. 1904. The history of anthropology. In *The shaping of American anthropology, 1883–1911: A Franz Boas reader*, ed. G. W. Stocking, Jr., 23–36. New York (1974).

Bock, K. 1956. *The acceptance of histories: Toward a perspective for social science*. Berkeley.

Bryson, G. 1945. *Man and society: The Scottish inquiry of the eighteenth century*. Princeton.

Burrow, J. 1966. *Evolution and society: A study in Victorian social theory*. Cambridge.

Condominas, G., et al., eds. 1979. *L'Anthropologie en France: Situation actuelle et avenir*. Paris.

Diamond, S., ed. 1980. *Anthropology: Ancestors and heirs*. The Hague.

Evans-Pritchard, E. E. 1964. *Social anthropology and other essays*. New York.

———. 1970. Social anthropology at Oxford. *Man* 5:704.

Foucault, M. 1970. *The order of things: An archaeology of the human sciences*. New York.

Gerholm, T., & U. Hannerz, eds. 1982. The shaping of national anthropologies. *Ethnos* 47 (I/II).

Harris, M. 1968. *The rise of anthropological theory: A history of theories of culture*. New York.

Henson, H. 1974. *British social anthropologists and language*. London.

Kuklick, H. 1978. The sins of the fathers: British anthropology and African colonial administration. *Res. Soc. Knowl. Sci. Art*. 1:93–119.

Leopold, J. 1980. *Culture in comparative and evolutionary perspective: E. B. Tylor and the making of* Primitive Culture. Berlin.

Lewis, I. M. 1984. The future of the past in British social anthropology. *Vienna J. Anth*. (In press.)

Loizos, P. 1977. Personal evidence: Comments on an acrimonious argument. *Anth. Forum* 4:1–8.

Merz, J. T. 1904. *A history of European thought in the nineteenth century*. 4 vols. London.

Mühlmann, W. 1968. *Geschichte der Anthropologie.* 2d ed. Frankfurt.

Radcliffe-Brown, A. R. 1958. *Method in social anthropology.* Chicago.

Rivière, P. n.d. Changing shapes and directions: The decade ahead. Unpublished manuscript.

Schrempp, G. 1983. The re-education of Friedrich Max Müller: Intellectual appropriation and epistemological antinomy in mid-Victorian evolutionary thought. *Man* 18:90–110.

Stocking, G. W., Jr. 1973. From chronology to ethnology: James Cowles Prichard and British anthropology, 1800–1850. In Prichard, *Researches into the physical history of man.* Chicago.

————. 1981. Apes, grandfathers, and Rubicons: Some thoughts on an enduring tension in anthropology. Symposium on "Anthropological implications of evolutionary theory," Chapel Hill, March 2.

————. 1982. Afterword: A view from the center. *Ethnos* 47 (I/II):172–86.

Trigger, B. 1980. *Gordon Childe: Revolutions in archaeology.* New York.

THE FUNCTIONAL
REDUCTION OF KINSHIP
IN THE SOCIAL THOUGHT
OF JOHN LOCKE

THOMAS DE ZENGOTITA

Thirty years ago, Meyer Fortes distinguished two traditions in sociocultural anthropology: a "sociological" one he associated with Maine, Morgan, Mc-Lennan, and their structural-functionalist descendants; a "cultural" one he associated with Tylor, Frazer, and the Boasian School. Quite properly, he claimed kinship studies for the sociological tradition (Fortes 1953:11–14; Fortes 1969). That claim has since been challenged from a revivified cultural point of view, as mounting ethnographic evidence from Oceania, the Middle East, and New Guinea has threatened virtually every substantive claim in functionalist theories of kinship (Firth 1957; Murphy & Kasdan 1959; Barth 1954; Khuri 1970; Leach 1961, and 1971; Sahlins 1965; Barnes 1962). The ablest theoretical minds in the cultural camp—some of them converts to it—have found in this evidence and the ensuing critique of functionalist theories of kinship a larger implication: the whole idea of a natural science of society, upon which functionalism ultimately depends, has been opened to doubt (Needham 1971; Sahlins 1976).

So comprehensive a critical task demands an answer to this question: if functionalism is in some sense a mistake, then how did it come to dominate the social sciences? How, in particular, could functionalist theories of kinship have been accepted by generations of anthropologists? The most obvious an-

---

Thomas de Zengotita is Adjunct Assistant Professor in the School of Continuing Education at New York University. His previous publications include "Après Jonestown" (in *Le Genre Humain*), and he is currently completing a study of kinship ideas in the social thought of the French Enlightenment.

swer is in terms of the venerable phenomenon of projection. Proposed sources for functionalist projections range from a straightforward selectivity imposed on data by theory (Keesing 1972) through a transfer of models based on one ethnographic area onto others (Leach 1961; Barnes 1962) to the subtler problem of anthropologists' native cultural models (Schneider 1972:50). Sahlins has suggested a deeper, essentially historical explanation, in which the "modern mind" itself is held responsible (Sahlins 1976). If this is true nothing less than a full-scale culture history of anthropology's formation can bring our projections to consciousness and free us from their insensible sovereignty.

Although few anthropologists venture beyond the discipline's boundaries or into its predisciplinary past, most of those who have are agreed that anthropology "is a child of the Enlightenment and bears throughout its history and today many of the characteristic features of its ancestry" (Evans-Pritchard 1951:21; cf. Harris 1968:9). This agreement would come as no surprise to intellectual historians, for the consensus among them is that "rich and weighty as were the legacies bequeathed to us by old Greece and Rome, by the Middle Ages and the Renaissance, the fact remains that it is the eighteenth century of which we are lineal descendants" (Hazard 1954:xvii). It follows that if we replace subject matter we now call anthropological in its Enlightenment context we may uncover the foundations of its situation in modern thought. Kinship, because of its privileged position in social life, provides an especially pointed instrument for such an effort.

John Locke and the Moral Sciences

Science, its associated technologies, and the attitudes and values essential to them are the distinguishing features of the eighteenth century's Enlightenment. Bernard le Bouvier de Fontenelle, in his *Discourse on the Ancients and the Moderns* (1688), made the Enlightenment's break with the Renaissance official as it was occurring when he declared that, in the sciences and the useful arts, the moderns had surpassed the ancients, thus transcending the classic model that had previously served as modernity's ideal and limit. General acceptance of this judgment produced a completed concept of progress in which the modern mind found its characteristic value (Manuel 1962; 98–116; Bury 1932).

From the very beginning, natural science and its technologies obsessed thinkers in what were once called the "moral sciences." The example of medicine especially inspired the nascent social and psychological sciences and their applications (Gay 1969:12–20). In a study of science as a cultural idea, Jacques Barzun shows why the mere fact that "the appliance works" became "the great argument that has redirected the western mind" (1964:19). This "argument" was so persuasive precisely because it was not an argument, but rather the central social experience of the rising middle class of Europe in early modern times. Natural science and its applications are not merely historians' criteria; they were the axis for a transformation of our *Weltanshauung*—and the inference followed: since the bodies of nature, our own precious bodies too, were the better governed as they were understood scientifically and manipulated accordingly, why not our psychosocial bodies as well? The moral sciences were explicitly conceived from this point of view, and whatever "characteristic features of its ancestry" social anthropology retains today derive from it. The crisis in functional social anthropology *is* a crisis for the idea of a natural science of society.

Classical natural science reached an apogee in Newton, and in the Newtonian cosmology the Enlightened form of modern consciousness is distilled. After Newton "nature became a clock from which one argued back to the clockmaker" (Cobban 1929:27). On the basis of this archetypal image, in which the relation of the technologist to his device was represented on the screen of Creation itself, the "new philosophers" took as their essential task the discovery of natural law. Like other cosmologies, Newton's offered its constituency a divine ideal of itself. The "Great Artificer" had an industrious human analogue who aspired—in all reverence, at the outset—to look upon the Maker's world from the Maker's point of view. On this basis, Europe's "productive classes" might induce the laws of nature's design and eventually make (or let) nature, even human nature, serve human designs.

If the moral sciences of the Enlightenment had a Newton to inspire them, he was John Locke (Berlin 1956). Locke's thought was a cardinal moment in the history of the idea of a natural science of society, the moment in which the subjective position symbolized by Newton's cosmology was successfully assumed in relation to human nature. Acknowledgments of Locke in the softer social sciences—to say nothing of social history itself—tend understandably to vagueness compared to acknowledgments of Newton in the precise sciences. But contemporary disciplines that bear upon our nature and history routinely admit the pervasive impact of a Lockean tradition, and histories of such disciplines can pick out specific threads of influence (Abraham 1973; Kantor 1969; Letwin 1965). Similarly, in anthropology, we will see that Frazer's typology of homeopathic and contagious magic is an application of Locke's laws of association; that the axiomatic nineteenth-century equation of savages and children can be traced to Locke's selection of pragmatic rationality as the defining characteristic of the mature human being; that the progressive role assigned to modalities of property in Morgan, Maine, and Lubbock derives from Locke's contrast of commons and waste, with the value of individual labor justifying the right of appropriation; and that the paradigmatic opposition in the nineteenth century between backward societies based on status and progressive societies based on contract, while it was immediately due to Maine, derived ultimately, and much more deeply, from Locke.

More generally, with the whole liberal tradition in modern thought in mind, we will interpret these particular threads as part of a fabric of influence in which Locke's tabula rasa psychology provided the perfect object for modern technologies of government and education, even as it gave natural science its empiricist epistemology; in which Locke's social and political ideas gave orienting expression, in widely acceptable and efficacious form, to modernity's prerogative of "merit"; in which reason claimed the right to govern according to nature rather than custom, to construct society according to its understanding of how human nature worked just as it constructed technological devices according to how the rest of nature worked. Locke, that is, articulated the modern alternative to the traditional order for the age that first realized it; and a proper understanding of the impact of the Lockean tradition on anthropology begins with the replacement of anthropological material in the moment of transformation crystallized in Locke's social philosophy.

Fortes attributed the sociological tradition's dominance of kinship studies to the "comparative jurisprudence" practiced by disciplinary founders like Maine and Morgan. In this essay sociological functionalism will be traced back to Locke's epochal *Second Treatise of Government* (1690a), where the "comparative jurisprudence" at issue was no scholarly exercise but a great political conflict of paradigms of legitimacy in the West. In that work Locke attacked what progressives saw as a traditional confusion between paternity and monarchy, between the family and the nation; modern social ideology took shape through an effort to separate kinship and politics in a demystifying reduction of both to their proper functions on rational and empirical grounds. Contemporary functionalist theory in anthropology, a tiny and proximate current in the great river of thought and value that flowed through Locke, has come to its particular crisis at the point of general departure. The reality of kinship in primitive social thought has been the unintended victim of modernity's original attack on the medieval social thought that primitive social thought resembles in fundamental ways.

Tribal *gemeinschaft* would one day be inaccessible to the style of mind that arose in opposition to feudal *gemeinschaft*, for both these forms of "natural will" take the values and meanings of social things to be as inherent in them as colors and textures in material things. When the young John Locke, inspired by the "new philosophy" of Cartesian natural science, turned to medicine, the most prestigious and socially suggestive science of them all, he freed himself to look at our bodies "objectively," evacuated of inherent meaning by mechanistic dualism. When, in his maturity, Locke became political advisor to the Whig leader Lord Shaftesbury, he was engaged to cast a physician's eye upon the body politic with intent to cure. Like a doctor, he developed an image of his object functioning as it was made to. Like a doctor, he compared that image with the facts of the case, with an analysis of impaired functioning under the Stuart kings. Like a doctor, he prescribed a remedy in the *Second Treatise*, a corrective intervention, which history seemed actually to apply successfully.

The Glorious (because peaceful) Revolution brought the House of Hanover to England's throne and for a century served the Western world as a model of rational social progress (Martin 1953). Locke's *Second Treatise of Government* was a blueprint for *gesellschaft* that, because of Britain's spectacular progress under the constitutional monarchy, appeared as the basis for an extension of the "argument of the device" to the social world. *Gesellschaft's* "rational will," which devises means to practical ends, triumphed over "natural will" in our history long before it became a concept of our sociology (Tönnies 1887). Long before contemporary anthropology looked upon primitive societies as if they were functional devices and nineteenth-century anthropology looked upon them as dysfunctional devices, modern society was itself conceived as a functioning device and governed accordingly.

A Division of Ages, a Collision of Symbols

The *First Treatise of Government* was written so that "The False Principles and Foundation of Sir Robert Filmer," taken from the Book of Genesis and presented in *Patriarcha: or the Natural Power of Kings* (1680), might be "Detected and Overthrown." The *Second Treatise* would show "The True Original, Extent, and End of Civil Government," and propose, on that basis, a replacement for overthrown tradition (Locke 1690a).[1] Although now forgotten, *Patriarcha* was a worthy opponent in its day. By the time of the Glorious Revolution, it had "very nearly become the official state ideology" of the displaced House of Stuart (Schochet 1975:193). Filmer had argued for the divine right of kings by appealing to the "lordship which Adam by creation had over the whole world," which "by right descending from him the Patriarchs did enjoy," and which, after the flood, descended through "the three sons of Noah" who "had the whole world divided amongst them" as both family heads and princes (Filmer 1680:58–59).

Filmer's account of political legitimacy cannot be taken as a detailed representation of "medieval political thought." Indeed, as the doctrine of a Reformed nation and an absolute monarchy, it stood consciously opposed to much of that thought. Nevertheless, the fact that "the careful and self-conscious work-

---

1. Title page. *Second Treatise*. Further references to Locke's *Two Treatises* are to paragraphs as numbered in the Laslett edition.

ing out and enunciation of this [patriarchal] view signalled the beginnings of its demise rather than its validity" (Schochet 1975:57) suggests how we may appropriately take Filmer to represent the premodern West in all sorts of different particular contexts—Protestant, Catholic, Monarchical, Aristocratic, and Republican: he was a last representative of the *gemeinschaft* type in modern history. "The core of [Filmer's] persuasiveness lay in that ineffable incoherence in which God's power was paternal and the King's power religious, in which the family was a kingdom and a kingdom a family and all duties were one" (Dunn 1969:75–76). That sort of "incoherence" has been a staple anthropological concept at least since Durkheim distinguished mechanical and organic solidarity. When Schochet says the real task of the *Second Treatise* was to "complete the destruction of the symbol" of the patriarchal family, he suggests by implication the point of access most suited to anthropologists willing to consider Locke's social thought as a moment in their culture history. Schochet concludes that Locke replaced the symbol of the family with a familiar array of modern ideas and values like individualism, utility, conventionalism (1975:267–76). But this essay will argue that Locke evoked an image that embraced modern ideas and values as inclusively and half consciously in its context as the family had in its own; traditional kinship as the social archetype meets more than new ideas and values in the *Second Treatise*; it meets the very image of the "rational will" in the archetype of the device. Modern functionalism begins with that encounter.

Power and Reason in the *Second Treatise*

Assuming that Filmer's biblical foundation had been destroyed by the *First Treatise*, Locke promised "another original of Political Power, and another way of designing and knowing the Persons that have it" through a rational examination of its basis in nature (II, 1). Proposing what was in effect the sociological distinction between status and role, Locke moved to clear up the "ineffable incoherence" in Filmer's patriarchy:

> the power of a Magistrate over a Subject, may be distinguished from that of a Father over his Children, a Master over his Servant, a Husband over his Wife, and a Lord over his Slave. All which distinct Powers happening sometimes in the same Man, if he be considered under these different Relations, it may help us to distinguish those Powers one from another . . .
>
> (II, 2)

What did Locke mean by these "Powers" he wished to distinguish under natural law? The polemical *Second Treatise* does not say; there, with political persuasion in mind, Locke appealed to an immediate intuitive grasp of basic concepts. But Locke's great philosophical work, the *Essay Concerning Human*

Understanding (1690b), which was written during the same period, gave an exhaustive treatment of the general notion of "Power." There power was defined as either passive or active, as "able to make or able to receive any change" (1690b:159, 309). The understanding (perception) is the passive power of man and, while it is involved in activity and is of vital epistemological importance, it is subordinate, in matters of action, to the will. The will is man's power to make changes, and it is determined by a goal evaluated in terms of pleasure or pain—the only innate principle allowed in the *Essay* (1690b:313–29). Locke singled out the will's capacity to forbear, to "suspend" action, as the source of the misnomer "free will." Moral choice thus became a calculation of contingencies—albeit a calculation that, in Locke, still included eternal pleasure and pains. Willed action was automatically determined by the outcome of these "considerations."

This was the focal point of transformation in Locke's moral philosophy; here modern reason and natural law emerged from the medieval chrysalis. Sanctions of pleasure and pain made law, and reason's considerations of these sanctions determined the forbearing will. There was no positive problem of evil, but only the failure of reason properly to inform the will, because passion could delude it into overestimating immediate pleasures. The Fall was reconceived as the original failure of this sort, a fall from that "state of perfect obedience" that was the immediate integration of natural reason and natural law in Eden. Original sin was a miscalculation, and the misery of human history reflected the release of passion from the government of a reason that rightly sees the sanctions of natural law, that knows the way through the hierarchy of earthly goods to the greatest good, which is divine pleasure. Man's will was alienated from God's will through reason's failure, and Man's duty is to reason his way back (1690b:353–59). When the *Treatise* appeals to reason in so-called "nativist" terms—as the "voice of God within us"—it does not contradict the *Essay*; reason in an unfallen state would apprehend natural law immediately. But in a fallen state reason has the more difficult job of inducing God's laws indirectly from evidence of his design in the world.

The collapse of the medieval consensus, the great wars of religion, appeared to the early moderns like another Fall. In Locke, we find natural reason obliged to abstract itself from the fullness of an immediate apprehension of natural law, obliged to abandon Eden-like fusions, which only multiplied with conflicting sects, and to look down upon humanity from a position apart, from ever more narrowly defined and abstract "considerations" upon possible good and evil consequences of human action in an increasingly intricate world. Locke's behaviorist theory of value was modern reason's abstract response to the collapse of tradition, and modern natural law was its form. Historical forces encouraged the detachment that the scientific and technological style of subjectivity invited.

So "Power" in the *Second Treatise* should be understood in terms of the

Essay, despite Locke's reliance on "self-evident" medieval formulations. Power is will, the capacity to make changes. The particular powers Locke distinguished are all relations of authority; they involve some human wills "changing" other human wills by means of formative sanctions. Locke's purpose was to reason rightly about these powers, to inform human wills how to determine each other in ways conforming to the will of the Maker. That is why Locke proceeded by showing us God's creations as God designed them to function; in the "state of nature." In this way, the way of a new "right reason," he aimed to return us all to a state as near to that of "perfect obedience" as is humanly contrivable in a sinful world. We shall see how far Locke travelled into the future in search of the past.

Human Artifact, Earthly Steward

"To understand Political Power right and derive it from its original, we must consider what State all Men are naturally in" (II, 4). Locke organized his state of nature so that Filmer's patriarchal and authoritarian arguments would be untenable. His strategy was to show that kinship's functions were as distinct as possible from those of civil government. To begin with, political power, "the Right of making Laws with Penalties of Death, and consequently all less Penalties," was not to be authorized in any institutional form by natural law (II, 3). That premise, assumed from Locke's point of view, was the essence of social contract theory in modern political thought; as far as politics is concerned, the state of nature was a "State of Perfect Freedom" (II, 4). But, though there was no man-made artifact of government, no human system of sanctions for determining individual wills, Locke's state of nature was "not a State of License," not a Hobbesian anarchy; "it has a Law of Nature to govern it, which obliges everyone: and Reason which is that Law . . . teaches all Mankind who will but consult" what God's laws are. In the state of nature God's laws, not man's, determine the forms of human authority, and these forms are familial, not political. Locke laid his foundation in this way: "For Men being all the Workmanship of one Omnipotent, and infinitely wise Maker; all the Servants of one Sovereign Master, sent into the World by his order and about his business, they are his Property, whose Workmanship they are" (II, 6).

Upon this seminal image of man as a device of God's making in the state of nature the whole structure of the *Second Treatise* and Locke's account of kinship depend (Schochet 1969:84). Upon it, too, depends the history of the idea of a natural science of society in the Lockean tradition; for the gradual replacement of God's designs with nature's adaptations did not deflect the quest for functions or for human control of them. The right of self-preservation, which was the atheist Hobbes' only natural law, became, under Locke's image of the human artifact, the overriding natural duty; for man did not ultimately own himself, and suicide was robbery of God; likewise, a man could not sell himself into slavery (II, 23). Health and even property were natural rights prior to man-made government, and derived from the duty to preserve God's property in human lives (II, 25). The absence of political subordination, the central democratic claim of "the equality of Men by Nature" that the *Treatise* was written to establish, was based on the artifactual image. God made men "furnished with like Faculties, sharing all in one Community of Nature" and therefore "equal in His eyes" (II, 5, 6).

An obligation to preserve others was derived from the greaty duty to the Maker as well—except when it was necessary to "do Justice to an Offender" (II, 6). This exception is only an apparent one, because offenders against natural law were no longer really human. They became like "one of those wild Savage Beasts," for they have "quit the Principles of Human Nature" by "having renounced Reason," and nothing made their irrational inhumanity clearer than their willingness to risk the associated sanctions (II, 7–13).

The *Treatise*'s first statement of the new reason's importance was also the strongest. The capacity for self-government through detached calculation of long-term self-interest had gained the name of reason and, with it, the power to define human being. Through all the changes in future accounts of its genesis and development, that much did not change. Philosophers of eighteenth-century France and Benthamites of nineteenth-century Britain might claim that reason could be shaped in a generation, given only the political will. Conjectural historians in eighteenth-century Scotland and nineteenth-century evolutionists might conceive of reason as the hard-won fruit of epochs of struggle. But all would see—for such was the manifest power of the new reason to transform the world—that here was the difference between us and the less than, or not yet, human.

Notice that Locke placed political power, the "Power of the Magistrate," in each man's hands as God's "executioner of the Law of Nature" against less than human criminals in the state of nature. This was his intended point; political power must be given over to the state in a social contract; it proved "convenient" to do so, because all fallen men were ill-equipped to judge and police the natural law in cases involving their own interests. Civil government was made by men who were alienated from their artifactual destiny, but not so alienated that they would not seek an artificial substitute for it in a disinterested human governor (II, 13). This quintessentially rational act stands out in the *Treatise* like a promise of redemption. Man is not too far fallen to attempt self-government through an institutionalized detachment of the new reason, and the special prerogatives and duties of those who led the way are implied by the new reason's criterial status. The absent Maker of the Newtonian Cosmos was appointing, in his human analogues, a diligent steward to cultivate his property in human lives.

Later anthropological critics of social contract theory correctly condemned Locke's account as ahistorical (if we read him as claiming contractual origins for the first human societies). But the conscious "constitution" of society was an outstanding fact of *modern* history, and Locke's appeal to "original" contracts must be seen as its ideological expression. Locke's influence on nineteenth-century evolutionists who criticized his history can only be appreciated when we notice that they never questioned the superiority of contractual societies any more than they questioned the superiority of the other, technological, devices of the new reason. Henry Maine concluded his most famous passage with a statement expressing the social judgment of his age: "the movement of progressive societies has hitherto been a movement from status to contract" (1861:100). Maine used the word "status" to refer to precisely the kind of kinship-based society Filmer defended and Locke attacked; he even excused himself from detailed description of patriarchal societies in the primitive world by referring his readers to their dispute (1861:72). But Locke, effecting the structure of progress Maine would describe, based his account of the family, not on history, but on the same artifactual image of man he had used to establish the claims of democracy. Finding positive injunctions for God-made natural institutions rather than the space for man-made political ones, he sketched a design for family life adapted to contractual society. The Newtonian Maker's designs, here as elsewhere, set the functional standard.

Mere Begetting

Filmer had attacked earlier contractualist positions for implying that the state of nature entailed equal rights for children. The artifactual image enabled Locke to grant parents authority over their children in the state of nature without contradicting the principle of equality. "Parents have a sort of Rule and Jurisdiction over them when they come into the World and for some time after," Locke allowed; because, although born free and rational, children could not yet exercise these capacities—"age that brings one brings the other too." Thus Locke could maintain that "Natural Freedom and Subjection to Parents may consist together and both are founded on the same principle"— on the same grounds that "Lunatics and Idiots are never set free from the Government of their Parents" (II, 55, 60, 61).

In other writings, Locke also excluded the laboring poor and the indigent from civic participation, because they obviously lacked the reason to govern even their own lives, let alone the society's (MacPherson 1962:222–38). In the nineteenth century property still testified to a governing rationality marking

the fully developed civic person—as is clear in debates on universal male suffrage, women's rights, poor laws, and slavery; progressives were distinguished
from reactionaries primarily by a faith in the malleability of human nature
and the power of education. This whole framework was reflexively applied
to savages in the imperial context, and debates over colonial policy were conducted in precisely the same terms as debates over undeveloped domestic dependents. Nineteenth-century evolutionism took this framework for granted,
not as theory but as social historical experience, and "connecting and arrang-
ing in their order the stages of human advancement" (McLennan 1865:5) was
simply the obvious thing to do. The savage, the vulgar, and the child, rationally undeveloped and incomplete, were literally *perceived* in this framework;
controversy among evolutionists concerned only the stages of development
and their order (cf. Tylor 1881:407–8).

Even before the child reached the age of reason and became really human,
Locke saw parental authority as strictly limited by obligations to the Maker.
Even paternal authority, let alone monarchical, was not naturally absolute.
Filmer was thus twice "o'erthrown." For parental authority was an "Obligation
to preserve, nourish and educate the Children, they had begotten, not as their
own Workmanship, but the Workmanship of their own Maker, the Almighty,
to Whom they were but accountable for them." Children were held in trust
by parents as if by a steward (II, 56, 58). Thus did John Locke break with
traditional thought about kinship. Long before the priority of Pater over
Genitor was given "scientific" expression in British social anthropology, Locke
established it in his watershed polemic against the "natural power" of beget-
tors. To be sure, he intended parents to function as stewards for God; but
just as Locke himself had removed political society from the purview of God's
positive laws, the day would come when God, to whom Locke granted a manu-
facturer's dominion over domestic society, would lose that sovereignty as well.
Domestic society would be left, conceived as Locke described it, under functional natural laws; the relation of parent and child could never again be an
inward, mystical union of spiritual substance embodied in tangible permea-
tions and emanations of sex and birth, a relation derided by Locke as "the
bare act of begetting." It could only be conceived rationally, as "Care, Nourishment and Education," the conduct of the relation—the parental function (cf.
Schochet 1969:86).

So God was not the only subjectivity Locke was detaching from the world.
The severance of that begetting link testifies to a breakdown of the tangible
connections between people's minds, an absence of reciprocally embodied
selves. Educated moderns are accustomed to thinking of this as "individualism," as a liberation of human potential from the fetters of tradition, superstiti-
tion, and accidents of birth. For "men of merit" replaced "men of blood" only
when blood became incidental to social position. Modern individualism nec-

essarily devalued kinship, and, as a by-product of that necessity, modern individuals who happened to become anthropologists failed to appreciate the reality of kin-based societies. Even Henry Maine, of all evolutionary social thinkers the most influenced by German historicism and therefore the most sympathetic to kin-based communities, could conceive of them only as morally retarded (1861:179–83).

The Pageant of Error

To confound the claim of a specifically patrilineal line of inheritance from Adam to James II, Locke substituted "parental authority" wherever Filmer spoke of paternal authority. Sometimes the "Words and Names that have obtained in the World" led men into mistakes. This particular misnomer had made "Absolute Dominion and Regal Authority when under the Title of Paternal Power" seem appropriate; but it would "have ill supported the Monarchy" if by the very name it appeared that fundamental authority "was not placed in one, but two Persons Jointly" (II, 52, 53).

Although Locke's interest in the "Gross Mistakes" into which abused words had led men was limited, these remarks provide a striking insight into his view of history in general; there are important parallels with his account of the abuse of words. For Locke, history was a pageant of error, an arena dominated by passion and habit, by fallen man's abuse of reason, with all its miseries punishments for God's violated laws. At the same time, Locke recognized that history had some sort of secondary "nature" of its own, that passion and habit worked in regular ways, like diseases. The state of nature stood beside and behind history as the basis for evaluation and corrective action, a sketch of God's design, capable of guiding a rational reformation—a cure of history (II, 4, 89). The later concept of "natural history," which contained the basis of anthropological evolutionism, was thus prepared.

First in a context of pure deism, later in the context of God's death, a transformation of the ingredients in Locke's thought took place. The design connotations of Locke's state of nature would be promoted to the governing end of history—as man-made political utopia or naturally determined state of cosmic maturity, or both. Simultaneously, the historical process lost the theme of punishment for original sin while retaining that of irrational error, inefficiency, and injustice. Reason's corrective role remained, but with only its own nature and history to guide it.

So, for example, Benthamite radicals, resisting the despair that the age of revolution brought to so many of the Enlightenment's heirs, sought to reform the "abused words" of public life at a stroke in their massive codification of human psychology into law. Later, evolutionists like Tylor simply sketched the gradual and natural development of language from primitive grunts and signs toward the representational perfection of the phonetic alphabet and English syntax (Tylor 1881:131–81). Natural history was still a tale of gross mistakes, and rationality still represented its redemption. The bilateral nuclear family was to the matrilineal gens in moral life what the phonetic alphabet was to a whine in communication (Lubbock 1870:50, 113)—the superior device of an earthly steward who had become the sole proprietor of himself, his various dependents, and the world. The same enlightened condescension for primitive thought and institutions survived in twentieth-century anthropology in an insistence on seeing their real significance, not in terms of their own being, but in the latent functions it is the special province of anthropological reason to disclose. The underlying unity is one of subjective posture; behind the varying content of specific judgments, a detached subject observes; if he intervenes, it is not to participate but to teach, to manage, or to govern. Twentieth-century functionalism repudiated the stages of evolutionism but not the social devices that it classified.

A Woman's Place: Natural Design or Natural History?

Although Locke argued that whatever obligation "the right of generation lays on children it must certainly bind them equally to both concurrent causes of it," he took a somewhat ambiguous position on woman's God-given rights. His views on the natural relation between men and women were contained in his discussion of "conjugal society," not parenthood; and there the husband's authority over the wife was clear. But it was also sharply limited, and its "naturalness" appears to have more to do with secondary natural habits of history than with natural law proper. Like all "societies" that precede civil government, conjugal society was governed directly by God's design, which in this case was very simple: "the continuation of the species." Otherwise it was subject to the terms of individual contract or the "Customs or Laws of the Country." And marriage was contract, "made by a voluntary compact between Man and Woman" (II, 78, 82).

So far Locke's account was consistent with his artifactual use of natural law concepts, and there was no basis for the husband's authority. But no matter what the contract's terms, husband and wife would have "different understandings" and "different wills," and since it is "necessary that the last Determination, i.e. the Rule, should be placed somewhere, it naturally falls to the Man's Share as the abler and the stronger" (II, 82). Locke limited this authority to "common interest and property," leaving the wife "in full and free Possession of what by Contract is her peculiar Right." Having assumed women to be capable of contract, to possess—unlike children, idiots, beggars, lunatics, and criminals—the capacity for natural reason, Locke extended considerable natural liberty as well. Only the end of procreation made it "necessary" to place "the last Determination" in someone's hands.

But the "naturalness," in the natural law sense, of the husband's right to it is not clear. That this use of "naturally" contrasts with Locke's overall natural law usage is especially evident in his treatment of "Eve's Subjugation" in the *First Treatise*. Locke's reading of the Bible had woman's subjugation deriving from God's curse upon Eve as a "Helper in the Temptation." But it was an "accidental" and limited subjugation. God's words:

> [I]mport no more but that Subjugation that [women] should ordinarily be in to their Husbands. But there is here *no* Law to oblige a Woman to such subjugation, if the Circumstances either of her Condition or Contract with her Husband should exempt her from it, than there is, that she should bring forth her Children in Sorrow and Pain, if there could be found a Remedy for it, which is also part of the same Curse upon her . . .
>
> (I, 47)

God, said Locke, did not oblige women to submit to this curse, but merely foretold "what should be the Woman's Lot, how, by his providence, he would order it so that she should be subject to her Husband as we see generally the Laws of Mankind and the Customs of Nations have ordered it so" (I, 47). The medical possibility of "Remedy" is revealing. What God caused providentially did not carry the same force as his natural designs. Man's dominion falls "naturally" to him as "abler and stronger," the way a woman's labor pains fall "naturally" to her. Either might be changed, because neither is necessary to their true nature as rational, free, and nonpolitical beings, as originally designed. How, after all, could this particular "foundation in nature" possibly be traced to artifactual natural law when it governed the "state of perfect obedience" and Eve's subjugation was a consequence of the Fall? Locke's embryonic "natural history" had to be Providence-governed simply to preserve the idea of the divine Proprietor's omnipotence. But earthly stewards were already entitled, perhaps even authorized, to improve their "natural historical" lot so long as they did not violate the laws of their design. As the divine Proprietor faded from the picture, the Steward's prerogatives and duties would expand.

So Locke's subsumption of marriage under contract in the state of nature would be reconceived by evolutionists as the culminating moment in the development of legal codification. The Lockean conception of marriage was taken by evolutionists as a moment in moral development as well (Maine 1861: chap. ix). For codification was both an instrument and an expression of an increased refinement of the earthly steward's emotional and moral sensibilities under the regime of the new reason. When Lubbock, the most widely read and popularly influential of the evolutionists, declared that "the great advantages of civilization" could not be "more conclusively proved than by the improvement which it has effected in the relation between the sexes" (1870: 50), he echoed the judgment of evolutionists and developmentalists generally. The fully secularized natural history began with the "last determination" falling to the man as "abler and stronger" in the crudest sense—McLennan's caveman clubbing his intended and dragging her off. But it progressed to the marital contract and the "civilization" of male dominance, through the cultivation of manners and sentiment—through "self-government" in the broadest sense of the word.

Accidental Monarchs

The pregnant relation in Locke's thought between what "happens naturally" in history and what the laws of nature specify becomes even clearer when he ignored God's providential role. Locke gave a brief account of how hereditary and absolute patriarchal monarchies could have developed without a natural warrant. As with "abused words," here, too, reason's failure made possible the development by which "the natural Father of Families, by insensible change, became the Politick Monarchs of them too" (II, 76). "It is obvious to conceive how easy it was in the First Ages of the World, and in places still, where the thinness of People gave Families leave to separate into unpossessed Quarters . . . for the Father of the Family to become Prince of it." After all, "he had been a Ruler from the beginning of the Infancy of his Children and since without some Government it would be hard for them to live together," it only remained, to consolidate matters, for the father to have "chanced to live long, and leave able, and worthy Heirs, for several Successions" (II, 74–76).

Locke proposed two specific avenues for this development. Both involved the misapprehension of natural law by fallen reason in a way that tended "naturally" toward patriarchal monarchy. Here, as elsewhere, God's human artifacts were subject to a kind of repeating malfunction along certain plausible lines once they made an original miscalculation. The first avenue involved a child's natural obligation to honor parents even after reaching a majority, even though obedience was no longer required: "The want of distinguishing these two Powers; viz. that which the Father hath in the right of Tuition, during Minority, and the right of Honor all his Life, may have perhaps caused a great part of the Mistakes in this Matter" (II, 66, 67). Locke corrected this error of history by appeal to evidence of design in Nature. Whether or not they were also princes, fathers had the same powers over their children and owed the same honor to their parents. This showed how "perfectly distinct and separate," with "different foundations" and "different ends" the two kinds of power were. In insisting on this functional distinction, Locke showed a characteristic indifference to the inward, qualitative resemblances between kinds of social relations; he did not recognize a phenomenological kind, "authority," that persists in its various forms. Anticipating his successors, he saw only confusion in analogic thought, which was the source of the pernicious, unenlightened practices he was opposing.

Later evolutionists would look down upon analogic thought from the summit of the new reason's spectacular achievements as upon a long-vanquished foe, with a certain sympathy and, under Romanticism's influence, even nostalgia. But Frazer spoke for his age when, after a thirty-year study of how Locke's laws of thought (the associational principles of similarity and contiguity) ramified through the ancient and primitive worlds, he found in their gradual progress from unconscious, undirected to conscious, governed use a lesson "of hope and encouragement, to be drawn from the record of human error and folly" (1890:711). By then the horizons of natural history had expanded to include all of reality; its features had multiplied a thousandfold; and man stood alone in the landscape. But Locke's effort to redeem the pageant of error through functional understanding and utilitarian intervention was still underway, and anthropology was there to keep the record of the progress from magic to religion to science.

The Earthly Steward and the Fruit of his Labor

The second avenue for the naturally unwarranted (but historically "natural") development of monarchy out of paternity brings us to the most famous of all Locke's arguments: his effort to show that private property is a natural right. A principle of ownership perfectly suited to his immediate purpose and profoundly resonant with the historical moment was already sanctified in God's proprietary relation to the creature He had made in His image. From the claim that natural law gives each man ownership of his labor and its fruits, it followed that a man has the power to dispose of his possessions as he sees fit; there was no natural law governing inheritance, and children have no natural connection with a father's property. In history, however, given "the Power Men generally have to bestow their Estates on those who please them best," it "passes in the world for a part of the Paternal Jurisdiction" and the child's expectation (II, 72). Again, Locke devalued a crucial embodiment of kinship in the service of his political argument. In a way that parallels his opposition to begetting as the basis of parenthood, Locke here opposed individual labor— productive conduct, economic function—to that permeative, corporate dominion of kin group over things and places that subsists in virtue of manifold and traditional communion. Like the practical, economic reason it served, labor "puts distinctions" in the world and made it governable; labor thus drew the line against a collapse by insensible degrees into substantial participation. Again, middle-class modernity was served by an expulsion of subjectivity from the tangible world in favor of functional relations with it. Members of Locke's party worked, while lines of kings blended with the commonwealth and claimed it all. But labor put more than distinctions in the world; it gave value to things as it shaped them. God made the world for his analogous creature, for the "use of the Rational and Industrious" (II, 34), and therefore "the intrinsick Value of things depends only on their usefulness to the Life of Man," which is next to nothing prior to the exercise of man's labor (II, 37). Locke went on for pages on the benefits of "Industry," of the value labor brings to the "almost worthless materials" that "Nature and Earth furnished." He composed the melody for the hymn to a socioeconomic system the classical economists later orchestrated and performed so lavishly:

> . . . [F]or all that Bread, of that Acre of Wheat, is more worth than the Product of an Acre of good Land, which lies waste, is all the Effect of Labour. For 'tis not barely the Plough-man's Pains, the Reaper's and Thresher's Toil, and the Baker's Sweat, is to be counted into the Bread we eat; the Labour of those who broke the Oxen, who digged and wrought the Iron and Stones, who felled and framed the Timber imployed about the Plough. Mill, Oven, or any other Utensils, which are such a vast Number, requisite to this Corn, from its being seed to be sown to its being made Bread, must all be charged to the account of Labour; and received as an effect of that: Nature and Earth furnished only the almost worthless materials, as in themselves.
>
> (II, 43)

C. B. MacPherson (1962) offered an influential interpretation of Locke's enduring impact on modernity in terms of a "possessive individualism" that made men "proprietors of labor" in a "progressive market society." But he focussed on contemporary political and economic issues, missing the complex relation between the Maker and the Steward and other forms of selfpossession only implicit in Locke's thought. Our focus on anthropology and kinship permits us to see the framework that contains his argument.

A complete understanding of Locke's impact on modern man's view of man (which anthropology can claim to be) turns on the profound relation between his view of human labor and property and his view of the Maker and His human property. The full significance of this relation remains obscure until it is viewed in the light of the tabula rasa psychology; Locke would not see the implications, but history would realize them. The empiricist psychology held that the human mind is an empty cabinet as it comes from the hand of the Maker and is only "furnished" by experience. Without a providential supervision of that experience, human natures prior to cultivation—children, savages, and the vulgar—are left as "almost worthless materials, as in themselves" like other natural things. It only remained for the Steward to complete, in the great labor of improving civilization, a general appropriation of humanity, a usurpation of the Maker's position. The "Wastes" of America stood to the cultivated fields of England as American savages stood to cultivated English gentlemen. The prerogatives and duties of the "self-made" men—who embodied in their "polished" persons, and in other devices, the value that "rude" persons and devices so manifestly lacked—were simply obvious.

Conclusion

The history of the image of man in the eighteenth and nineteenth centuries can be given as the story of the several ways in which the substitution of proprietorship prefigured in this essay took place. John Locke best represents the initiating moment; but a culture history of social anthropology that would systematically expose the sources of functionalism's projections waits upon a completed reconstruction. Even on the basis of an initial step, however, it may be shown why an extended effort to reconstruct anthropology is essential to the anthropological reconstruction of other social worlds. Let us recall kinship as it has been conceived by two leading members of the cultural camp who oppose, in their own ways, Fortes' sociological functionalism.

In his contribution to *Kinship Studies in the Morgan Centennial Year* (1972), David Schneider asked "What is Kinship All About?" and concluded that it "is a non-subject, since it does not exist in any culture known to man." The operative word was "culture," for the point of the paper had been to "systematically and rigorously distinguish culture from the social system," to isolate the "symbolic devices [that] define the units and their relationship" in native culture itself, and so to study culture "uncontaminated" by the social system as the latter is defined by the "classic" sociological query: "How Does This Society Organize to Accomplish Certain Tasks?" (Schneider 1972: 58–60).

I choose these scattered formulations from among many similar ones, because they convey us most directly to what Schneider thinks he is doing: "I, too, am a functionalist" he declares, with a "functionalist explanation to offer." It is, he says, just a matter of a "different functional question" appropriate to the "system of symbols" and to the part of that system in the "total sociocultural system." Schneider is, he reminds us, still "following Parsons" and his "cultural system" (which "can be easily abstracted" from the "normative system" as it was "abstracted" from "concrete, observable patterns of behavior"), is still the cell in Parsons' famous four-function paradigm that performs the task of pattern maintenance in the general theory of action (Schneider 1972: 37–40). Parsons' general theory has rightly been called "the most perfect expression of functionalism" in our social thought (Rocher 1975:42, 155), and its capacity to maintain its imperial grip on its colonies in the realm of meaning testifies to that perfection.

But when we encounter the empirical work on American kinship for which Schneider is so justly admired by students of culture, the suspicion arises that all his multiplying "analytic levels" and "planes" with their variously "articulated units" of meaning are not so much the framework for a theory of culture as they are an improvised scaffold that has allowed Schneider to escape the functionalism he claims to serve. In application Schneider's theoretical categories amount to little more than spaces on the table where the historian of contemporary culture has arranged the more and less general objects and qualities of human experience which are the stuff of his interpretation. At this point, Schneider, the participant observer, the evoker, the intuiter, and, yes, the moral philosopher, takes over and proposes those nuanced generalities in which we recognize ourselves. And the view given here of the place of kinship in Locke's thought both reenforces and is reenforced by Schneider's account of contemporary American kinship. What else is his "order of law" rationally governing his "order of nature" but a legacy—described as a system—from Locke's proprietorial steward (Schneider 1968)?

Writing as chairman of a conference of British anthropologists who were *Rethinking Kinship and Marriage* (1971), Rodney Needham summarized his view of its results in the same absolute terms Schneider would use: "there is no such thing as kinship," and "it follows that there can be no such thing as kinship theory." "Constant professional attention extending over roughly a century" has been distorted by "some initial defect in the way we approach the phenomena." Social anthropology suffers a sort of mental illness due to what Wittgenstein called a "craving for generality" and to a "lingering delusion of a natural science of society." Needham prescribed a "conceptual therapy" requiring "unrelenting moral application" and "austere self-criticism" that would lead to a "completely new start" free of all "a priori assumptions." Social anthropology, now understood as the "disciplined interpretation of forms of human experience," could then "rely more directly on indigenous categories," and so "take each case as it comes" (Needham 1971:2–5, xvii–xx). To all of this the culture historian can say, "Amen."

But Needham's conception of the task at hand seems purely philosophical, as if a mere analysis of our professional language can discipline the biases out of our interpretations—though they extend back undetected for at least a century. But the cultural frame that gives meaning to the language game Needham uses to talk about kinship is not accessible to a mere analysis of sense and reference; it is the frame bequeathed us by our culture history.

To Needham it seems transparently appropriate to take as the barest "minimal premise" that "kinship has to do with the allocation of rights" to things like "group membership . . . office . . . residence . . . type of occupation and a great deal else." He is going to show that genealogy is not related in necessary ways to these "jural systems and their component statuses." But we are in a position now to see how impossible it was for Needham to avoid bias simply by a discipline of terminology without also the discipline of culture history (Needham 1971:3–4). Are concepts like "jural system" and "component status"—to say nothing of "office" and "type of occupation"—so obviously more open to a case-by-case interpretation than "sibling," "spouse," or "mother"? In fact, has not Needham inherited these categories from the very descendants of Fortes' "comparative jurisprudence" he most wishes to oppose? Even more fundamentally, has not he—like all of us—assumed the position that we necessarily assume as modern individuals, the position that suggests, and was suggested by, the very peculiar idea of studying "how human societies *work*" in the first place? Jural concepts come into being with consciously constituted society, and they are an important aspect of the initial defect in our approach to societies that were not *made* to work, but simply *do*.

References Cited

Abraham, J. H. 1973. *The origins and growth of sociology.* Harmondsworth.

Barnes, J. A. 1962. *Three styles in the study of kinship.* Berkeley.

Barth, F. 1954. Father's brother's daughter marriage in Kurdistan. *Southwest. J. Anth.* 10:164–71.

Barzun, J. 1964. *Science: The glorious entertainment.* New York.

Berlin, I. 1956. *The age of enlightenment.* Boston.

Bury, R. J. 1932. *The idea of progress.* New York.

Cassirer, E. 1961. *The philosophy of the enlightenment.* Princeton.

Cobban, A. 1929. *Edmund Burke and the revolt against the eighteenth century.* London.

Coulborn, R., ed. 1956. *Feudalism in history.* Princeton.

Douglas, M. 1970. *Natural symbols.* New York.

Dunn, J. 1969. *The political thought of John Locke.* Cambridge.

Evans-Pritchard, E. E. 1951. *Social anthropology.* London.

Filmer, R. 1680. *Patriarcha: Or the natural power of kings.* In *Patriarcha and other political works,* ed. P. Laslett. Oxford (1949).

Firth, R. 1957. A note on descent groups in Polynesia. *Man* 57:4–8.

Fortes, M. 1953. *Social anthropology at Cambridge since 1900.* Cambridge.

———. 1969. *Kinship and the social order.* Chicago.

Frazer, J. 1890. *The golden bough.* New York (1922).

Gay, P. 1969. *The science of freedom.* New York.

Harris, M. 1968. *The rise of anthropological theory.* New York.

Hazard, P. 1954. *European thought in the eighteenth century.* New Haven.

Kantor, J. R. 1969. *The scientific evolution of psychology.* Chicago.

Keesing, R. 1972. Simple models of complexity: The lure of kinship. In *Kinship studies in the Morgan centennial year,* ed. P. Reining, 17–31. Washington.

Khuri, F. I. 1970. Parallel cousin marriage reconsidered. *Man* 5:597–616.

Leach, E. R. 1961. *Pul Eliya: A village in Ceylon: A study of land tenure and kinship.* Cambridge.

———. 1971. *Rethinking anthropology.* London.

Letwin, W. 1965. *The origins of scientific economics.* New York.

Locke, J. 1690a. *Two treatises of government,* ed. P. Laslett. Cambridge (1967).

———1690b. *An essay concerning human understanding,* ed. A. C. Fraser. New York (1959).

Lovejoy, A. 1957. *The great chain of being.* Cambridge, Mass.

Lubbock, J. 1870. *The origin of civilization and the primitive condition of man,* ed. P. Rivière. Chicago (1978).

MacIver, R. 1969. *Politics and society,* ed. D. Spitz, New York.

McLennan, J. F. 1865. *Primitive marriage,* ed. P. W. Rivière. Chicago (1970).

MacPherson, C. B. 1962. *The political theory of possessive individualism.* Oxford.

Maine, H. 1861. *Ancient law.* London (1917).

Mandrou, R. 1979. *From humanism to science.* New York.

Manuel, F. 1962. *The prophets of Paris.* Cambridge, Mass.

Martin, K. 1954. *The rise of French liberal thought.* New York.

Murphy R. F., & L. Kasdan. 1959. The structure of parallel cousin marriage. *Am. Anth.* 61:17–29.

Needham, R. 1971. *Rethinking kinship and marriage.* London.

Rocher, G. 1975. *Talcott Parsons and American sociology.* New York.

Russell, B. 1945. *A history of Western philosophy.* Chicago.

Sahlins, M. 1965. On the ideology and composition of descent groups. *Man* 65:104–7.

———. 1976. *Culture and practical reason.* Chicago.

Schneider, D. 1968. *American kinship: A cultural account.* Englewood.

———. 1972. What is kinship all about? In *Kinship studies in the Morgan centennial year,* ed. P. Reining, 32–63. Washington.

Schochet, G. 1969. The family and the origins of the state in Locke's political philosophy. In *John Locke: Problems and perspectives,* ed. J. Yolton, 81–98. Cambridge.

———. 1975. *Patriarchalism in political thought.* New York.

Tönnies, F. 1887. *Gemeinschaft und Gesellschaft.* Leipzig.

Trevelyan, G. M. 1938. *The English revolution 1688–1689.* London.

Tylor, E. B. 1881. *Anthropology: An introduction to the study of man and civilization.* New York (1913).

Young, R. 1970. *Mind, brain and adaptation in the ninetetenth century.* Oxford.

ROBERTSON SMITH AND JAMES FRAZER ON RELIGION

Two Traditions in British Social Anthropology

ROBERT ALUN JONES

The impressive, even spectacular contributions of eighteenth-century Scotland to the study of human nature and social institutions are well-known (Bryson 1945). Less well-studied are the contributions of the late-Victorian Scots who literally revolutionized the scientific study of religion, a field their predecessors (with the noteworthy exception of Hume) were wont to avoid out of deference to the Westminister Confession. Indeed, in the discussion of totemism and primitive religion that extended from 1870 to the First World War, few names loom so large as John Ferguson McLennan, Andrew Lang, William Robertson Smith, and James Frazer. The relationship between Smith and Frazer is of particular interest: first, because their intellectual association extended over a ten-year period during which each produced the first edition of an eventual "classic" in the scientific study of religion—Smith's *Lectures on the Religion of the Semites* (1889) and Frazer's *The Golden Bough* (1890); second, because despite the common ground this association assumed, there were important differences between them that were reflected in the larger history of British social anthropology.

The events that led to Smith's and Frazer's simultaneous presence at Cambridge were somewhat fortuitous. While a Master of Arts candidate and budding classicist at Glasgow University, Frazer had planned to go to Balliol College, Oxford; but as a Free Church Presbyterian, his father was suspicious of Oxford's High Church tendencies. In December 1873, Frazer therefore

---

Robert Alun Jones is Associate Professor of Sociology and Religious Studies at the University of Illinois. His previous publications include "On Understanding a Sociological Classic" and "The New History of Sociology." He is presently writing a book on the intellectual context of Durkheim's *Elementary Forms of the Religious Life*.

Fellowship photograph of James G. Frazer, 1879 (courtesy of the Master and Fellows of Trinity College Cambridge).

competed for and won an Entrance Scholarship to Trinity College, Cambridge, where he continued to study classics and, after winning a fellowship in 1879 for a thesis on *The Growth of Plato's Ideal Theory* (1930), stayed on for life (Downie 1970).

Robertson Smith's arrival in Cambridge was a later, somewhat more dramatic consequence of Free Church orthodoxy. As the leading Scottish expert on the "Higher Criticism" of the Old Testament, Smith in 1875 contributed the articles "Angel" and "Bible" to the second volume of the ninth edition of the *Encyclopedia Britannica*. Although neither expressed views different from those Smith had presented for five years in scholarly journals and lectures, their appearance in a volume intended for more popular consumption led to the charge that he had undermined the authority of scripture. After the last successful heresy trial in Great Britain, Smith was formally removed from his chair of Hebrew and Old Testament Exegesis at Aberdeen University on May 26, 1881. Through the influence of friends, Smith then became co-editor of the *Britannica*, writing more than two hundred essays for the remaining volumes. Two years later, through the influence of William Aldis Wright, a fellow Scot and Adams Professor of Arabic at Cambridge, whom he had come to know on the Committee for the Revision of the Authorized Version of the Bible, Smith was appointed Lord Almoner's Reader in Arabic at Cambridge; and by Christmas of 1883, Smith had joined Frazer at Trinity College (Black & Chrystal 1912).

In view of the comparison that follows, it is important to recognize that Frazer's shift from classical antiquity to anthropology was not the consequence of Smith's influence alone. On the contrary, Frazer's interest had first been aroused by E. B. Tylor's *Primitive Culture* (1871), to which his attention had been drawn by a Cambridge friend, the philosopher and psychologist James Ward, and which he later said had "marked an epoch in his life" (1885:103). But as Frazer himself remarked in the preface to *The Golden Bough*, "it is a long step from a lively interest in a subject to a systematic study of it; and that I took this step is due to the influence of my friend W. Robertson Smith" (1890:x).

The friendship began only weeks after Smith's arrival in Cambridge, when Frazer, contrary to his custom, went to the Combination Room, and Smith engaged him in conversation about the Arabs in Spain. Though Frazer knew little about the matter, he nonetheless attempted an argument. He was "immediately beaten down, in the kindest and gentlest way." Never afterward did he dispute the mastership Smith "thenceforth exercised . . . by his extraordinary union of genius and learning." Soon establishing the habit of afternoon walks together, by September 1884 they were on holiday in the Highlands with Smith's eventual biographer, James Sutherland Black (Black & Chrystal 1912:476). Back at Cambridge, Frazer heard Smith deliver the three lectures later enlarged to form *Kinship and Marriage in Early Arabia* (1885), a work in whose second and posthumous edition (1903) Frazer had an active hand (Black & Chrystal 1912:481, 484). That same year, Smith asked Frazer to write some shorter classical articles for the *Britannica*—"Penates," "Praefect," "Priapus," "Proserpine," etc.—and, when the results proved satisfactory, he gave Frazer the more difficult charge of "Pericles" (1885). Frazer later recalled that, when he had trouble finding a satisfactory opening, Smith "actually came to my rooms and began to write the article with his own

Portrait of William Robertson Smith, 1888 (courtesy of the Master and Fellows of Christ's College).

hand at my dictation or from my notes to oblige me to make a start with it" (1897).

Similar collaborative efforts followed, despite Smith's move from Trinity to Christ's College in January 1885. Frazer later recalled that perhaps the "keenest moments of intellectual enjoyment" in his life were when Smith, "burning with some new idea," came over from Christ's: "a sort of electrical discharge of thought seemed to take place between us, while we turned up one passage after another in book after book, each new passage suggesting something fresh, till at last he went away, leaving my study table buried under a pile of books . . . and my head throbbing with the new ideas he had sent through it" (1897).

In this spirit of active editorial supervision, Smith turned Frazer from classical to anthropological topics for the twenty-third volume of the *Britannica* (1888); the results were "Taboo" and "Totemism," which in turn became foundations of both *The Religion of the Semites* and *The Golden Bough*. These, too, were to some degree collaborative efforts. Smith acknowledged his obligation, not only for access to Frazer's unpublished collections on "the superstitions and religious observances of primitive nations in all parts of the globe," but more generally to his "intimate familiarity with primitive habits of thought" (1894:ix). The first edition of *The Golden Bough* was in turn dedicated to Smith, acknowledging a debt "to the vast stores of his knowledge, the abundance and fertility of his ideas," and to his unwearied kindness in offering "many valuable suggestions which I have usually adopted" (1890:x–xi).

Smith in fact read proofs for Frazer while bedridden with tuberculosis, which had forced him to return to Edinburgh in 1890. There his energies were devoted largely to the second, revised edition of *The Religion of the Semites*, completed just two weeks before his death in 1894. But even in these last years, Frazer reported that Smith "was always keenly interested in hearing what I had to tell him about my own work" (1897).

Thus, for a full decade, the relationship between Smith and Frazer was one of active, productive, and almost constant mutual intellectual stimulation. Nonetheless, several historians have recently suggested that Frazer's views on primitive religion, even in this period, were fundamentally different from those of Smith. As J. W. Burrow has observed, Frazer "wrote anthropology like Tylor, not like Robertson Smith" (1966:241, n2; cf. Ackerman 1975; Turner 1981:115–34; Stocking n.d.). This essay will explore these differences through systematic summary comparisons of various aspects of their writings on the scientific study of religion.

The Aims and Uses of the Comparative Method

Both in their immediate purposes and ulterior motives, *The Religion of the Semites* and *The Golden Bough* were very different works. Distinguishing between the *positive* religion of the Old Testament and the *unconscious* religious tradition that preceded it, for example, Smith justified his focus on the latter by suggesting that the Hebrew religion could establish itself only by appealing to religious susceptibilities already shared by Semitic peoples generally. Biblical criticism thus led Smith directly to comparative religion, but not because he sought to reduce positive religion to its unconscious antecedent. On the contrary, as in *The Prophets of Israel* (1882), his goal was to contrast the ethical and spiritual religion of the Old Testament with its materialistic forebears, and thus to reaffirm the authenticity of divine revelation (1894:1–4). Frazer's declared purpose was the explanation of "one particular and narrowly limited problem"—that rule of the Arician priesthood whereby a candidate "could only succeed to office by slaying the priest, and having slain him . . . held office till he was himself slain" (1890:I, 2; cf. 1900a:I, xvii). But Frazer's real interest, like that of Max Müller and Wilhelm Mannhardt before him, was in the larger question of the primitive religion of the Aryan peoples generally (1890:I, viii). Where Müller had relied on comparative philology, however, Frazer, like Smith, turned to comparative religion; and as the evidence gathered from Greece and Rome, Mannhardt's European peasants, and eventually the Australian

Aboriginals accumulated, Frazer acknowledged that his goal, like Tylor's, was to describe the evolution of human thought itself from savagery to civilization (1908:159–60; Downie 1970:56).

There were also important differences between Smith's and Frazer's use of the comparative method. As Frazer observed (1894:202), Smith had become acquainted with the method through McLennan, whom he had met in October 1869; but before meeting McLennan, Smith had been influenced by the "Higher Criticism" of the Old Testament and the comparative study of Semitic languages, had read Maine's *Ancient Law* (1861) and possibly Fustel de Coulanges' *La Cité antique* (1864). Smith's comparative method was thus more cautious and historical than McLennan's, Tylor's, or Frazer's, generally avoiding comparisons between Semitic and non-Semitic cultures, or between Semitic societies representing different evolutionary stages (cf. 1885:v–vi; 1894: 14–15). When dealing with an utterly primitive stage in social evolution, however, Smith was willing not only to compare the Arab *jinn* or "demon" with the "goblins" of the northern Semites, but also to deny any "inherent" differences between the earliest Semitic and Aryan religions, and to ascribe their subsequent divergence to "the operation of special and local causes" (1894:32). The *general* type of Semitic religion based on totem-kinship was the *original* type from which all other religions, Semitic or Aryan, had emerged. Babylonian, Greek and Roman religions were unfit for comparison with the early Semites, therefore, not because they were non-Semitic, but because they represented subsequent stages of social evolution. They were incompatible with Smith's reasons for adopting the comparative method in the first place, which had less to do with the evolution of human thought than the discovery of the general and permanent features of ancient religion with which the revelations of the later prophets might be effectively compared.

In contrast, Frazer was convinced that such religions had not only similar origins but also similar evolutionary stages for, like Tylor, he believed that the human mind was everywhere the same. Confronted with similar customs in different societies, we might therefore reasonably assume that the motives of those performing them were also similar and use the customs to "mutually illustrate and explain each other" (1894:199; cf. Ackerman 1975:1212). Frazer's commitment to this method and its assumptions is especially clear in his reaction to those "well meaning but injudicious friends of anthropology" who argued that such comparisons should be limited to neighboring races. "Radium," Frazer responded, "is alike on the earth and in the sun; it would be absurd to refuse to compare them on the ground that they are separated by many millions of miles." No other science would impose on itself "the restriction which some of our friends would inflict on anthropology" (1922c:240–41; cf. 1922a:380).

The study of the primitive religion of the Aryans, Frazer thus argued, should begin with the similar beliefs and observances of the European peasantry, rather than the higher literature of classical Greece and Rome. In this sense, Frazer's peasants stood in approximately the same relationship to the primitive Aryans and the subsequent literature of the Greeks and Romans as Smith's Arabs stood in relation to the primitive Semites and the subsequent, higher literature of the Old Testament. But unlike Smith, Frazer drew comparisons between European peasants and peoples in the savage state *generally*, regardless of time, place, or even state of evolutionary development. Frazer thus saw in the classic description of the Australian *intichiuma* ceremonies (Spencer & Gillen 1899) "a close and striking analogy to the spring ceremonies of European peasants," despite the fact that the *intichiuma* was practiced by hunters and gatherers, while the rites of the peasantry were intimately bound up with agriculture; and since the Aboriginal, unlike the peasant, could recall the purpose of his ritual, the Australian data could be used to "illustrate and explain" the European practice (Frazer 1900b:199–200).

The Relative Priority of Myth and Ritual

Smith's argument concerning myth and ritual was based on two distinctions: the first, between religious *beliefs* and religious *rituals*; the second, between *mythological* beliefs and *dogmatical* beliefs. Guided by the preconceptions of Western Christianity, most studies of ancient religion had attempted to find a primitive creed or dogma from which religious practices were presumed to follow. Against this approach, Smith argued that ancient religions "had for the most part no creed," but rather consisted of "a body of fixed traditional practices, to which every member of society conformed as a matter of course" (1894:20). In so far as ancient religions *did* involve beliefs, moreover, these took the form of myths rather than dogmas—stories about the gods adopted voluntarily, rather than obligatory creeds enforced by social sanctions. The "most widespread and most permanent" features of ancient Semitic religion Smith sought could thus be neither dogma nor myth, because dogma was not ancient, and myth was not permanent or obligatory; in contrast, ritual was widespread, permanent, and obligatory. Smith therefore discounted the explanatory value of mythology: since "in almost every case the myth was derived from the ritual, and not the ritual from the myth," study must begin "not with myths, but with ritual and traditional usage" (18).

Smith thus discarded both the "euhemerist" interpretation, whereby myths were explained as accounts of real events and real persons (1894:18), and Tylor's "cognitionist" account of myths as primitive philosophical reflections on the nature and origin of the universe (19). Applying his "ritualist" theory to ancient Semitic sacrifice, Smith insisted that the earliest piacular rituals "were not forms invented . . . to express a definite system of ideas" but rather "natural growths, which were slowly developed through many centuries"; as such, they lacked the ethical and spiritual significance of their Judaic and Christian descendants (399, 439). Smith's ritual theory of myth was based on political analogues; just as political institutions are older than political theories, so religious institutions are older than religious theories; just as we are less interested in individual politicians and governments than in types of government, so we are less interested in individual gods and religions than in the types of "divine governance"—what place "the gods held in the social system of antiquity, and under what general categories their relations to their worshippers fell" (22). Smith's ritual theory also insisted that, because speculation and metaphysics had no place in ancient religions, they should have no place in the study of such religions. To ask about the types of "divine governance" was to raise a question, not about the metaphysical nature of the gods, but about their social office and social function. The study of ancient religion was thus one of institutions rather than ideas, by means of history rather than philosophy.

It was this theory of myth that led to that transformation of classical scholarship wrought by the "Cambridge ritualists" Jane Harrison, F. M. Cornford, and A. B. Cook, as well as the Oxonian Gilbert Murray; to the distinctive mythic elements in the works of Yeats, Eliot, Lawrence, and Joyce; and to the "myth and ritual" school of literary criticism represented by Stanley Edgar Hyman (cf. Turner 1981:77–134; Vickery 1973; Hyman 1974). Almost without exception, however, the source acknowledged by these writers was *The Golden Bough* rather than *The Religion of the Semites*. The irony here, as Ackerman has demonstrated, is that Frazer "emphatically was not at all a ritualist through most of his career, and it is indeed debatable whether, with the exception of a few early years, he might ever have been accurately so identified" (1975:115–16). Hyman has similarly suggested that Frazer "was never content with the theory of ritual origins," found some of its implications "emotionally upsetting," and, in particular, sought a euhemerist theory to replace it (1974: 216–17).

There is some evidence of a ritual theory of myth in Frazer's early essay on burial customs (1885:80), and again in the first edition of *The Golden Bough* (1890:I, 62; II, 245–46). As for the second and third editions, the situation is complicated by their palimpsest character. Frazer changed his mind frequently, but in doing so deleted neither the "theories" he no longer believed nor the "facts" he had gathered to support them. As a result, the third edition can be read as a history of the development of Frazer's mind—a history filled with "fossils" embodying the ritualist, euhemerist, and cognitionist "stages" of his thought (Ackerman 1975:123; cf. Hyman 1974:239; Frazer 1915: VI, 158; IX, 374; XI, 315).

The clearest indication of Frazer's position lies in two letters written to R. R. Marett in 1911 (cf. Ackerman 1975:126–29). In the second edition of

The Golden Bough, Frazer argued that magic and religion were distinct stages in the evolution of thought based upon opposite presuppositions. Magic assumed man's capacity to coerce and constrain natural forces to his own ends, while religion assumed the existence of powers superior to man that required propitiation and conciliation; the latter, which grew out of the repeated failures of the former, thus represented the "birth of humility." In his 1910 inaugural lecture at Oxford, Marett agreed with Frazer that humility was the distinctive characteristic of religion, but rejected the attempt to derive it from failed magic as too "intellectualistic," too inclined to treat emotion "as the offspring of thought instead of as its parent." Among the resources Marett brought to this argument was Smith's ritual theory of myth: social anthropology was "but today beginning to appreciate the psychological implications" of the "cardinal truth" that ritual was "historically prior to dogma" (1914:169, 181).

Frazer's response insisted that Smith had not said that ritual was "historically" prior to dogma, but only that many dogmas are historically posterior to the rituals they profess to explain. Far from assuming the irrationalist position Marett ascribed to him, Smith had always insisted that *some* dogma was prior to myth, and that the object of anthropological investigation was to find the idea on which the ritual was based. Savage ritual, Frazer argued, had "the imprint of reflexion and purpose stamped on it just as plainly as any actions of civilized man." Marett's immediate response cited Smith's distinction between myth and dogma (i.e., "theory or *reasoned* belief"), adding that Smith spoke of ancient religions emerging under the influence of "unconscious forces." He went on to suggest that "every psychologist in Europe" would reject the idea that "reflexion" and "purpose" underlay savage ritual. Though impressed by Marett's citations, Frazer still felt that "every ritual is preceded in the minds of the men who institute it by a definite train of reasoning, even though that train of reasoning may not be definitely formulated in words and promulgated as a dogma"—and he felt that Robertson Smith would have agreed (Ackerman 1975:127–29).

In fact, Smith would have assented to no such thing; and Frazer, in any case, was soon defending positions that would have been anathema to his Cambridge friend. In 1921 Frazer alternately embraced both euhemerist and cognitionist interpretations of myth, with all their rationalist implications, while simultaneously denouncing their ritualist counterpart (1921:xxvii, xxviii, n1); and in 1930 his rationalism extended to the assertion that such myths contained "a substantial element of truth" (v, 201–2).

The Relationship of Magic and Religion

A "natural society," Smith observed, was one to which each member belongs, without choice, simply by birth and upbringing. In the ancient world such societies included gods as well as men. A man was thus born into fixed relations with certain gods just as he was born into fixed relations with certain men, and "religion" was simply that part of his overall conduct determined by the former relationship. A man did not choose his religion or shape its views for himself, for "it came to him as part of the general scheme of social obligations and ordinances"; but neither was there intolerance nor religious persecution, for "religion did not exist for the saving of souls but for the preservation and welfare of society." The earliest communities were either clans based on blood-kinship or, where several clans had joined together in mutual self-interest, a state. In the first, the god was represented as "father," and in the second, as "king," in the literal sense of both terms; thus, as father, the god was literally of the same blood as his worshippers, with whom he engaged in reciprocal familial duties, while as king, the guidance of the state was in his hands, and provision was made for consulting his will in foreign and domestic matters (1894:28–30).

The more traditional approach to the study of ancient religion had suggested that divine "fatherhood" and "kingship" were merely figurative expressions, that the central problem was to know why gods could do things for their worshippers that fathers and kings could not, and that we must thus ask about the nature of the gods and the class of natural phenomena or moral activity over which they presided. Against this approach, Smith argued that the help of the gods was in fact sought in all matters, without distinction, which were "objects of desire and could not certainly be attained by the worshipper's unaided efforts"; moreover, the worshipper sought such help from "whatever god he had a right to appeal to," a question settled, not by the abstract nature of the god, but by the relation in which the god stood to the worshipper. Finally, citing Frazer's discussion of primitive magic, Smith observed that some of the things ancient worshippers asked of their gods were in fact conceived as within the reach of ordinary mortals, and certainly of kings (1894:81–83; cf. Frazer 1890:I, 13 ff., 44 ff.).

But the earliest form of Semitic kinship had not been based on "fatherhood" at all. Invoking the arguments of McLennan's *Primitive Marriage* (1865) and his own *Kinship and Marriage in Early Arabia* (1885), Smith suggested that the mother's blood formed the original bond of kinship, and that, where the deity was conceived as the parent of the clan, she was a goddess rather than a god. This worship of female deities appealed to the "emotional side of Semitic heathenism"; and only when it was replaced by the more austere worship of male gods did the concepts of divine "authority" and of reverence and service due the god enter Semitic religion. In contrast with the absolute legal authority of the Roman father, however, Smith emphasized the limited, non-despotic character of Semitic fatherhood, which was reflected in the relatively benign authority of Semitic gods. Early Semitic kingship was as little absolute as Semitic fatherhood; and thus the god as "king" was not yet the Old Testament agent of unremitting divine justice (1894:52–64).

Quite aside from their relations with the men of Smith's "natural religious community," the gods also had fixed relations with the natural environment. All acts of ancient worship had certain spatial, temporal, and material limitations, chosen neither by gods nor worshippers, but set by immemorial tradition. This utterly primitive conception, Smith argued, resulted from the inability of savages to distinguish between phenomenal and noumenal existence, between organic and inorganic nature, and between animals and plants. Reasoning wholly by analogy, therefore, savages ascribed to all material objects a life similar to their own; and "the more incomprehensible any form of life seems to them, the more wonderful and worthy of reverence do they take it to be" (1894:86).

This argument was more "irrationalist" than Frazer's in at least three respects. First, according to the "animistic hypothesis" of Tylor and Frazer, sacred animals, plants, and other objects were the habitation, rather than the embodiment of the gods; and though Smith was not unattracted to this argument, he felt that the drawing of animistic inferences from dreams and their extension to all parts of nature belonged to a later stage in religious evolution. Smith's notion that the sacred object was the embodiment of the god himself belonged to a much earlier stage "in which there was no more difficulty in ascribing living powers and personality to a stone, tree, or animal than to a being of human or superhuman build" (1894:87). Second, while Frazer interpreted "transformation myths" (i.e., stories of sacred animals changing into one another) as "grotesque anticipations of the modern theory of evolution" (1909b:33–34), Smith refused to regard such myths even as allegories, let alone anticipations of scientific theories, on the ground that they belonged to a totally different mode of thought. Finally, Frazer's argument that religious ritual arose out of fear of such unknown spirits (1885:64–65) provoked Smith to declare publicly that "Mr. Frazer goes too far in supposing that mere fear of ghosts rules in all these observances. Not seldom we find also a desire for continued fellowship with the dead, under such conditions as make the fellowship free from danger" (1894:370, n1; cf. also 54–55, 336 n2).

Smith did not deny Frazer's notion that the savage experienced fear of the unknown, nor did he deny that this fear gave rise to efforts at appeasement; but he did deny that such fears and efforts were in any way "religious"; and this leads us to Smith's distinction between religion and magic. In primitive thought, divinity was extended, rather indiscriminately, to virtually everything, and the "range of the supernatural" was thus too broad for any single religion to deal with all its manifestations. Religion proper thus dealt only with the gods—"a definite circle of supernatural powers whose relations to men were established on a regular friendly basis and maintained by stated rites and fixed institutions" (1894:90). But beyond the circle of the gods was an "undetermined mass" of demons, who were distinguished from the gods only by their lack of such relations, and who could thus be approached only through magic and sorcery. Precisely because religion was a public, social matter, it held no selfish utility for the individual. Those needs and desires for which religion would do nothing were thus pursued by magical ceremonies addressed to demoniac powers; and for the same reason, magic was regarded as illicit by every well-ordered Semitic community (90, 264).

Like Smith, Frazer was fascinated by the ancient belief in "divine kingship," whereby kings were not only priests but gods, able to bestow on subjects and worshippers certain blessings supposed to be beyond the reach of men (1890:I, 8; cf. Smith 1894:83); also like Smith, Frazer placed the origin of this belief in a primitive stage of thought in which ordinary mortals possessed supernatural powers (1890:I, 8–9). But unlike Smith, Frazer based his early religious conception of the "man-god" on the rational cogitations of Tylor's "primitive philosopher," which also gave Frazer the first of his three theories of totemism. Since the analogy between sleep and death implied that even the temporary absence of the soul from the body involved risk, this risk could be reduced or eliminated if the soul were deposited, temporarily or permanently, in the body of an animal thenceforth regarded as divine (II, 296–97). Conjoined with Tylor's notion that the earliest gods were originally the souls of dead relatives, the same animistic principle underlay the religious conception of the "man-god," who "derives his divinity from a deity who has taken up his abode in a tabernacle of flesh" (I, 12).

Even in 1890, however, Frazer's religious conception of the "man-god" had a magical counterpart, "another conception in which we may detect a germ of the modern notion of natural law" (I, 9). This counterpart was "sympathetic magic," whereby a desired effect could be produced simply by imitating that effect or some of its qualities; and since the effect was supposed to follow the imitative rite necessarily and invariably, without intervention of supernatural agency, sympathetic magic was not a religious conception at all, but rather a primitive form of science. Insofar as he employed this means of influencing nature, the "man-god's" supernatural powers were drawn, not from the indwelling of some spirit, but from "a certain physical similarity with nature" (I, 12). By 1899, Frazer had accepted Spencer and Gillen's evidence that among the Aboriginals of Australia "magic is universally practiced, whereas religion, in the sense of a propitiation or conciliation of the higher powers seems to be nearly unknown" (Frazer 1905:162). In the second edition of *The Golden Bough*, therefore, Frazer insisted on "a fundamental distinction and even opposition of principle between magic and religion": "in the evolution of thought, magic, as representing a lower intellectual stratum, has probably everywhere preceded religion" (1900a:I, xvi).

But whether he regarded magic as a lower form of religion or as its independent, evolutionary antecedent, in neither case did Frazer view magic and religion as did Robertson Smith. Indeed, one of the many reasons why Frazer so admired Malinowski's *Argonauts* was his hope that its account of magic in the Kula would dispel "the erroneous view that magic, as opposed to religion, is in its nature essentially maleficent and anti-social, being always used by an individual for the promotion of his own selfish ends and the injury of his enemies, quite regardless of its effect on the common weal" (1922b: 395–96). One can scarcely conceive a more succinct description of Smith's conception of magic, subsequently turned to such powerful effect in Durkheim's *Elementary Forms of the Religious Life* (1912:57–61).

These differences on magic and religion were ultimately based on different preconceptions about the mind of primitive man. Smith emphasized the unconscious and irrational character of primitive peoples; for Frazer, as for Tylor, the human mind was fundamentally the same everywhere, and the differences between savage and civilized thought were those of degree rather than kind. Frazer thus criticized Lucien Lévy-Bruhl's suggestion that primitive thought was "pre-logical" and "mystical" on the grounds that civilized peoples also maintain supernatural conceptions of cosmic forces; that savages do not ignore relations of cause and effect; that savage society contains "skeptics" as well as "mystics"; that civilized peoples frequently ignore and even defy the law of contradiction; and that savages, though less given to abstractions, are quite capable of reasoning and arguing logically (1923:417–18).

Taboo and the Idea of the Holy

Albeit at Smith's behest, "taboo" was the one major anthropological topic to which Frazer made a significant contribution before his Cambridge friend. Having assumed that taboo was a system peculiar to Polynesia, Frazer was convinced by his research for the *Britannica* article that it was a worldwide phenomenon of considerable importance in the evolution of society and morality, a view subsequently reflected in Smith's *Religion of the Semites* (Frazer 1931:v–vi).

According to Frazer, "taboo" originally meant "marked thoroughly" in the sense of "sacred." But Frazer, like Smith, denied that the word had any moral implications; it merely referred to a "connexion with the gods or a separation from ordinary purposes and exclusive appropriation to persons or things considered sacred" (1888:15). Although he distinguished between religious and civil taboos, spontaneous and artificial taboos, and taboos of privilege and disability, Frazer was more interested in the fact that the same rules were observed in every case; like Smith and Durkheim, therefore, Frazer insisted that these distinctions were the result of subsequent evolutionary differentiation from an original "root idea" of taboo, "by reference to which alone their history and mutual relations are intelligible." For Frazer, this idea was the animistic belief that spirits occupied certain persons or objects, which was artificially extended by the avarice and ambition of priests and chiefs into more modern conceptions of private property and the sanctity of marriage. Frazer thus argued that the moral sentiments of civilized peoples, insofar as they are sentiments rather than inductions from experience, derive much of their force from primitive superstition (1888:16–17).

To private property and the sanctity of marriage, Frazer might easily have added, as he later did in *Psyche's Task* (1909c), respect for governmental authority; for the immediate significance of taboo in *The Golden Bough* was that it shed light on the network of prohibitions surrounding the man-god–king. The course of nature was seen as dependent on the life and independent of the will of such kings, and they were therefore surrounded by a network of prohibitions designed to ensure the healthy presence of the life-giving soul. Violation of these prohibitions had disastrous consequences not only for the king, but for the society at large, and was subject to severe punishment. Thus the king came to be viewed, not merely as sacred, but also as a source of danger, as "electrically charged with a powerful spiritual force which may discharge itself with fatal effect on whatever comes into contact with it" (1890:I, 167). At their origin the concepts of holiness and pollution were thus indistinguishable (1890:I, 171; II, 242–43).

The influence of Frazer's essay on *The Religion of the Semites* was well-acknowledged; but the place of taboo in Smith's social evolutionary theory, as well as his explanation of its origin, was quite different. Frazer's focus was on holy persons, as manifested in the concept of divine kingship. For Smith, the holiness of places was the special form of sanctity amenable to independent study; for holy persons, things, times, and even gods all seemed to presuppose the existence of such places at which persons minister, things are set aside, times celebrated, and gods reveal themselves. The idea of holiness is less an attribute of things than one of relations; and since the relations between man and sacred things "are concentrated at particular points of the earth's surface, it is at these points that we must expect to find the clearest indications of what holiness means" (1894:142).

Where Frazer found the origin of taboo in animism, Smith refused to find it altogether: "That the gods are not ubiquitous but subject to limitations of time and space . . . is the universal idea of antiquity and needs no explanation" (1894:114). Each god had his home and each demon his haunt, and both were taboo. The real question was why some spots rather than others became the sites of sanctuaries; Smith's answer was a theophany, which immediately became the occasion for a sacrifice, which in turn established the precedent of regular worship at that location. Smith acknowledged how difficult it is for us to believe in such visible manifestations of a god; but he added that "when all nature is mysterious and full of unknown activities, any natural object or occurrence which appeals strongly to the imagination, or excites sentiments of awe and reverence, is readily taken for a manifestation of divine or demoniac life" (119).

Though Smith agreed with Frazer that both pollution and holiness involved taboos, he argued that rules of uncleanness arose from fear of unknown, hostile demons (magic), while rules of holiness emerged from respect for known, friendly gods (religion). Magic and religion, Smith then argued, have played conflicting roles in social and moral progress. Being founded only on fear, precautions against mysterious, hostile powers have acted "merely as a bar to progress and an impediment to the free use of nature by human energy and industry." Precautions founded on respect for the gods, by contrast, "contain within them germinant principles of social progress and moral order" (1894:154).

In his least antireligious moods, Frazer too could point to the positive role played by "superstition" in social progress; but it was a role based on fear, and one well replaced by reason (1909c). For Smith, religion was "progressive" precisely because it had nothing to do with fear, but enabled man to transcend it, to "convert" the demons of the wilderness, approachable only through magic, into the beneficent gods of the community, whose relations with man were the essence of religion itself.

The Origin and Function of Totemism

That the earliest societies consisted of totemic clans had been suggested by McLennan in 1867 and again in 1869, and Smith became familiar with the argument almost immediately through his association with McLennan in the Edinburgh Evening Club. Later convinced by Julius Wellhausen's *Geschichte Israels* (1878) that the canonical order of the Old Testament books was nearly the reverse of the events of Hebrew history, Smith began to suspect that Semitic polytheism had its origin in totemism. Although the important Arabic texts were unavailable to Smith in Aberdeen, he gave a "provisional statement" of his views in 1880, which, after travels in Arabia, he elaborated in *Kinship and Marriage in Early Arabia* (1885). While he asked Frazer to write the *Britannica* article "Totemism" (1888), Smith himself took "much personal pains with it, guiding Frazer carefully in his treatment"; and when Frazer's materials expanded beyond the constraints set by the *Britannica*, Smith interceded with its publishers to secure the publication of a small volume even before the article itself appeared (Black & Chrystal 1912:494–95).

In it, Frazer attempted to "collect and classify all the main facts, so far as they are at present known," considering questions like the characteristic features of totemism, its generality, and its origin (1887:v). Like Smith, Frazer stressed the mutual beneficence of the relation between a man and his totem: "The totem protects the man, and the man shows his respect for the totem in various ways, by not killing it if it be an animal, and not cutting or gathering it if it be a plant" (1887:2). On the generality of totemism, Frazer was somewhat restrained, describing it as "almost universal" among the Australians and "widely prevalent" among North American Indians, but acknowledging that competent authorities had failed to find it in the northwest United States and among the Alaskan Eskimo. But the evidence for totemism in Egypt was "compelling," and Smith's argument for the early Semites "highly probable." As to its origin, Frazer dismissed previous attempts to explain totemism, including those of Herbert Spencer and Sir John Lubbock, as utterly implausible (1887:9–15).

Smith's discussion of totemism in *The Religion of the Semites* followed directly from his discussion of magic and religion. As opposed to the demon, the local god had fixed relations both to a group of men and a definite sphere of nature; and through his relations with such gods, man was brought "into stated and permanent alliance with certain parts of his material environment which are not subject to his will and control" (1894:124). Smith then cited Frazer's discussion of "mutual beneficence" to show that, in the earliest stage of savage society, precisely the same thing was effected through totemism. In both cases, the primary function of the belief was "the emancipation of a society of men from the dread of certain natural agencies, by the establishment of a physical alliance and affinity between the two parts." Smith had no more explanation for totemism than Frazer had in 1887, nor did he immediately argue that the local gods must have "evolved out of ideas or usages which also find their expression in totemism, and therefore must go back to the most primitive stage of savage society" (1894:125). For Smith totemism was thus the key to the origin of social progress itself.

In *The Golden Bough*, Frazer remained skeptical of the universality of totemism despite evidence from the European peasantry that appeared to confirm Smith's hypothesis of a "totem sacrament"; and when the Durkheimians Henri Hubert and Marcel Mauss linked Frazer's views on totemism to those of Smith, Frazer replied that he had never assumed its universality: "The worship of trees and cereals, which occupies so large a space in these volumes, is neither identical with nor derived from a system of totemism" (1900a:I xix–xx; cf. Hubert & Mauss 1899). Where totemism did exist, Frazer was still content to explain it on animistic principles, as a means of "externalizing" and protecting the human soul by placing it in the body of the totem animal. Under the influence of Spencer and Gillen's description of the Australian *intichiuma*

ceremonies, Frazer dismissed this explanation in favor of the view that totemism was "simply an organized and cooperative system of magic" contrived to
secure a plentiful supply of food (1899a:282). The evidence for "soul transfer-
ence" among the Central Australians was "slight and scanty"; and its purpose
was "not so much to deposit the man's life in a secure place as to enable him
to control the totem for his own and the common good" (1899b:844).

With the publication of Spencer and Gillen's *Northern Tribes of Central Australia* (1904), however, Frazer discovered a more primitive form of totemism
that suggested still a third origin theory. Among the least developed Australian tribes, there were "totem centres" haunted by souls of a single totem.
Wherever a pregnant woman first felt the child in her womb, she thought
that a spirit of the nearest totem center had entered her; the child was thus
traced to that totem. Because it ignored the role of sexual intercourse in reproduction and the maternal as well as paternal bond of blood-kinship, Frazer
regarded this "conceptional" form of totemism as "the most primitive known
to exist at the present day," and an "astounding" ignorance of natural causation as its putative cause (1905:453–56).

Despite their apparent differences, each of Frazer's three theories presupposed an animistic belief in the separation of the soul from the body, as well
as a decidedly rational series of inferences whereby the soul was presumed
to get from one body to another. Even the utterly primitive "conceptional"
totemism was itself a "theory" used by the Australians to "account for" the
phenomena of pregnancy and childbirth; and Frazer took pains to show his
readers how very reasonably such a theory might be arrived at. Regardless
of which particular explanation of totemism he was defending, totemism, for
Frazer, was consistently an intellectual solution to a cognitive problem posed
by some otherwise inexplicable natural phenomena.

Sacrament as Communion and Propitiation

For Smith, the origin and meaning of sacrifice was "the central problem of
ancient religion," for it was an institution "shaped by the action of general
causes, operating very widely and under conditions that were common in
primitive times to all races of mankind" (1894:27, 214). It was thus a problem
amenable to the comparative method, an approach further encouraged by
the "fragmentary and unintelligible" character of much of the Semitic evidence.
As Wellhausen (1878) had made clear, the older pre-Exilic literature had little
to say about the rules of ritual, while the more detailed laws of Leviticus were
clearly post-Exilic, and thus represented merely "an antiquarian resuscitation
of forms which had lost their intimate connection with the national life, and
therefore had lost the greater part of their original significance." Since an ex-

clusive reliance on the Semitic evidence would thus have been "unscientific and misleading," Smith defended his right to "call in the sacrifices of other nations to confirm or modify the conclusions to which we are led" (1894: 214–16).

Smith developed an elaborate evolutionary argument that animal offerings preceded vegetable offerings; that offerings simply set upon the altar preceded the burnt offering or "holocaust"; and that the "communion" sacrifice, in which god and worshippers shared in the consumption of the sacrificial animal, preceded the "gift" sacrifice made over to the god alone. He concluded that the determining characteristic of ancient religion was that religious occasions and festal seasons were identical, a view "proper to religions in which the habitual temper of the worshippers is one of joyous confidence in their god, untroubled by any habitual sense of human guilt, and resting on the firm conviction that they and the deity they adore are good friends, who understand each other perfectly, and are united by bonds not easily broken" (1894:255). The bonds thus continuously reaffirmed were those of kinship—"participation in a common mass of flesh, blood, and bones"—which, among the Arabs, depended heavily on commensality; and since the god was also construed as a kinsman, the communion sacrifice was a primitive, materialistic form of atonement, a periodic reconciliation of man with god.

Because such sacrifices were public acts of the clan and forbidden to private individuals, and because the only class of actions to which this description applied were those involving an invasion of the sanctity of tribal blood, Smith then argued that the sacrificial victim was itself a kinsman, was sacred, and was therefore a totem. The result was the single, most powerful idea of *The Religion of the Semites*—the theory of a primitive *totemic sacrament*:

> The same blood is supposed to flow also in the veins of the victim; so that its death is at once a shedding of the tribal blood and a violation of the sanctity of the divine life that is transfused through every member, human or irrational, of the sacred circle. Nevertheless the slaughter of such a victim is permitted or required on solemn occasions and all the tribesmen partake of its flesh, that they may thereby cement and seal their mystic unity with one another and with their god. . . . This cement is nothing else than the actual life of the sacred and kindred animal, which is conceived as residing in its flesh, but especially in its blood, and so, in the sacred meal, is actually distributed among all the participants, each of whom incorporates a particle of it with his own individual life.
>
> (1894:313)

The subsequent evolution of sacrifice proceeded in two directions: in the ordinary sacrificial meal, the original notion of the holiness of the victim gradually faded away; while in extraordinary, piacular sacrifices, the inviolable character of the victim became so intensified that even a religious participation in the flesh became regarded as impiety, thus giving rise to the "holocaust" and eventually the sacrificial "gift" wholly made over to the god.

One variation of the more exceptional rite is of special interest, since by Frazer's own account it was the stimulus for "the central idea" of *The Golden Bough*—the conception of "the slain god." Smith argued that many primitive peoples, regardless of their mode of subsistence, observed certain "annual piacula" involving the slaughter of a theanthropic animal, whose original, purely naturalistic significance was that "the mystic unity of life in the religious community is liable to wear out, and must be revived and strengthened from time to time" (1894:405-6). Oblivious to this original unconscious meaning of the rite, the primitive worshipper explained it mythologically, suggesting that the god himself was not exempt from the universal law of decay and death, and had ordered this truth to be commemorated annually. With the development of agriculture and the conception that harvest involved the extinction of a particle of the divine life, these piacula were brought into a cycle of agricultural feasts whose neglect meant disaster; and with the decline of the national religions, the original gaiety of the rites gave way to fearful lamentations (415). Such rites, however, had no share in the development of the higher sense of sin and responsibility which characterized the literature of the Old Testament.

Though he acknowledged his debt to this discussion of the annual piacula, Frazer added that Smith was "in no way responsible" for his general explanation of those rites. Indeed, for Frazer, the slain man-god was a magical rather than a religious conception. Because the course of nature was viewed as dependent on the man-god, his gradual enfeeblement and ultimate death were fraught with terrors. These could be averted only by killing the man-god and transferring his soul to a successor before it deteriorated. This explained both the rule of the Arician priesthood and the periodic slaying of vegetation-spirits among the European peasantry; and thus the annual cycle of agricultural feasts, in which Smith had seen the unconscious survival of a mystical, theanthropic sacrifice, became a rational utilitarian means to promote the growth and revival of vegetation (Frazer 1890:I, 248).

Similarly, while Frazer appeared to confirm Smith's hypothesis of the "totem sacrament," his utilitarian explanation of the rite emphasized the savage's belief that, by thus "eating the god," he acquired the god's physical, moral, and intellectual qualities (1890:II, 84-85); and consistent with his early reservations concerning the universality of totemism, Frazer doubted that the gods thus eaten were totems (1894:206). Decisive proof that savages ate their totems sacramentally appeared only with Spencer and Gillen's description of the Australian *intichiuma* (1899); and while Frazer then acknowledged that Smith's "wonderful intuition" had been "strikingly confirmed after the lapse of years" (1900b:202), he added that it was a long step from the Australian

intichiuma to the universal practice of the totemic sacrament (1900a:I, xix).
Even the *intichiuma* was not precisely what Smith had expected:

> The sacrament he had in his mind was a religious rite, the sacrament we have
> found is a magical ceremony. He thought that the slain animal was regarded
> as divine, and never killed except to furnish the mystic meal; as a matter of
> fact, the animals partaken of sacramentally by the Central Australians are in
> no sense treated as divine; and though they are not as a rule killed and eaten
> by the men and women whose totems they are, nevertheless they are habitually
> killed and eaten by all the other members of the community; indeed the evi-
> dence goes to show that at an earlier time they were commonly eaten also by
> the persons whose totems they were, nay, even that such persons partook of
> them more freely, and were supposed to have a better right to do so, than any-
> one else. The object of the real totem sacrament which Messrs. Spencer and
> Gillen have discovered is not to attain a mystical communion with a deity, but
> simply to ensure a plentiful supply of food for the rest of the community by
> means of sorcery. In short, what we have found is not religion, but that which
> was first the predecessor, and afterwards the hated rival, of religion; I mean magic.
> (Frazer 1900b:202)

To his earlier utilitarian explanation that one ate the god to acquire his qualities, Frazer thus added the equally utilitarian explanation that the sacrament
was designed to secure a plentiful supply of food.

The historical significance of Smith's "communion theory" of sacrifice was
that it replaced—or at least counterbalanced—Tylor's "gift theory" (Tylor 1871:
II, 375 ff.; cf. Jones 1981:186–90). But here Frazer's sympathies remained entirely with Tylor. "Influenced probably by his deeply religious nature," Smith
had underestimated the role of fear and overestimated that of the benevolent
emotions in molding early religion: "Hence his view of sacrifice as mainly a
form of communion with the deity instead of a mode of propitiating him and
averting his anger"—of which the latter was to Frazer the "substantially correct" view (Black & Chrystal 1912:518).

Evolution and Social Progress

According to Smith, in the earliest stage of religious evolution, the earth was
literally "parcelled out" between demons, who haunted the untrodden wilderness regions, and the gods, with whom men had established relations at familiar sanctuaries. Religious progress thus paralleled economic progress, for
the cultivation and irrigation of previously barren lands was accompanied
by the "conversion" of erstwhile demons into beneficent local gods; and the
belief in such gods in turn provided the confidence required for the subjugation of nature. As higher religions developed, these gods might in turn be

reduced to the demons of foreign superstition; and in this sense, the earliest religious communities were henotheistic, believing in the existence of many gods, but worshipping only those with whom they had established relations of kinship (1894:121–24, 39).

The formation of communities based on the common interests of neighboring clans rather than kinship led to the state, which was thus an artificial agency based on practical necessity and liable to dissolution in its absence. When intermittent danger gave way to prolonged warfare, the need for a permanent leader to restrain clan feuds and lead the army against enemies led to the institution of kingship, which became hereditary when only the king's household could bear the cost of warfare. This gradual process of social fusion was in turn reflected in two forms of religious fusion: where the attributes and titles of local gods were similar, the merging of clans frequently led to the merging of gods; and where the gods were more distinct, they continued to be worshipped side by side as allied deities—Smith's explanation for Semitic and Aryan polytheism. As the local king grew stronger, the standard of his judicial authority was gradually raised above the consideration of which disputant had the stronger kin; similarly, the god became "the champion of right against might, the protector of the poor, the widow and the fatherless, of the man who has no helper on earth" (1894:72–73).

This evolutionary development was common to both Semitic and Aryan societies; Smith was determined to explain the subsequent divergence of their religion as the effect of local historical causes rather than "innate tendencies." The decisive factor was the emergence of private property, wealth, and economic inequality, which the king, fearing the growth of a powerful aristocracy, sought to resist. The resulting conflict ended differently in East and West: among the Greeks and Romans the kingship fell before the aristocracy, and religious evolution was thus "towards a divine aristocracy of many gods, only modified by a weak reminiscence of the old kingship in the not very effective sovereignty of Zeus"; among the Semites, the kingship remained strong and even despotic, and thus the national god "tended to acquire a really monarchic sway" (1894:73–74). The "natural tendency" of Semitic religion toward ethical monotheism was thus nothing more than a consequence of the alliance of religion with monarchy.

In Smith's mind, therefore, the greatest differences lay, not between Aryan and Semitic religious conceptions, but between ancient religion generally and the prophetic religion of the Old Testament and Christianity. While he emphasized the social and historical influences that led to the religious divergence between East and West, Smith was the first to admit—indeed, insist upon—their impotence in accounting for the unique features of Old Testament religion. The ethical teachings of the prophets, for example, could not be "explained" by Semitic social and political history any more than they could be explained by race; for prior to the prophets, the ethical difference between Eastern and Western religion was one of degree rather than principle: "All we can say is that the East was better prepared to receive the idea of a god of absolute righteousness." Similarly, since neither early Semites nor Aryans came near the Old Testament conception of monotheism, the differences between East and West permit little beyond the suggestion that Semitic institutions were better prepared to accommodate that conception (1894:74–75). Finally, while Smith's discussion of the evolution from religious particularism to universalism focussed entirely on Semitic societies, Smith regarded that evolution among heathen Semites as retrogressive—it "seemed only to widen the gulf between the deity and man," and "to weaken the moral ideas of nationality without bringing in a higher morality of universal obligation." Only the Hebrew ideal of a divine king had better things to offer—specifically "the unique conception of Jehovah as a God whose love for His people was conditioned by a law of absolute righteousness" (81).

It is customary to date Frazer's mature view of religious evolution from 1900 when, influenced by Spencer and Gillen's data, he asserted the evolutionary priority of magic over religion, and described the universal development of human thought as one from magic, to religion, to science. However, while the first edition of The Golden Bough (1890) did suggest that magic and religion were "parallel" in the earliest stage of thought, the evolutionary argument was otherwise identical to the second edition—supernatural agents were regarded as scarcely superior to man; they could be frightened and coerced by man into doing his will; and the world was thus a "great democracy," in which gods and men stood on "a footing of tolerable equality." With the growth of human knowledge, man gradually learned to recognize his impotence in the face of nature; resigning his hope of directing natural forces through magic, he increasingly looked to the gods as "the sole repositories of those supernatural powers which he once claimed to share with them." Religion thus eclipsed magic; sacrifice and prayer became the primary activity of "the pious and enlightened portion of the community"; magic and sorcery, "the refuge of the superstitious and ignorant." Finally, the conception of elemental forces as personal agents gave way to the recognition of natural law; and "magic, based as it implicitly is on the idea of a necessary and invariable sequence of cause and effect, independent of personal will, reappears from the obscurity and discredit into which it had fallen, and by investigating the causal sequences in nature, directly prepared the way for science" (1890:I, 30–32).

There was perhaps no topic among Frazer's anthropological concerns where one is more tempted to simply endorse Burrow's judgment that Frazer "wrote anthropology like Tylor, not like Robertson Smith" (1966:241, n2). Not only was Frazer's reliance on the "growth of human knowledge" as an independent variable more consistent with Tylor's "primitive philosopher" than with Smith's emphasis on the "unconscious" evolution of religious institutions, but the impetus behind Tylor's evolutionism—his opposition to the "degenerationists"—was adopted intact by Frazer (1922c:237–38; cf. Stocking 1968). Similarly, Frazer presented his theory of social evolution as the necessary "corollary" of its biological counterpart (1922c:237). By contrast, Smith, who was virtual co-author of *The Unseen Universe* (Tait & Stewart 1875)—one of the last great efforts of Victorian science to reconcile divine intervention with natural law—opposed all "materialist" versions of the "development hypothesis," and drew his evolutionary notions from German theology rather than natural science (Black & Chrystal 1912:80, 161–65).

Smith, Frazer, and the Demise of Scottish Philosophy

In sum, Smith's and Frazer's views on virtually every facet of primitive religion were different if not downright opposed. For all their misleading simplicity, dichotomous categories like rational versus unconscious, fear versus affection, cognition versus conation, belief versus institution, individual versus collectivity, intellectual progress versus spiritual progress immediately suggest themselves. But these differences simply reflect a more fundamental disagreement, or rather mutual incomprehension, on the nature of religion itself; and the basis for this incomprehension had been laid long before Smith and Frazer met in the Combination Room at Trinity College.

Their common point of departure was the philosophy of Sir William Hamilton, the last great representative of the Scottish "Common Sense" philosophy of Thomas Reid, and the first to have a thorough knowledge of continental philosophy, and especially Kant. Elected to the chair of logic and metaphysics at Edinburgh despite powerful evangelical opposition in 1836, Hamilton had opposed the Disruption that created the Free Church in 1843, and his presence at Edinburgh was a primary reason for the independent chair in philosophy created by the Free Church at New College Theological Seminary. Though himself devout, Hamilton's philosophy marked the end of all distinctively Scottish apologetics, and laid a foundation for late-Victorian agnosticism.

To think of something, Hamilton argued, is to think of a thing of some sort. Thought thus imposes conditions on its object, and only that which is thus "conditioned" can become an object of knowledge. That which is "unconditioned" (the Infinite, God, Absolute, etc.) is thus inconceivable, not because it does not exist, but because it is beyond the limits of human reason; but if we cannot know *what* such things are, we can know *that* they are. The existence of God is at least a natural inference, although the attributes of God must remain "unknowable." This argument was extended by H. L. Mansel to suggest that even the moral terms we apply to God do not mean what they mean as applied to men (1858). This provoked John Stuart Mill's *Examination of Sir William Hamilton's Philosophy*, which objected that terms not used in their usual sense ought not to be used at all and, more strongly, that a God whose acts are not sanctioned by human morality is unworthy of worship (1865). Though disciples of Hamilton survived to the end of the century, Mill's *Examination* effectively destroyed the Scottish philosophy as a foundation for religious belief.

Rural Aberdeenshire was pervaded by the "apathetic agricultural Moderatism" that had provoked the Scottish Evangelical Revival and the Disruption itself; as the child of a Free Church minister, Robertson Smith was first educated wholly within the manse, had a conversion experience before he was twelve, and had committed himself to the Free Church ministry before he was sixteen. Even among other students at New College, Smith was conservative in theology, suspicious of Moderates, pro-Sabbatarian, and opposed to the union of the Free Church with the "voluntary" United Presbyterians; upon reading Mill's *Examination* early in 1867, he found "the bitterest hostility to Christianity" of a "simply shocking" degree. In Bonn the following summer to study theology, German, and Hebrew, Smith encountered representatives of the *Vermittlungstheologie*, an attempt to find a *via media* between Confessional orthodoxy and scientific, philosophical, and biblical rationalism; and Smith adopted their arguments in his early defense of biblical miracles (1869). But by the summer of 1869, Smith was in Göttingen, where he came under the influence of Albrecht Ritschl, the most important German theologian between Schleiermacher and Barth.

Earlier a disciple of the *Vermittslungtheologie* and then the more radical, Hegelian Tübingen School, by 1869 Ritschl was in the midst of an attempt to define religion independently of morality, metaphysics, and subjective feeling. The most common tendency in all religions, he discovered, is the effort to transcend, by spiritual means, the determinism of both our own and external nature. Religious knowledge is thus not theoretical but pragmatic; it satisfies, not intellectual curiosity, but practical necessity; and this tendency is epitomized in Christianity, the only "completely spiritual and ethical" religion, and the standard by which all other religions are judged. Over the centuries however, Christianity had acquired alien philosophical accretions, dogmas, and metaphysical propositions of which it must be purged. Invoking the Kantian distinction, Ritschl thus argued that theology must dismiss speculation about God's nature (noumena), and focus instead on what God has revealed to man (phenomena) through Christ; and, because even Christ cannot be known "in Himself," our only resource is that consciousness of Christ which existed in the early Christian community. History thus replaced philosophical speculation, and the Bible was less a source of dogmatic propositions about God than the historical record of that state of mind which His revelation inspired. And the lesson of that record was that God's grace is extended to men, not individually, but collectively, for the transcendence of the individual self that the religious life presumes is possible only in the context of society (Ritschl 1870–74).

"I have never heard anything . . . so interesting on a theological subject as Ritschl's lectures," Smith wrote on May 24, 1869. Admiring Ritschl's condemnation of Protestant sects, his defense of infant baptism, and his attack on speculative metaphysics, Smith saw him as a "strong Calvinist," whose "lectures are of a kind that will be directly useful in Scotland." By July 1870, Smith had begun an eleven-year correspondence with Ritschl and was actively introducing his ideas in lectures and essays; and when the *Britannica* article "Bible" caught the attention of the Free Church, it was Ritschl whom Smith called "the father of the Aberdeen heresy."[1]

Frazer's parents were also Free Church Presbyterians of "unquestioning orthodoxy"; but unlike Smith's, they were well-to-do members of Glasgow's merchant class. Frazer thus owed his introduction to Greek and Latin to two of the early Scottish "academies" whose function, utterly inconsistent with the older tradition of "the democratic intellect," was to avoid "mixing" with children of the urban-industrial working class, and to secure entrance to the more prestigious English universities (Drummond & Bulloch 1973:189; cf. Davie 1961). Frazer continued his work in classics at Glasgow University, where he also studied physics with Sir William Thomson (later Lord Kelvin) and logic and metaphysics with John Veitch. From Kelvin's class, Frazer carried away "a conception of the physical universe as regulated by exact and absolutely unvarying laws of nature expressible in mathematical formulas," which became "a settled principle" of his thought (1932:123). Veitch's family, like Smith's and Frazer's, had gone into the Free Church in 1843, and Veitch himself entered New College three years later to prepare for the ministry. However, lured to the university by Hamilton's lectures, Veitch found himself repelled by Free Church orthodoxy, became Hamilton's assistant and, on Hamilton's death, the most ardent among his waning disciples. As professor of logic and rhetoric at Glasgow for the last thirty years of his life, Veitch was viewed as an eccentric, out of touch with the more prominent mainstreams of evolutionary materialism and Hegelian idealism; but his influence on Frazer was undeniable. Veitch's teaching, Frazer recalled, "opened up an intellectual vista of which I had never dreamed before, and which has never since been wholly

---

1. Ritschl's correspondence with Smith extended from July 6, 1870, to December 31, 1881, and comprises Add., 7449, D596–D610 of the W. R. Smith Collection in the Cambridge University Library, Cambridge, England. The letters have been superbly translated by Sarah Glenn Demaris. Cf. also C115, C116, F55.

closed or obscured by later and very different studies" (1932:123). Unlike Smith, Frazer was neither a philosopher nor a theologian, and it is doubtful that he held any religious beliefs with depth or precision; but the most reasonable description is that he was a Hamiltonian agnostic.

If questions remain over the source of Smith's and Frazer's differences on primitive religion, there is no question about their significance. Frazer's "psychological-intellectualist" view of religion left him relatively indifferent to those developments in psychology wrought by McDougall, Lévy-Bruhl, and Freud, which emphasized emotional, conative, and unconscious influences on human behavior; and in the subsequent reaction against Frazer led by Marett, Smith was cast as an early prophet of this more "emotionalist" approach. A similar reaction led by Durkheim, Harrison, and Radcliffe-Brown insisted on sociological rather than psychological influences; and here again, Smith, along with Maine and Fustel de Coulanges, was repeatedly cited as an early seer (Evans-Pritchard 1965). Ironically, the foreseeable future of social anthropology belonged to the master, and only the past to the protégé.

Acknowledgments

I am grateful for the assistance provided by Research Grant SOC 78-07311, Program in the History and Philosophy of Science, Division of Social Sciences, National Science Foundation.

References Cited

Ackerman, R. 1975. Frazer on myth and ritual. *J. Hist. Ideas.* 36:115–34.

Black, J. S. & G. Chrystal. 1912. *The life of William Robertson Smith.* London.

Bryson, G. 1945. *Man and society: The Scottish inquiry of the eighteenth century.* Princeton.

Burrow, J. W. 1966. *Evolution and society: A study in Victorian social theory.* Cambridge.

Davie, G. E. 1961. *The democratic intellect: Scotland and her universities in the nineteenth century.* Edinburgh.

Downie, R. A. 1970. *Frazer and the Golden Bough.* London.

Drummond, A. L., & J. Bulloch. 1973. *The Scottish church, 1688–1843.* Edinburgh.

Durkheim, E. 1912. *Les Formes élémentaires de la vie religieuse: le système totémique en Australie.* Paris. Trans. J. W. Swain as *The elementary forms of the religious life: A study in religious sociology.* New York (1915).

Evans-Pritchard, E. 1965. *Theories of primitive religion.* Oxford.

Frazer, J. G. 1879. *The growth of Plato's ideal theory: An essay.* London (1930).

———. 1885. On certain burial customs as illustrative of the primitive theory of the soul. *J. Anth. Inst.* 15:64–104.

———. 1887. *Totemism.* Edinburgh.

————. 1888. Taboo. *Encyclopedia Britannica*. 9th ed. 23:15–18.

————. 1890. *The golden bough: A study in comparative religion*. 2 vols. London.

————. 1894. William Robertson Smith. In 1920:194–209.

————. 1897. Letter to J. F. White, December 15, 1897. In *Two professors of oriental languages*, by J. F. White, 19–34. Aberdeen (1899).

————. 1899a. Observations on Central Australian totemism *J. Anth. Inst.* 29:281–86.

————. 1899b. The origin of totemism. *Fort. Rev.* 45:647–65, 835–52.

————. 1900a. *The golden bough: A study in magic and religion*. 2d ed. 3 vols. London.

————. 1900b. On some ceremonies of the Central Australian tribes. In 1931:198–204.

————. 1905. The beginnings of religion and totemism among the Australian aborigines. *Fort. Rev.* 84:162–72, 452–66.

————. 1908. *The scope of social anthropology*. In 1909c:159–76.

————. 1909a. Fison and Howitt. In 1920:210–59.

————. 1909b. Some primitive theories of the origin of man. Reprinted as "Creation and evolution in primitive cosmogonies," in 1935:3–34.

————. 1909c. *Psyche's task: A discourse concerning the influence of superstition on the growth of institutions*. 2d ed. London (1920).

————. 1915. *The golden bough: A study in magic and religion*. 3d ed. 12 vols. London (1915).

————. 1920. *Sir Roger de Coverly and other literary pieces*. London.

————. 1921a. Ernest Renan et la méthode de l'histoire des religions. Reprinted as "Address to the Ernest Renan Society," in 1931:266–78.

————. 1921b. Introduction, in *Apollodorus: The Library*, ix–xliii. 2 vols. London.

————. 1922a. The Andaman islanders. In 1931:376–81.

————. 1922b. Preface, B. Malinowski, *Argonauts of the western Pacific*. In 1931:391–98.

————. 1922c. The scope and method of mental anthropology. In 1931:234–51.

————. 1923. Primitive mentality. In 1931:413–18.

————. 1930. *Myths of the origin of fire: An essay*. London.

————. 1931. *Garnered sheaves: Essays, addresses, and reviews*. London.

————. 1932. Speech on receiving the freedom of the City of Glasgow. In 1935:117–218. (April 22, 1932.)

————. 1935. *Creation and evolution in primitive cosmogonies and other pieces*. London.

Fustel de Coulanges, N. D. 1864. *The ancient city: A study on the religion, laws, and institutions of Greece and Rome*. Baltimore (1980).

Hamilton, W. 1829. On the philosophy of the unconditioned. *Edin. Rev.* 1:194–221.

————. 1852. *Discussions on philosophy and literature, education and university reform*. London.

————. 1859–60. *Lectures on metaphysics and logic*. 4 vols. Ed. H. L. Mansel and J. Veitch. Edinburgh.

Hubert, H., & M. Mauss, 1899. Essai sur la nature et la fonction du sacrifice. Trans. as *Sacrifice: Its nature and function*. Chicago (1964).

Hyman, S. E. 1974. *The tangled bank: Darwin, Marx, Frazer, and Freud as imaginative writers*. New York.

Jones, R. A. 1981. Robertson Smith, Durkheim, and sacrifice: An historical context for *The Elementary Forms of the Religious Life*. *J. Hist. Beh. Scis.* 17:184–205.

McLennan, J. F. 1865. *Primitive marriage: An inquiry into the origin of the form of capture in marriage ceremonies.* Edinburgh.

Maine, H. S. 1861. *Ancient law: Its connection with the early history of society and its relation to modern ideas.* Boston (1963).

Mansel, H. L. 1858. *The limits of religious thought.* 1st American, ed. Boston (1866).

Marett, R. R. 1914. *The threshold of religion.* 2d ed. London (1914).

Mill, J. S. 1865. *An examination of Sir William Hamilton's philosophy.* 2 vols. Boston.

Ritschl, A. B. 1870–74. *Die Christliche Lehre von der Rechtfertigung und Versöhnung.* 3 vols. Bonn.

Smith, W. R. 1869. Christianity and the supernatural. In *Lectures and essays of William Robertson Smith,* ed. J. S. Black & G. Chrystal, 109–36. London (1912).

———. 1882. *The prophets of Israel and their place in history to the close of the eighth century B.C.* Edinburgh.

———1885. *Kinship and marriage in early Arabia.* Cambridge.

———. 1894. *Lectures on the religion of the Semites.* 2d ed. New York.

Spencer, B. & F. J. Gillen. 1899. *The native tribes of Central Australia.* London.

———. 1904. *The northern tribes of Central Australia.* London.

Stocking, G. W., Jr. 1968. *Race, culture, and evolution: Essays in the history of anthropology.* New York.

———. n.d. Social evolutionism and social theory: The epigoni. Unpublished manuscript.

Tait, P. G., & B. Stewart. 1875. *The unseen universe, or physical speculations on a future state.* London.

Turner, F. M. 1981. *The Greek heritage in Victorian Britain.* New Haven.

Tylor, E. B. 1871. *Primitive culture: Researches into the development of mythology, philosophy, religion, language, art and custom.* 2 vols. 1st American ed. Boston (1874).

Veitch, J. 1869. *Memoir of Sir William Hamilton, Bart.* Edinburgh.

Vickery, J. B. 1973. *The literary impact of The Golden Bough.* Princeton.

Wellhausen, J. 1878. *Prolegomena zur Geschichte Israels.* 2d ed. Berlin (1883).

TRIBAL EXEMPLARS

*Images of Political Authority
in British Anthropology, 1885–1945*

HENRIKA KUKLICK

This essay examines six decades of British anthropology with the object of deciphering a particular feature of its successive messages: its contributions to and reflection of a sustained national debate about the structure of ideal political order. The period is bracketed by significant developments in the political history of Britain, as well as by benchmarks in the history of British anthropology. The age of modern, class-based politics began with the passage of the Third Reform Bill of 1884 and the Redistribution Act of 1885, which instituted virtual manhood suffrage (although measures implementing truly universal suffrage, including the enfranchisement of women, were very gradually introduced thereafter). An era of enthusiasm for imperialism began with Britain's occupation of Egypt in 1882, which signalled the opening of her participation in the "Scramble for Africa"; this era came to an end in 1945, when the newly elected Labour government began the practice of development administration in the colonies in order to prepare them for independence in the near future. And during our period anthropology was professionalized, transformed from an amateur pursuit into an academic discipline. In 1884 E. B. Tylor became both reader in Anthropology at Oxford and first President of the newly created Section for Anthropology of the British Association for the Advancement of Science (Section H). By 1946, anthropology had become a thoroughly academic occupation: unlike anthropological societies founded earlier, the Association of Social Anthropologists restricted its mem-

Henrika Kuklick is Janice and Julian Bers Assistant Professor in the Department of History and Sociology of Science, University of Pennsylvania. She is the author of *The Imperial Bureaucrat: The Colonial Administrative Service in the Gold Coast, 1920–1939*, and is currently working on a history of the social uses of British anthropology from 1885 to 1945.

bership to those who had earned Ph.D.'s in anthropology or could present evidence of equivalent qualifications.

Conquest and Polity in Folk Political Theory

But though the events of our period made consideration of certain political questions especially urgent, the debate over these questions was framed by persistent British cultural assumptions about the range of possibilities of structuring the social order. These assumptions are conspicuous in popular culture and can be abstracted into a "folk political theory"; but they have also been prominent in the discourse of high culture, in the debates on the nature of the state conducted by political philosophers since the revolutionary period of the seventeenth century. Well before 1885, extrapolation from these assumptions had led to the elaboration of two, antithetical, ideal-typical models of political organization, each made up of a set of social elements in an interdependent complex. In extremist political argument of both the conservative and radical sort, it was granted that these two models exhausted the possibilities of constitutional choice, that the elements of each did not permit of independent assortment, although other moderate political theorists developed hybrid varieties of these schemes.

If it is assumed that the capacity for rule, and indeed for achievement of any sort, derives from inborn talents possessed by only a small fraction of the population, then the legitimate form of government is a centralized polity, dominated by an hereditary aristocracy. Social integration takes organicist shape: unequal individuals cooperate to advance collective ends, accepting as just the measure of status and material rewards that they are dealt in proportion to the power they exercise. Although this political philosophy exemplifies the tradition of Western conservative thought persuasively described by Karl Mannheim (1953; cf. Manuel 1956), the British variant of this social philosophy has a particular emphasis. The strong polity is created when a superior band of conquerors forces the consolidation of diverse peoples, none of which has previously been capable of developing culturally advanced forms of social organization. The alien conquerors retain a monopoly on the use of force within the state; this monopoly permits them to establish themselves as hereditary rulers, compel general obedience, and subordinate individual interests to the needs of the state. The character of such a state's international relations is consistent with its internal constitution: the state seeks to expand its territorial domain, and does so by military means. Evidently, the rhythm of life in such a state is punctuate: the stable order will be altered only under special circumstances by persons of peculiar genius.

If, on the contrary, it is assumed that talent is distributed fairly—if not perfectly—uniformly throughout the human race, a legitimate political order must be an egalitarian, contractual union of atomistic individuals. The British folk-model of such a state is premised on the assumption that the use of force to achieve political ends is illegitimate. The polity must be based on voluntary alliances, a principle that extends to foreign affairs as well as domestic; the sovereignty of other nations must be respected, and peaceful relations effected with them, usually through the medium of economic exchange. The social stratification system of the polity may not be thoroughly egalitarian, but it must be meritocratic; individual social status must be based on personal achievement, rather than birth into an hereditary caste. Above all, political leaders can retain their offices only with the consent of the governed, for the function of the state is the satisfaction of popular desires and the protection of individual liberties. If this liberal state is considered the natural order of things, it is also assumed that social changes occur constantly but gradually, the products of small innovations made everywhere, everyday, by ordinary beings.

British political debate was not, of course, conducted in the abstract. It was shaped by the national experience, and in particular by reactions to significant historical events subject to diverse interpretations. From the period of constitutional revolution of the seventeenth century, the Norman Conquest of the Anglo-Saxon people was a major historical reference point of political argument. The results of the Conquest could be represented as justification for the conservative folk model of the state outlined above, as the events necessary to the foundation of the English nation, which was destined to extend its jurisdiction into the territories constituting Great Britain and beyond. Hence, the Conquest could be offered as but one illustration of the theory advanced by seventeenth-century defenders of the established order: submission to conquerors is in accordance with the providence of God, the salvation of a divided and confused people from anarchy (Franklin 1978). Thus, King James asserted that the Norman Conquest had disciplined the previously dissolute Anglo-Saxons (Hill 1958:52). This argument was to be echoed in the years to come. In 1762 David Hume wrote that until the Norman Conquest the Saxons had been "very little advanced beyond the rude state of nature" (Skinner 1965:155). And a number of nineteenth-century historians agreed with Carlyle that without the benefit of alien rule the English would have remained "a gluttonous race of Jutes and Angles, capable of no grand combinations; lumbering about in pot-bellied equanimity; not dreaming of heroic toil, and silence, and endurance, such as leads to the high places of this universe" (Burrow 1981:143). By the middle of the nineteenth century, the Norman Conquest represented a paradigm for British colonialism: it had welded a disparate population into a master race destined to bring the benefits of civilization to peoples as backward as the Saxons had been (Hill 1958:120).

Critics of established order ranging from liberal to radical could hardly deny that many governments were based on force. But as Locke argued in 1689, government rested on a voluntary compact between autonomous individuals; though natural societies might elect kings, they would permit them to reign only so long as they ruled properly, and many simple societies functioned without kings except during periods of military conflict. Portrayed in terms such as Locke's, the government established through the Norman Conquest was illegal, an abrogation of the natural democracy of the Saxons. Anglo-Saxon precedent was repeatedly invoked by supporters of causes ranging from radical to liberal, from the seventeenth-century Levellers and Diggers, through the followers of Thomas Paine at the turn of the eighteenth century, to the defenders of Lloyd George's redistributive "People's Budget" of 1909 (Briggs 1966:7–8). The constitutional ideal supposedly embodied in Anglo-Saxon society could be evoked without specific reference to the "Norman Yoke," however. It clearly informs the middle-class radicalism of the nineteenth-century free-traders Richard Cobden and John Bright, who envisioned a social order maintained by voluntary cooperation and economic exchange, with minimal government interference. And in the latter half of the nineteenth century, this sustained tradition of social thought was translated into the formulae of Herbert Spencer, who argued that while social evolution could be realized in "militant" or "industrial" form, the "industrial" order was the more natural, and thus preferable, form of society; Spencer's models corresponded to the conservative and liberal ideal types here outlined (Peel 1971:192–223).

Historically, there was one conspicuous attempt to reconcile conservative and radical models of the polity: the "Whig" historical tradition, which stresses the continuity of English history, arguing that the Conquest little altered the pattern of English life. Though originally a conservative argument made in the sixteenth and seventeenth centuries by those who appealed to the "ancient constitution" in order to resist royal innovation, the "Whig" interpretation became an essentially liberal position. The Normans may have triumphed through force, but they could not reign without the consent of the governed, and therefore could not suspend Saxon liberties. Some "Whig" historians even suggested, as did one eighteenth-century writer, that William the Conqueror could not have ruled had he not "founded his Right upon the Election of the People" (Skinner 1965:174). Subsequent historical scholarship discredited such fictitious accounts, but many nineteenth-century historians agreed with E. A. Freeman that the Conquest was only a "temporary overthrow of our national being"–"in a few generations we led captive our conquerors" (Burrow 1981:102). "Whig" historians did not necessarily insist on Norman reaffirmations of the democratic Saxon constitution. Like Turner, they could argue that Anglo-Saxon society had been no less socially stratified than post-Conquest England (118). "Whigs" were, however, distinguished by their denial that force could effect disjunctive historical change.

Evolutionary Anthropology and Political Development

Evolutionist anthropologists of the late nineteenth and early twentieth centuries described political development in the terms of liberal British thought, although, as we shall see, evolutionist schemes could subsequently be turned to different purposes. But because anthropology was by no means a professionalized academic discipline at the turn of the century, the evolutionist thought of this period virtually defies systematic summary. The loosely defined anthropological community tolerated a diversity of opinion, and, indeed, evolutionary ideas were to be rendered in their most schematic form by those determined to reject them. Nevertheless, one can abstract from the intricacies of anthropological discussion two interrelated postulates on which the evolutionist faith in universal human progress and the practicability of the "comparative method" of "armchair anthropology" were predicated. The first of these postulates, grounded in Enlightenment beliefs in human equality, was the "psychic unity" of mankind: Human beings everywhere possessed identical faculties of reasoning. The second was the "recapitulation hypothesis": the development of each individual, and of every society, normally followed a single pattern. Individuals and societies were distinguished from one another by the *stage* of maturity they had attained, the *rate* at which they had evolved, and variations which could be explained primarily as functions of environmental factors. The "comparative method" followed from this model of development: no matter what their historical and geographical locations, peoples gauged in the same evolutionary "stage" were essentially identical, and whatever was known about any one of them could be used in analysis of the others (Bock 1978).

Evolutionist assumptions permitted the ranking of societies all over the world, as well as people within society, according to a single, meritocratic standard—the degree to which they had achieved high levels of rationality and morality in all forms of behavior, and with these the technical mastery of their environment. By this standard, it was possible to equate contemporary primitives, ancient European peoples, and the people living in less-developed sectors of modern societies—rural residents and the "dangerous classes." All of these relationships were analogous: tribesmen to Europeans; children to adults; women to men; the poor to the elite. The last group was of course the vanguard of evolutionary advance. These relationships held because physical evolution and cultural evolution were interdependent. Racial characteristics were both dependent and independent variables, not only determinants of culture but themselves determined by all aspects of individuals' and peoples' environments—their willful behavior, their traditional practices, their material possessions, and their natural surroundings. As W. H. Flower remarked, "The physical characteristics of race, so strongly marked in many cases, are probably always associated with equally or more diverse character-

istics of temper and intellect" (1894). If physical development and mental development were correlated, these were also associated with social status. Many
anthropologists agreed that the rulers of tribal societies resembled British
gentlemen in manners and attitudes, while the lower orders in Britain dis-
played primitive physical capacities of strength and endurance their social su-
periors lacked (e.g., Beddoe 1891; Harley 1887; Hose 1894; Roth 1892; Venn
1888).

Belief in this social scheme was threatened at the turn of the century by
new biological ideas—August Weismann's theory of the "germ plasm" and Gregor Mendel's rediscovered work on the laws of inheritance. This variant of
social evolutionism was predicated on the neo-Lamarckian assumption that
acquired characteristics were inherited. A number of figures prominent in the
anthropological community at the end of the nineteenth century were quick
to accept the new biology, although their judgments of its implications varied.
It was possible to believe simultaneously that acquired characteristics were
not inherited and that many apparent racial differences were produced by
environmental rather than biological factors (Turner 1889). It was possible
to argue that new findings on the mechanism of inheritance were entirely
compatible with the observation that a people transplanted from one location to another could become physically adapted to their new environment,
although the new biology suggested that the process of adaptation might require a greater period of time than had previously been thought. It was possible to argue, as Francis Galton did most notably, that the new biological
knowledge would permit deliberate acceleration of human evolution (1885).
And it was possible to argue that the new model of heredity did not in itself
entail judgments of the relative superiority of some races over others, or
eliminate the possibility that the dominance of some races over others was
caused by environmental rather than biological factors (Campbell 1886). It
should be stressed, however, that those who most readily embraced strict
hereditarianism were those whose primary anthropological interest was the
explanation of physical variations.

Evolutionist anthropologists concerned to maintain the integration of physical and social anthropology could not so readily abandon Lamarckism, however, for their theoretical synthesis seemed to require it. Few remained as un-
abashedly Lamarckian as William Ridgeway, who insisted on the importance
of "the effects of the environment in changing racial types, and that, too, in
no long time. The change in the type of the American of New England from
that of his English ancestor and his approximation to the hatchet face and
thin scraggy beard of the Red Indian have long been remarked" (1908:525).
A. C. Haddon's defensive response to new biological theories was more cautious; he advanced a modified Lamarckism, arguing that while some physical
characteristics, such as headform, were not modified by environmental influ-

ences, other characteristics, such as stature, were (1900). Haddon's revisionist approach was characteristic of a number of anthropologists. They agreed that some racial types were more stable than others, that some physical characteristics were more susceptible to environmental modification than others, that some climatic conditions had greater impact on physical characteristics than others (Beddoe 1889; Clouston 1894; Conder 1887; Flower 1884; Petrie 1906; Ridgeway 1910).

The new biology threatened the basis of the assumption of the "psychic unity" of all of the world's peoples, and with it the postulate that peoples everywhere were capable of "independent invention" of higher civilization. This is not to suggest that evolutionists were unwilling to explain cultural innovation as a consequence of contact between peoples. Indeed, in 1884, E. B. Tylor cautioned that, before the anthropologist fell "back on the extreme hypothesis of independent origins," he had to entertain the possibility that cultural similarities between peoples were products of "diffusion" (1884: 451). But evolutionist anthropologists agreed that different peoples who had attained the same level of social development also reasoned in identical fashion, so that cultural similarities need not be assumed to indicate diffusion (e.g., Brabrook 1898). And, as John Rhŷs argued, a people would only accept diffused cultural elements appropriate to their level of development, even when they had been forced to submit to alien rule; he "proceeded on the principle that each successive band of conquerors has its race, language and institutions essentially more or less modified by contact with the race, language and institutions of those whom it has conquered" (1900). Cultural advance could not be forced, but the "psychic unity" of mankind made the gradual development of all of the world's peoples inevitable. The view of social change embodied in evolutionary gradualism evidently represented a liberal, not radical, political outlook, and, indeed, was explicitly identified as such (Pitt-Rivers 1888).

Evolutionary anthropologists' explanations of the origin of the state were consistent with their liberal outlook, for the polity was the spontaneously generated product of peaceful, *natural* human drives. The rise of the state was based on the biological imperative of reproduction, for the state grew from progressive extensions of kinship ties. Anthropologists differed over the details of this process. Some argued that the most primitive society was a promiscuous horde, which by degrees accepted the discipline of monogamous family life; others countered that the nuclear family was the primordial form of social organization. But whether they believed that families derived from or merged into clans, anthropologists agreed that clans fused into tribes and tribes into nations (Gomme 1887; Lang 1905; Thomas 1906). The inevitability of state formation followed from the universal practice of exogamy, a practice variously explained as a consequence of the incest taboo instinctive to those reared together (Westermarck 1891:544), the rational decision to regulate reproduction for the biological good of the community (Howitt 1888), or the recognition that marital ties could be used to effect political alliances (Tylor 1888). Furthermore, primitive government was expected to serve popular needs, although it did not do so in a manner civilized man would regard as rational. The function of primitive government was control of natural resources; but it was the superior physical and moral condition of its archetypal leader, the "divine king"—rather than instrumental action—that supposedly ensured his people's prosperity (Frazer 1900:I, 208–10). Anthropologists recognized that there were instances of state formation that deviated from this ideal pattern of its "independent invention" through the elaboration of voluntary alliances. Cultural patterns had been diffused; and the political consolidation of peoples had been effected through force: The strong triumphed over the weak—a process that might have some biological justification. But societies organized through peaceful cooperation would be more successful societies because they adhered to the most natural social form (Haddon 1889:387).

Diffusionism as the Migration of Conquering Races

At the beginning of the twentieth century, the climate of social opinion in British anthropology began to change. Emblematic of this change was the rise of the "diffusionist" school, whose most prominent members were G. Elliot Smith, W. J. Perry, W. H. R. Rivers, and A. M. Hocart, whose theoretical loyalties lay with the diffusionists more than with any other school. The conspicuously lunatic aspects of diffusionism, and the disrepute into which it fell in the 1930s, should not blind us to the school's earlier importance. And if we are to understand the diffusionists' role in British anthropology, we must appreciate the features of their scheme that gave it broad anthropological appeal during this period (after World War I the diffusionists were to emphasize different aspects of their model).

A new model of race underlay the new anthropological explanations of the development of modern civilization, including diffusionist explanations. This model did not derive from the new biology, however, but from the new paleontology—the excavation and analysis of ancient human remains. Elliot Smith figured prominently in the discovery of key pieces of evidence—the remains of approximately six thousand individuals who lived in Egypt from the predynastic period to the early Christian era, excavated during 1907 and 1908, as well as the fraudulent Piltdown remains, "discovered" in 1912 by Charles Dawson. Regardless of the provenance of these pieces of evidence, they were taken as proof that the races of mankind had remained unaltered for millenia (Anon. 1911). Anthropologists' changed understanding of race might have

W. H. R. Rivers and Malekulan natives, 1914 (courtesy of the University Museum of Archaeology and Anthropology, Cambridge).

led them to eliminate racial factors from their explanations of cultural differences, as post-World War I anthropologists were to do. Instead, they revised their interpretation of the relationship between race and culture. They continued to believe that physical and behavioral traits were correlated, defining the perpetuation of culture from one generation to another as a biological process. The assumption that every race had a fixed cultural character, which would be sustained in the absence of unwonted constraints upon its behavior, entailed several propositions: geographical dispersal would not modify the behavior of members of a single race; cultural diversity within an area was prima facie evidence that its inhabitants were a racially diverse collection of migrant settlers; the global distribution of races reflected the inherent migratory propensities of members of different stocks, not the effects of the environment (Beddoe 1905; Cunningham 1902; Haddon 1920; Hall 1904; Parsons 1919; Pearson 1903; Seligman 1924).

For both those who accepted the new hereditarianism and those who rejected it, then, the crucial anthropological problem was the causes and consequences of migrations (Myres 1909). If the diverse races of mankind did not possess in equal measure the capacity to invent independently the elements of civilization, evolutionary advance had to be the product of "the clash and contact of peoples" (Crooke 1912). For the social forms of modern civilization were, as Elliot Smith declared, "artificial and unnatural" (1915:167). This was not to say that modern civilization was not a great achievement, but that it was the product of historical accident and special genius—whether of gifted individuals or inherently superior races. Significantly, even Frazer enunciated an essentially diffusionist position in 1908:

> The more we study the outward workings of society and the progress of civilisa-
> tion, the more clearly shall we perceive how both are governed by the influence
> of thoughts which, springing up at first we know not how or whence in a few
> superior minds, gradually spread until they have leavened the whole inert lump
> of a community or of mankind. The origin of such mental variations, with all
> their far-reaching train of social consequences, is just as obscure as the origin
> of those physical variations on which, if biologists are right, depends the evolu-
> tion of species, and with it the possibility of progress.

Smith and Perry's diffusionism now seems undeniably bizarre: the origin of modern civilization was a culture-complex that had been developed in the unique conditions of ancient Egypt, and from there spread by migrants who were searching for precious substances. But we must recognize that certain features of their scheme were widely accepted. The initial reception of their work was positive (Anon. 1916), and even those like Haddon and Bronislaw Malinowski, who was later to ridicule diffusionism in all of its aspects, greeted early diffusionist work respectfully (Haddon 1918; Malinowski 1924). And the diffusionists' early success must have been due in no small measure to their ability to sustain anthropology's charter mission—the integration of social analysis with archeological and biological findings (Rivers 1922)—for the diffusionists brought to bear upon social analysis new evidence about man's biological evolution, as we have seen, as well as archeological theories about the origin of civilization (Evans 1896).

During this period it was assumed that force was a necessary component of evolutionary advance, and that evolution occurred in unpredictable, disjunctive leaps rather than through the steady accretion of small advances. Conquest was essential to the creation of the state; when two peoples came into contact, the superior one would inevitably establish dominance over the inferior one, forcing the latter to adopt a more civilized mode of behavior. This pattern of cultural change obtained everywhere—in the ancient societies of Greece, Rome, and Egypt, in prehistoric Europe, and among contemporary primitives (Johnston 1913; Keith 1916; Migeod 1917; Naville 1907; Peake 1917; Rivers 1913; Seligman & Seligman 1930; Smith 1915; Werner 1911). Class divisions were legacies of military pacification and of interracial competition for niches in the social hierarchy, not the result of the ever-elaborating division of labor that accompanied economic growth, as late nineteenth-century anthropologists would have had it (Keith 1915; Migeod 1919; Torday & Joyce 1906). Some anthropologists specifically invoked the Norman Conquest as an exemplar of the process by which societies were brought to a higher level of evolution (cf. Raglan 1956).

Significantly, perennial anthropological problems were reanalyzed to suit the new intellectual fashion. Such a problem is the origin of the social form called the "dual organization," which has been observed all over the world: a people conceptualizes all cultural and natural phenomena in dichotomous terms, which may be antithetical or complementary, and assigns them to one or another set of related phenomena; and the population is divided into two groups, each of which has a special relationship to one of these dichotomous inventories. Whereas the "dual organization" had been explained as the product of an internally generated split within an evolving group, in the early twentieth century anthropologists described it as a fundamental class division resulting from the conquest of one people by another (Gomme 1909; Perry 1923:326; Rivers 1914: II, 562–64).

Functionalism and the Anglo-Saxon Model

The political orientation of British anthropology changed after World War I. The shift in anthropological opinion was marked by the rise of the functionalist school, led by Bronislaw Malinowski and A. R. Radcliffe-Brown. Prominent among their disciples were E. E. Evans-Pritchard and Meyer Fortes. In technical terms, functionalism represented a dramatic departure from earlier styles of anthropological practice, but the political message embodied in functionalism was also conveyed by evolutionists and diffusionists after World War I, albeit to a lesser degree. The majority of anthropologists no longer presumed that conquering peoples were culturally superior to defeated ones, that race and culture were interdependent, that the state was the highest and best form of political organization, that the current character of Western civilization represented an evolutionary yardstick by which to measure the developmental level of all other cultures. Perhaps most important, they no longer assumed that those societies that were most technologically advanced and politically organized would also adhere to the highest moral standards. The virtue of Western civilization itself seemed questionable. In 1929 Elliot Smith chose to emphasize the negative rather than positive aspect of the diffusionist account of the world's history, writing that "when mankind acquired culture" it developed "with it social unrest, dangerous practices, and methods of cruelty" (Smith 1929: xviii). R. R. Marett could no longer equate material evolution and progress, wondering "whether it is possible to be both civilized and good?" (1935:21). Postwar anthropologists granted their predecessors' premise: the strong state and an elaborated status hierarchy would not be developed in the absence of technological sophistication and material wealth. But they denied the merits of such achievements. Meyer Fortes, for example, stated that the social relationships of the Tallensi were harmonious because their society was distinguished by "the almost complete absence of economic differentiation, by occupation or by ownership of resources, and, in particular, the absence of both material or technological possibilities for capital accumulation or for technological advance" (1945). As Hocart said of ostensibly undeveloped peoples, "True it is that such societies cannot form big nations, maintain disciplined armies, lay networks of roads and railways, or suffer economic crises on a colossal scale; but they can exist, and quite successfully too, if success consists in surviving with happiness" (1936:128).

Evidently, postwar anthropology was a vehicle for liberal criticism of Western society. Paradoxically, by some measures it seemed conservative. It retained the model of social change implied in a positive interpretation of the Norman Conquest: change did not derive from the internal dynamics of a society but was necessarily stimulated by contact with some outside agents. Functionalists portrayed traditional cultures as perfectly integrated societies, inevitably static because all of their institutions were mutually reinforcing, their peoples united in consensual agreement. Certainly, their social organicism represented a rejection of the traditional liberal view of society as an aggregate of atomistic individuals—the view embodied in late nineteenth-century anthropology. But in the early twentieth century, British liberalism was reinterpreted by the proponents of the "New Liberalism," who argued for an increase in state power on the grounds that in modern society the average man was now powerless to protect himself against all manner of threats to his welfare. Unlike traditional conservatism, however, their collectivism did not entail subordination of individual interests to the needs of the state. As the New Liberal L. T. Hobhouse wrote in 1911, social harmony was the end of progressive evolution, effected in a voluntarist manner through the growth of altruism and the sense of social responsibility; in an integrated society, "an individual right . . . cannot conflict with the common good" (Collini 1979:126). Functionalist anthropologists projected the social condition that New Liberals saw as the end-state of evolution onto the simple societies they studied. Just as centuries of British radicals had invoked the mythology of Anglo-Saxon England, they were describing a lost golden age of mankind.

Certainly, there were anthropologists whose work contravened prevailing trends. The most important was C. G. Seligman, who in the 1930s continued to equate race with culture, and military success with cultural superiority. His "Hamitic Hypothesis" explained evolution in Africa in diffusionist terms:

[T]he history of Africa South of the Sahara is no more than the story of the permeation through the ages, in different degrees and at various times, of the Negro and Bushman aborigines by Hamitic blood and culture. The Hamites were, in fact, the great civilising force of black Africa.

(Seligman 1930:18)

In the late 1930s, Malinowski's student Margaret Read adopted a similar approach in her analysis of the Ngoni: Their superior moral qualities had been tested and shaped through their conquest of inferior peoples; they became the hereditary rulers of the state they formed through combat (1936). Significantly, though, Read became an academic, but not an anthropologist, and her views were unpopular in anthropological circles. By the time of World War II, the anthropological community had rejected the argument that the origin of the state lay in the conquest of one ethnic group by another—the conventional wisdom of the era of World War I (Nadel 1940:193). Indeed, for a time British anthropologists did not entertain speculations about the origin of the state, perhaps out of reluctance to conclude that force was necessary to political organization.

The anthropologists of the 1920s and 1930s turned for preference to the study of simple, "acephalous" or stateless societies, glorifying their way of life by virtue of the analytical model they adopted. A number of factors conspired to direct anthropologists' attention to such societies. They were the ideal subjects for a group then anxious to distinguish itself from its amateur predecessors, for trained expertise was necessary to discern the routinized patterns of behavior that sustained order in the absence of centralized government. Furthermore, owing to the dynamics of colonial pacification and rule, acephalous societies were likely to be relatively remote from colonial authority, and hence still-unexplored subjects for anthropological research; centralized polities were more common in thoroughly pacified areas, partly because consolidation of tribal authority was one of the typical responses to foreign invasion and partly because colonial rulers encouraged political centralization (Kuklick 1978). But anthropologists' selection of research problems also represented normative judgment, for it entailed recognition of sources of social stability and personal satisfaction ignored by previous generations of anthropologists. And anthropologists' judgments fitted a conventional form; acephalous societies were portrayed after the fashion of the folk model of Anglo-Saxon democracy.

Fortes and Evans-Pritchard's *African Political Systems*, published in 1940, summarized the approach of this era in anthropology. It is generally agreed that this book heralded and inspired a generation of anthropologists (Middleton & Tait 1958:1–3; cf. Mair 1975:8–9, 14–15), but it also constituted the culmination of a previous trend; for post-World War I anthropologists, not merely those represented in this collection, typically portrayed the simplest societies as the realization of a cultural ideal. Only minimal differences of power and status existed in economically undeveloped societies, and social order was maintained through informal cooperation and consensus. In contrast, powerful states were socially stratified, and the hereditary aristocracies that ruled them maintained their authority through force. In such simple societies as that of the Andaman Islands described by Radcliffe-Brown, community leaders were selected on the basis of talent, not inherited status (1922:45). Persistent relationships between individuals and groups were conceptualized in inherently egalitarian terms, seen as resting on cooperation and reciprocal obligations. Variations in social structure such as the "dual organization" were assimilated to this model, and institutionalized practices were identified as the "realization of the mutual interdependence of the various parts of the society" (Firth 1936:57). Even those political structures resulting from invasion and subsequent domination of one group by another did not necessarily breach the norm of consensual government, for different peoples could be integrated as virtual equals in the same social system, and a government framework created by a conquering people as an instrument of subordination could become irrelevant in these terms (Evans-Pritchard 1940:125). Such a denial of the importance of force is wonderfully reminiscent of the "Whig" interpretation of the Norman Conquest.

Anthropologists could not deny the existence of centralized states or of aristocracies, but they emphasized those features of traditional centralized polities that made these societies essentially democratic. Even in a society pervaded by consciousness of class distinctions, dominated by an hereditary aristocracy, the exigencies of survival required the ruling class to grant some measure of authority to persons of talent and achievement, for the adaptive capacity of a people depended on its acceptance of meritocratic standards (Evans-Pritchard 1937:203, 343). These anthropologists postulated a relationship between a people and its environment that their predecessors did not grant axiomatically: if a culture had survived, this indicated that a people had satisfactorily adapted to its environment; that it had adapted to its environment indicated that a people necessarily accepted meritocratic standards to some degree. Even in centralized tribal societies, leadership was evaluated by performance standards, for the function of political leadership was instrumental, not merely symbolic. A ruler had effective contractual obligations to his subjects, and indigenous tribal constitutions incorporated checks on chiefly power. A chief who failed to meet his obligations would certainly cease to be an effective ruler and might well be deposed. Nevertheless, the ideal society was one without centralized political leadership, in which minimal distinctions of power and status obtained.

The Nuer and the British Folk-Political Tradition

To appreciate the degree to which this normative political theory was manifested in anthropological analysis, we can examine the diverse findings of students of the Nuer; the task of the historian of anthropological ideas would
be easier if other peoples had been studied over and over again, but unfortunately the range of materials available on the Nuer is unusual, if not unique,
in the anthropological literature. The standard work on the Nuer is, of course,
that done by Evans-Pritchard. To Evans-Pritchard, the sustained interest in
the Nuer was a "tribute to the Nuer themselves. Twenty years ago they were
not so highly regarded; but little by little we have learnt . . . that they are
a people whose values are worth handing down to posterity" (1954:v–vi). We
are not, then, doing Evans-Pritchard an injustice if we describe his landmark
study, *The Nuer* (1940), as a brief for the Nuer way of life. But others who
have studied this people have described them in different terms.

According to Evans-Pritchard, Nuer social organization embodies the form
known as "segmentary society"; it is made up of equivalent, autonomous units,
which are not joined in a centralized hierarchy but act together only in opposition to some common enemy. The largest stable unit, which Evans-
Pritchard rather confusingly calls the "tribe," does not include all people who
consider themselves Nuer and display the Nuer pastoral culture, but is the
largest group of distinct communities that "affirm their obligation to combine
in warfare against others and acknowledge the rights of their members to compensation for injury." The critical feature of Nuer political organization is its
relative character. Loyalties are determined in the mode that is common to
all Nuer culture: a political group "is a group only in relation to other groups";
the political system "is an equilibrium between opposed tendencies towards
fission and fusion, between the tendency of all groups to segment, and the
tendency of all groups to combine with segments of the same order" (1940:
5, 147–48). Social equilibrium is not sustained among the Nuer because of
the absence of conflict, but each source of tension tends to be balanced with
a countervailing power, so that paradoxically conflict becomes a force for social integration.

The Nuer make some status distinctions. Each tribe has a dominant clan,
and has incorporated captured Dinka, people from the ethnic group traditionally preyed upon by the Nuer, who constitute at least half of the population. But the social distance between the classes is slim. Relations between
the sexes are as egalitarian as anywhere; the dominant clan in each tribe may
be the "owners of the land" as the descendants of the original settlers of the
area, but they have "prestige rather than rank and influence rather than power";
the Dinka are incorporated as equals in Nuer society. The Nuer possess no

E. E. Evans-Pritchard with a group of Azande, ca. 1928 (courtesy of the Pitt Rivers Museum, University of Oxford).

tradition of strong leadership of any sort: prophets arose among them after the Arab and European invasions, but they were religious figures with limited political authority; the men known as "leopard-skin chiefs" are only "ritual experts," persons from the commoner class who mediate but cannot arbitrarily resolve disputes. Furthermore, "the ordered anarchy in which they live accords well with their character, for it is impossible to live among the Nuer and conceive of rulers ruling over them" (1940:174, 181, 215, passim).

Evans-Pritchard's portrait of the Nuer is different from others' in several ways: it minimizes the importance of status distinctions in their society; it eliminates strong leaders from their political life, even as occasional figures; it minimizes those features of their society that reflect their history as a people who have expanded their territory by preying upon others. Certainly, there are common elements in all descriptions of Nuer culture: their democratic values, and the absence of a centralized, coordinated political system at all times in their history. But other anthropologists have argued that the Nuer have a tradition of strong leadership, particularly evident in times of crisis, although the power of such figures rests on their ability to articulate the popular will, not on the authority embodied in inherited status or routinized in an office. And they have seen the "leopard-skin chief," a constant character in Nuer society, as having more power than Evans-Pritchard was willing to grant (Howell 1954:28–34; Huffman 1931; Seligman 1934:23–34). Indeed, these patterns may be elicited from Evans-Pritchard's own material, although he did not emphasize them (Gough 1971). In some part, we may see Evans-Pritchard's interpretations as strategic, designed to counter the view of the colonial officials of the Sudan Political Service; like other members of his professional generation, he was determined to prevent colonial rulers from subverting traditional institutions to serve their own ends (Powdermaker 1966:43). And like British colonial officials everywhere, those in the Sudan were eager to find in indigenous political institutions an orderly system of leadership which they could employ; thus they were critical of Evans-Pritchard's analysis because it denied them such useful agents (Howell 1954:28–29). But another disputed component of Evans-Pritchard's analysis serves no such immediate tactical purpose: his critics have argued that he saw the same egalitarian relations between social classes everywhere in Nuerland; whereas in the parts of Nuerland recently acquired through predatory expansion, the social distance between aristocrats and commoners, and between commoners and captured Dinka, was greater than elsewhere (Gough 1971:89–90).

One can appreciate these anthropologists' differences in the context of the folk tradition of British political thought, in which societal variation is conceptualized in terms of a limited range of possibilities. Political and social stratification systems are interdependent, and a democratic society is necessarily egalitarian and stable—because social control is maintained without force, disjunctive change is impossible. The ideal-typical alternative, the hierarchical political order effected through force, is fundamentally aristocratic rather than democratic. The pattern evidenced in recently acquired areas of Nuerland is consistent with this tradition, for it incorporates the elements that have been seen as essential features of aristocratic government: military pacification; exaggerated divisions between social classes; inherited, not achieved, characteristics as requisites for political leadership. Because Evans-Pritchard cast his description of Nuer society in the mold of the archetypal democratic polity, there was no place in his account for cultural materials that did not fit the mold.

The particular character of Evans-Pritchard's perspective is brought into bold relief when it is contrasted to the visions of anthropologists who work in other national traditions and bring different expectations to their analysis of the Nuer. Americans might find it particularly revealing that an American anthropologist, Marshall Sahlins, has described Nuer society as ideally structured to make it a "successful predatory organization in conflicts with other tribes"; unlike Evans-Pritchard, he has no difficulty reconciling the "militantly egalitarian" character of the Nuer with their insatiable appetite for territorial acquisition and subordination of other peoples—notably the Dinka (1961: 323, 335, 343). And a French anthropologist, Louis Dumont, has taken Evans-Pritchard to task, along with the others of his anthropological generation, for ignoring the social realities of "order, interdependence, subordination, and hierarchy," while projecting the virtues of liberal individualism onto the peoples they studied, seeing "everywhere individuals in the modern sense of the term, people imbued with the values of liberty and equality" (1975:338).

Evans-Pritchard's rendition of the relations between dominant Nuer and subordinate Dinka in the language of mutual consent and benefit might be interpreted as an implicit apology for British colonial power, cast in the conventional formula of "Whig" liberalism. Anthropologists, no more than other British liberals in this period, could not rationalize colonial rule as necessary to the improvement of subject peoples. But by denying that a conquered people could be compelled to follow an unwonted way of life through the use of force, they in effect denied the reality of colonial domination. If the consent of the governed was essential to the maintenance of authority, by definition colonized peoples had accepted only those British colonial directives they recognized as legitimate, practicing various forms of subterfuge in order to maintain cultural practices they cherished (cf. Mair 1952:1). But because Evans-Pritchard and his generation also idealized these stateless societies, their work may perhaps be better appreciated as a paean to the merits of egalitarian democracy than as an apology for colonialism.

Anthropology and Society in Modern Britain

How can we explain the three phases of anthropological development described here? We must point to both national trends and changing opinion within the scientific community. In the late nineteenth century, the political opinions expressed through anthropology reflected the increasing importance of meritocratic standards in the determination of social status in Britain. Certainly, the advantages of inherited status were not altogether eliminated, but in the 1850s, 1860s, and 1870s the liberal professions, the civil service, the universities, and the military were made more meritocratic (Perkin 1983; Reader 1966). The new scientific occupations, anthropology among them, seemed to exemplify the meritocratic ideal. As new professions, they represented relatively open avenues for upward mobility. And the very nature of scientific activity seemed to preclude undeserved reputation within the scientific community. Hence, the leading propagandists for public support of science conventionally argued that scientific progress could not be made in any aristocratic society, but must be accomplished by the "industrious classes," as did Lyon Playfair in the 1870s (Turner 1978). The scientific population as a whole, anthropologists among them, can be broadly characterized as proselytizing secularists of provincial dissenting origins (Cardwell 1957:6). Not surprisingly, then, anthropological writing represented a brief for the meritocratic values that had altered the fortunes of the middle classes, and especially the dissenters among them.

At the turn of the century, anthropological thought was affected by the shifting national mood—a product of a hardening of class lines and changes in Britain's world role. In the first half of the nineteenth century, Carlyle and Disraeli had described the widening gulf between rich and poor, but the gap was more pronounced by 1900. Upward mobility had become more difficult, as the consolidation of firms into companies created an economic climate too harsh for the self-made entrepreneur. Attendant on the reorganization of industry was the divorce of management from ownership and the growth of a rentier class. At the other end of the social scale was a growing underclass or "residuum," in large part composed of urban in-migrants from the impoverished countryside, whose numbers were increased by an intermittent stream of agricultural crises between 1873 and 1886. Political radicals and conservatives alike predicted the imminent outbreak of a "serious war of the classes." By the first decade of the twentieth century, the conflict between the classes had become intense: the self-conscious defense or privilege was exemplified in the behavior of the House of Lords, which provoked a constitutional crisis between 1909 and 1911 with its obstruction of the reform measures of the Liberal government. The belligerence of the working class was manifested in a series of major strikes between 1910 and 1912. As class lines hardened and class antagonism grew, anthropologists began to think of race as a fixed attribute and of the lower races as inferior beings incapable of spontaneous cultural advance (cf. Lorimer 1978; Wohl 1968).

Imperialist enthusiasm translated upper-class attitudes toward the lower orders into international terms, and was a response to an increasing awareness of Britain's decline as a world power. In the international context, the population of Britain was one race, competing with other races for world domination. All parties to World War I sounded this theme, of course, but it was heard with increasing frequency from the time of the ill-managed South African War (1899–1902). Imperialism was now defended both because it was a means for improving the British race through conflict and because it would bring the benefits of civilization to inferior races, who would not advance unless forced to do so by a superior race. This argument represented a dramatic change from the earlier brief for imperialism, premised on the assumption that while Britain might gain economically from an expanded empire the peoples she conquered would necessarily be exploited (Semmel 1960).

It is not surprising that anthropological opinion again changed after World War I, for to many observers it seemed that the war marked the collapse of the old social order. Certainly, many prewar trends were sustained after the war. Relations between the classes remained uneasy. The postwar economic collapse brought trade union militancy, culminating in the General Strike of 1926; the growth of class consciousness also contributed to the first Labour Party victory in a General Election in 1924; the conditions of the Depression were to exacerbate class strife. Britain continued to lose ground as a world economic power, and her imperial authority was challenged in Ireland, India, and, to a lesser extent, in the other colonial territories; throughout the empire, varying concessions were made to nationalist demands. Finally, Hitler's triumph in Germany portended international conflict. Anthropologists were not alone in seeing these developments as evidence that the technical achievements of Western civilization had brought Western man neither moral improvement nor happiness (cf. Wersky 1978). Anthropologists in particular felt that Nazi excesses illustrated the destructive potential of race theories, doing public penance for what they saw as the misuse of their work (Smith et al. 1935).

The point of this exercise is that anthropologists' responses to national developments were not random. At the begining and end of the period, their work could be construed as cultural criticism, while in the pre-World War I period it was a celebration of established order and national glory. But whether their politics were critical or celebratory, anthropologists' observations were refracted through cultural lenses. Thus the history of British anthropological thought demonstrates the extraordinary persistence of the folk tradition of

British political theory. This conclusion is in some sense ironic, for the demonstration of continuities in political argument impacted in British anthropology illustrates—as many typically ahistorical anthropological studies cannot—the value of the anthropological notion of culture.

References Cited

Anon. 1911. The ancient inhabitants of the Nile valley. Review of *The archaeological survey of Nubia, report for 1907–08. Nature* 85:310–12.

———. 1916. Untitled news report. *Nature* 98:134–35.

Beddoe, J. 1889. Observations on the natural colour of the skin in certain Oriental races. *J. Anth. Inst.* 18:257–63.

———. 1891. Anniversary address. *J. Anth. Inst.* 20:348–59.

———. 1905. Colour and race. *J. Roy. Anth. Inst.* 35:219–50.

Bock, K. 1978. Theories of progress, development, evolution. In *A history of sociological analysis*, ed. T. Bottomore & R. Nisbet, 39–79. New York.

Brabrook, E. W. 1898. Presidential address, Section H, Brit. Assn. Adv. Sci. *Nature* 58:527–32.

Briggs, A. 1966. *Saxons, Normans and Victorians*. Bexhill-on-Sea, Sussex.

Burrow, J. W. 1974. The "village community" and the uses of history in late nineteenth-century England. In *Historical perspectives*, ed. N. McKendrick. London.

———. 1981. *A liberal descent*. Cambridge.

Campbell, G. 1886. Presidential address, Section H, Brit. Assn. Adv. Sci. *Nature* 34: 454–57.

Cardwell, D. S. L. 1957. *The organisation of science in England*. London.

Clouston, T. A. 1894. The developmental aspects of criminal anthropology. *J. Anth. Inst.* 23:215–25.

Collini. S. 1979. *Liberalism and sociology*. London.

Conder, C. R. 1887. The present condition of the native tribes of Bechuanaland. *J. Anth. Inst.* 16:76–92.

Crooke, W. 1912. The scientific aspects of folklore. *Folk-Lore* 23:31.

Cunningham, D. J. 1902. Right-handedness and left-brainedness. *J. Anth. Inst.* 32: 273–96.

Dumont, L. 1975. Preface to the French edition of Evans-Pritchard's *The Nuer*. In *Studies in social anthropology*, ed. J. H. M. Beattie & R. G. Lienhardt, 328–44. Oxford.

Evans, A. J. 1896. The Eastern question in anthropology. *Nature* 54:527–35.

Evans-Pritchard, E. E. 1937. *Witchcraft, oracles and magic among the Azande*. London.

———. 1940. *The Nuer*. Oxford.

———. 1954. Foreword. In P. P. Howell, *A manual of Nuer law*, v–vi. London.

Firth, R. 1936. *We, the Tikopia*. Paperback ed. Boston (1963).

Flower, W. H. 1884. On the classification of the varieties of the human species. *J. Roy. Anth. Inst.* 14:378–95.

———. 1894. Presidential Address, Section H, Brit. Assn. Adv. Sci. *Nature* 50:388.

Fortes, M. 1945. *The dynamics of clanship among the Tallensi*. London.

Fortes, M., & E. E. Evans-Pritchard, eds. 1940. *African political systems.* London.

Franklin, J. H. 1978. *John Locke and the theory of sovereignty.* London.

Frazer, J. G. 1900. *The golden bough.* 2d ed. London.

———. 1908. *The scope of anthropology.* London.

Galton, F. 1885. Presidential address, Section H, Brit. Assn. Adv. Sci. *Nature* 32:507–10.

Gomme, G. L. 1887. On the evidence for Mr. McLennan's theory of the primitive human horde. *J. Anth. Inst.* 17:118–33.

———. 1909. Sociology, the basis of inquiry into primitive culture. *Soc. Rev.* 2:317–37.

Gough, K. 1971. Nuer kinship: A reexamination. In *The translation of culture,* ed. T. O. Beidelman, 79–112. London.

Haddon, A. C. 1889. The ethnography of the western tribes of the Torres Straits. *J. Anth. Inst.* 19:387.

———. 1900. The evolution of European peoples. *Nature* 62:27–28.

———. 1918. The ethnological value of shells. *Nature* 100:482.

———. 1920. Migrations of cultures in British New Guinea. *J. Roy. Anth. Inst.* 50: 237–80.

Hall, R. N. 1904. The great Zimbabwe. *J. Af. Soc.* 4:295–300.

Harley, G. 1887. Comparison between the recuperative bodily power of a man in a rude and in a highly civilized state; illustrative of the probable recuperative capacity of men of the stone age in Europe. *J. Anth. Inst.* 23:171.

Hill, C. 1958. *Puritanism and revolution.* New York.

Hocart, A. M. 1936. *Kings and councillors.* Reprint ed. Chicago (1970).

Hose, C. 1894. The natives of Borneo. *J. Anth. Inst.* 23:171.

Howell, P. P., ed. 1954. *A manual of Nuer law.* London.

Howitt, A. W. 1888. Further notes on the Australian class systems. *J. Anth. Inst.* 18: 31–70.

Huffman, R. 1931. *Nuer customs and folk-lore.* London.

Johnston, H. H. 1913. A survey of the ethnography of Africa. *J. Roy. Anth. Inst.* 43: 375–421.

Keith, A. 1912. Modern problems relating to the antiquity of man. *Nature* 90:268–71.

———. 1915. The Bronze Age invaders of Britain. *J. Roy. Anth. Inst.* 45:12–22.

———. 1916. On certain factors concerned in the evolution of human races. *J. Roy. Anth. Inst.* 46:33.

Kuklick, H. 1978. The sins of the fathers: British anthropology and African colonial administration. *Res. Soc. Knowl., Sci. Art.* 1:93–119.

Lang, A. 1905. The primitive and advanced in totemism. *J. Roy. Anth. Inst.* 35:315–36.

Lorimer, D. 1978. *Colour, class and the Victorians.* New York.

Mair, L. 1952. *Native administration in central Nyasaland.* London.

———. 1975. How far have we got in the study of politics? In *Studies in African social anthropology,* ed. M. Fortes & S. Patterson, 8–20. London.

Malinowski, B. 1924. New and old anthropology. *Nature* 113:299–301.

Mannheim, K. 1953. Conservative thought. In *From Karl Mannheim,* ed. Kurt Wolff. New York (1971).

Manuel, F. 1956. From equality to organicism. *J. Hist. Ideas* 17:54–69.

Marett, R. R. 1935. *Head, heart and hands in human evolution.* New York.

Middleton, J., & D. Tait, eds. 1958. *Tribes without rulers.* London.

Migeod, F. W. H. 1917. The racial elements concerned in the first siege of Troy. *Man* 17:45–46.

———. 1919. Some observations on the physical characters of the Mende nation. *J. Roy. Anth. Inst.* 49:265–70.

Myres, J. L. 1909. The influence of anthropology on the course of political science. *Nature* 81:379–84.

Nadel, S. F. 1940. The Kede. In *African political systems,* ed. M. Fortes & E. E. Evans-Pritchard, 165–95. London.

Naville, E. 1907. The origin of Egyptian civilisation. *J. Roy. Anth. Inst.* 37:201–14.

Parsons, F. G. 1919. Anthropological observations on German prisoners of war. *J. Roy. Anth. Inst.* 49:20–35.

Peake, H. 1917. The racial elements concerned in the first siege of Troy. *Man* 17:80.

Pearson, K. 1903. On the inheritance of the mental and moral characteristics in man, and its comparison with the inheritance of the physical characters. *J. Anth. Inst.* 33:179–207.

Peel, J. D. Y. 1971. *Herbert Spencer: The evolution of a sociologist.* London.

Perkin, H. 1983. The pattern of social transformation in England. In *The transformation of higher learning, 1860–1930,* ed. K. H. Jarausch, 207–18. Chicago.

Perry, W. J. 1923. *The children of the sun.* London.

Petrie, W. M. F. 1906. Migrations. *J. Roy. Anth. Inst.* 36:189–232.

Pitt-Rivers, G. 1888. Presidential address, Section H, Brit. Assn. Adv. Sci. *Nature* 38:516–18.

Powdermaker, H. 1966. *Stranger and friend.* New York.

Radcliffe-Brown, A. R. 1922. *The Andaman islanders.* Cambridge.

Raglan, Lord. 1956. The class society, *J. Roy. Anth. Inst.* 86:2–3.

Read, M. 1936. Tradition and prestige among the Ngoni. *Africa* 9:453–83.

Reader, W. J. 1966. *Professional men.* London.

Rhŷs, J. 1900. Presidential address, Section H, Brit. Assn. Adv. Sci. *Nature* 62:519.

Ridgeway, W. 1908. The application of zoological laws to man. *Nature* 78:525.

———. 1910. The influence of the environment on man. *J. Roy. Anth. Inst.* 40:10–22.

Rivers, W. H. R. 1913. Report on anthropological research outside America. In *Reports upon the present condition and future needs of the science of anthropology,* ed. W. H. R. Rivers et al. Washington.

———. 1914. *The history of Melanesian society.* 2 vols. Cambridge.

———. 1922. The unity of anthropology. *Nature* 109:323–24.

Roth, H. L. 1892. On the signification of couvade. *J. Anth. Inst.* 22:204–6.

Sahlins, M. 1961. The segmentary lineage: An organization of predatory expansion. *Am. Anth.* 63:323–43.

Seligman, C. G. 1924. Anthropology and psychology: A study of some points of contact. *J. Roy. Anth. Inst.* 54:13–46.

———. 1930. *Races of Africa.* Reprint ed. London (1939).

———. 1934. *Egypt and Negro Africa.* London.

Seligman, C. G., & B. Z. Seligman. 1930. Note on the history and present condition of the Beni Amer (southern Beja). *Sudan Notes and Records* 8:83–97.

Semmel, B. 1960. *Imperialism and social reform*. London.

Skinner, Q. 1965. History and ideology in the English revolution. *His. J.* 8:155.

Smith, G. E. 1915. The influence of racial admixture in Egypt. *Eugenics Rev.* 7:163–83.

———. 1929. *Human history*. New York.

Smith, G. E., et al. 1935. *Race and culture*. London.

Thomas, N. W. 1906. *Kinship organization and group marriage in Australia*. Cambridge.

Torday, E., & T. A. Joyce. 1906. Notes on the ethnography of the Ba-Yaka. *J. Roy. Anth. Inst.* 36:39–59.

Turner, F. M. 1978. The Victorian conflict between science and religion: A professional dimension. *Isis* 69:356–76.

Turner, W. 1889. Presidential address, Section H, Brit. Assn. Adv. Sci. *Nature* 40:526–33.

Tylor, E. B. 1888. On a method of investigating the development of institutions applied to laws of marriage and descent. *J. Anth. Inst.* 18:267.

Venn, J. 1888. Cambridge anthropometry. *J. Anth. Inst.* 18:140–54.

Werner, A. 1911. The Akikuyu. *J. Af. Soc.* 10:447–58.

Wersky, G. 1978. *The visible college*. New York.

Westermarck, E. A. 1891. *The history of human marriage*. London (1894).

Wohl, A. S. 1968. The bitter cry of outcast London. *Int. Rev. Soc. Hist.* 13:189–245.

ENGLISHMEN, CELTS, AND IBERIANS

The Ethnographic Survey of the United Kingdom, 1892–1899

JAMES URRY

Popular Racial History and "Scientific" Race

Every educated Victorian knew in outline the "racial" history of the British nation. The ancient Britons encountered by the Romans were of unknown ancestry; the Britons had been invaded by Anglo-Saxons, who created the English nation; the Normans had then seized the country and ruled the Saxons rather than replaced them. Most Englishmen saw themselves as descended from Anglo-Saxons. The English language was Anglo-Saxon; and, more important, their culture, political institutions, and common law were Saxon in origin. In popular tradition, dating back many centuries, Saxon virtues had triumped over an alien Norman yoke (Hill 1954). Victorian historians, particularly those of Whiggish persuasion, gave a degree of scholarly legitimacy to the notion that English history was a triumph of Saxon values, a victory of superior racial character (Briggs 1966; Blaas 1978; Burrow 1981). Discussing in 1885 the influence of the Saxons on British character, Palmer argued that their "mental activity, acting on the contemplative Britons, brought about that combination of thought and action which has made the England of today, and from which has been evolved that comprehensive English intellect of which Shakespeare is the type" (1885:192).

As invaders from Germany, Anglo-Saxons were of Teutonic ancestry, and

James Urry is Lecturer in Anthropology at the Victoria University of Wellington, New Zealand. He has published a number of papers on the history of British anthropology and on aspects of Australian Aboriginal history, and is currently writing an account of the transformation of Mennonite life in Russia in the nineteenth century.

in mid-Victorian England "Teutomania" had important political implications both abroad and at home. By tracing their origins to Germany, Englishmen denied their links with the French, who were considered Celtic in origin, overlaid with Latin culture. Before its reunification in the last quarter of the century, when it began to pose a threat to British industrial and colonial ambitions, Germany was seen as a friendly group of states; in contrast, France had been Britain's enemy for centuries. Teutonic ancestry also allowed Englishmen to deny links with the Celtic peoples, who had retreated to the fringes of Britain after the Saxon invasion. In the nineteenth century English prejudice against the Irish Celts was based increasingly on appeals to racial and evolutionary criteria (Curtis 1968, 1971). But while opposition to the Irish intensified during the century, after 1870 new views of the Celts tempered such racial prejudice. A general revival of interest in Celtic culture, particularly of the Scots and Welsh, was supported by some Englishmen who objected to Teutomania and extreme Anglo-Saxonism (Arnold 1867; Allen 1880; cf. Faverty 1951). In the arguments which followed, more "scientific" evidence was marshalled to support opposing opinions.

By the 1870s, the problem of racial history was the subject of several modes of scholarly inquiry that had already achieved a degree of institutionalization (Bolt 1971; Stepan 1982). The results of these inquiries—some of which gave support to the Celtic cause—greatly complicated the popular racial history. Prominent among these studies was philology, which played a crucial role in "ethnological" speculation from the 1830s onwards, when it had been demonstrated that Celtic languages, like the Germanic, were Indo-European, or "Aryan" languages, as they were more commonly termed. Since these were thought to have been spread by the migration of a distinctive "Aryan" race, the Celts and Germans thus shared both a common racial and linguistic inheritance. By 1860, however, the philological dominance of "ethnology" was passing (cf. Stocking 1971, 1973), and the study of British racial history was strongly influenced by archeology, physical anthropology, and folklore.

Although as late as the 1890s many Victorian historians thought British history began shortly before Caesar's invasion (e.g., Church 1889), by 1870 a much greater antiquity had been established (Gruber 1965). In reconstructing its history, archeologists continued to think in terms of a succession of racial migrations by tribes with distinctive languages, customs, and physical features. What one writer has called an "invasion neurosis" became established among British antiquarians and historians (Clark 1966:172): successive waves of Celtic speaking peoples had pushed aside populations of more ancient lineage, who spoke non-Aryan languages and differed in physical form. Although the only non-Aryan language that had survived in Europe from this era was Basque, Thomas Huxley argued in 1871 that indications of an earlier race could be seen in the features of contemporary populations living in isolated areas, especially in western Britain (Huxley 1871).

The archeological study of British antiquity depended heavily on the Scandinavian "three-age" system for the classification of artifacts into "stone," "bronze," and "iron" stages, which were linked to successive racial invasions (Daniel 1975). In 1880 Boyd Dawkins proposed a set of British sequences. The earliest inhabitants were River Drift People with rough, crude artifacts and low, uncivilized manners. They were replaced by Cave-men (ancestors of contemporary Eskimos), who in turn were forced northwards by the invasion of a neolithic "Iberian race"—dark, long-headed, small in stature, possessing agriculture, and speaking a non-Aryan language. The Iberians were displaced by a new invasion of Celts—tall and round-headed, with light-colored hair and blue eyes, and using bronze implements—who were followed by Neo-Celts possessing iron. Thus when the Romans first invaded Britain they encountered three populations: Iberians, Celts, and Scottish Caledonians—the descendants of tall, red-headed Teutonic northern invaders (1880:487).

Among the data incorporated into Dawkins' synthesis were those of an emerging "physical anthropology" based on both the study of skeletal material from archeological sites and the detailed investigation of the contemporary British population. The study of skeletal remains, particularly the skull, played a crucial role in most nineteenth-century racial classifications (Jorion 1982). In Britain, the work of J. Barnard Davis and John Thurnham (1865) and later of Greenwell and Rolleston (1877) related skeletal remains to successive racial changes in the population. Long barrows contained burials of long-headed people with polished stone tools; round barrows contained round-headed people with bronze tools. The study of variation in contemporary populations provided complementary evidence to that provided by prehistoric remains. Early work in this field, based on obvious external features, produced a host of wild hypotheses on differences in character, mental ability, and cultural habit, often in derogatory terms—as many of the papers published by the Anthropological Society of London during the 1860s testify (e.g., Mackintosh 1866). But there were also more rigorous scholars, including particularly John Beddoe and Francis Galton.

Beddoe, a Bristol doctor, was a versatile scholar who produced a number of papers on human physical variation and a major synthesis of *The Races of Britain* in 1885 (cf. Beddoe 1910). Although Beddoe utilized the findings of anthropometry, prehistoric and recent skeletal remains, surnames, and sundry other evidence, such as historical accounts, folklore, and antiquities, he relied heavily on data he collected himself on variations in eye and hair color. He also utilized entries in *Hue and Cry*, a listing of military deserters that recorded the physical features of absconders, as well as data collected between 1875 and 1883 by the Anthropometric Committee of the British Association (BAAS 1883:253–356). Presented in detailed tables and distribution maps, Beddoe's findings seemed to confirm many speculations derived from other studies; but he could also identify finer variations, including the racial contributions of more recent invasions of Normans and Norsemen, as well as the settlement of later European migrants as refugees or specialized workers.

Galton, whose polymathic evolutionary interests included various aspects of anthropology, was another pioneer of large-scale anthropometric research in Britain. He played an important role in developing his own forms of measurement and statistical techniques to analyze material, and in the aftermath of the British Association Committee's survey, founded his own anthropometric laboratory in London in 1884 (Galton 1891; Forrest 1974:181–82). Although his interest in anthropometry was only partially concerned with identifying racial types, his methods and materials were used by others to this end.

In addition to philology, archeology, and physical anthropology—all of which in 1871 were included among the diverse interests of the Anthropological Institute (cf. Stocking 1971)—the study of folklore also contributed data for debates on racial history. Under the auspices of the Folk-Lore Society, founded in 1878, folklore moved from being a minor antiquarian concern to a subject of major importance in the study of man (Dorson 1968). Oral traditions became as significant as physical antiquities in the study of the past, and the "science of folk-lore" was considered by some as important as physical anthropology (Hartland 1891). Along with certain racial features, old ideas and customs, "arrested" during the development of culture, had survived in remote areas. Folklorists argued that if "incoming civilisations flowing over lower levels of culture in any given area have been many, there will be as many stages of arrestment in the folklore of that area, and in so far as each incoming civilisation represents an ethnic distinction, the different stages of survival in folklore would also represent an ethnic distinction" (Gomme 1892:12).

Nowhere could folklore be put to better use than in the areas of the Celtic fringe, where isolated populations maintained their oral traditions. In the early 1890s the eminent Welsh philologist and folklorist John Rhŷs (Parry-Williams 1954) gave influential lectures on early British ethnology, in which he argued that there were traces of three ancient populations in Britain: a non-Aryan neolithic people he called Ibero-Pictish, and two Celtic groups, the Goidels of the Bronze Age migrations and the Brythons of the Iron age (Rhŷs 1890, 1891a, 1891b, 1892; cf. Daniel 1954). The Goidels, who retained their guttural speech, were to become the Irish and Gaels, whereas the Brythons were the ancestors of the mellifluous Welsh. Folklore, as well as language, supported Rhŷs' argument: stories of fairies documented the existence of earlier races and their struggle with invading peoples (cf. Haddon as quoted in Rhŷs 1901:684n; Haddon 1898a:xxix).

Thus in the latter half of the nineteenth century, both popular tradition and "scientific" speculation had established a general outline of the racial history of Britain. Older ethnological concepts had been combined with later evolutionary ideas; the study of antiquities, physical anthropology, and folk-lore all contributed to the picture. But research was uneven and uncoordinated, and an overall synthesis of the accumulated material was lacking. During the late 1880s and early 1890s a number of these societies encouraged new research programs. Stimulated by the passing of the Ancient Monuments Protection Act in 1882, the Society of Antiquaries became involved in recording, county by county, sites scheduled under the act (Evans 1956:332–33). The Anthropological Institute underwent a renaissance; as president between 1886 and 1889, Galton encouraged research particularly in physical anthropology (Pearson 1924:334–96). A new edition of the Institute's research guide, *Notes and Queries on Anthropology*, was produced in 1892 (Urry 1972). The Folk-Lore Society also published a research guide (Gomme 1890), and members stressed the need to collect new material (Burne 1890). Recognizing that his own survey was provisional, Beddoe ended his major book with an open appeal for a new synthesis. The racial history of Britain would be "solved only by patient labour and by the co-operation of anthropologists with antiquarians and philologists; so that so much of the blurred and defaced inscription as is left in shadow by one light may be brought into prominence and illumination by another" (Beddoe 1885:299).

Haddon and the Genesis of the Ethnographic Survey

Early in 1892 representatives of the Anthropological Institute, the Society of Antiquaries, and Folk-Lore Society met in London "to discuss the possibility of making an ethnographic survey of the British Isles, and of ascertaining the anthropometric, archaeological, and customary traces of the various races that have inhabited these isles" (Folk-Lore 1892:270). They were responding to a suggestion (Brabrook 1893:262n, 1896:227) made by A. C. Haddon, then Professor of Zoology at the Royal College of Science in Dublin, who had become attracted to anthropology while researching zoology in the Torres Strait in 1888, and had joined the Anthropological Institute and Folk-Lore Society shortly after his return. Although Haddon subsequently abandoned zoology for ethnology, in 1892 he was still gaining a knowledge of anthropology (Quiggin 1942; Urry 1982). Trained in the new school of physiology in Cambridge (Geison 1978), he had maintained his links, and in 1892 moved back there to lecture on physical anthropology in the Department of Anatomy under Professor Alexander Macalister, who was himself to become president of the Anthropological Institute. Haddon soon acquired proficiency in contemporary physical anthropological methods, including the study of hair and eye color—an interest he derived from Beddoe's work. He particularly admired the French anthropologists Paul Topinard and René Collignon, who with others had made regional surveys of the French population (Haddon 1898a, 1898c), and may well have conceived the idea of a British survey from their example.

Despite his move to Cambridge, Haddon maintained his post in Dublin, and he soon took up anthropological research in Ireland. In 1891 he opened an Anthropometric Laboratory with D. J. Cunningham, Professor of Anatomy at Trinity College, and his assistant, Dr. R. Browne. Modelled on Galton's in London, the Dublin laboratory aimed to help "unravel the tangled skein of the so-called 'Irish Race'" (Cunningham & Haddon 1891:36). During long vacations the investigators travelled to remoter regions, including Aran Island, where in addition to making physical anthropological observations they studied "anthropography" (language, health, psychology, land holding, etc.), as well as folklore and the island's antiquities (Haddon & Brown 1893). Further regional investigations provided models for the type of work Haddon hoped a larger survey in mainland Britain could pursue (Haddon 1898a: 436–37).

The work on Aran reflected Haddon's broad vision of anthropology. Despite his natural scientific background, Haddon did not restrict himself to physical anthropology. For him, as for the Anthropological Institute, anthropology aimed at a "complete History of man" (Haddon 1890:638), and this involved the synthesis of physical anthropology, the study of customs, language, and antiquities to construct a total ethnographic account of a people or area. In Ireland Haddon studied ancient Irish crania (Haddon 1893a, 1894, 1898b), encouraged the collection of folklore (Haddon 1893b), and investigated the development of Irish carts (Haddon 1898a:chaps. 6–7). All of these different kinds of information assisted "ethnological" analysis, which included the reconstruction of racial history. It was an holistic vision of anthropology that continued the older tradition of ethnology in Britain, but utilized new methods and new ideas to analyze the material.

Instructions for a Delegated Ethnography

Although the three societies involved in the initial discussion for the establishment of an ethnographic survey were active in promoting research, they lacked the organizational abilities, funds, and personnel actually to conduct a survey. Therefore, after agreeing to support the survey, they turned for assistance to the British Association for the Advancement of Science. From the time of its founding in 1831, its peripatetic meetings were the major forum of scientific debate and the formulation and funding of research projects (Morrell & Thackray 1981; Howarth 1922). After a somewhat checkered history, anthropology was established in 1884 as Section H within the Association's hierarchy of sections that met annually to listen to papers and to appoint committees to investigate important issues; and by 1892 Section H had already established a number of research committees.

The idea that the Association support an Ethnographic Survey of the United Kingdom was proposed at the Liverpool meeting that year by E. W. Brabrook, a lawyer and a member of all three societies. Following a two-tiered research strategy deeply engrained in nineteenth-century British science, Brabrook suggested that the basic research should be carried out by members of the corresponding societies of the Association and that experts be appointed by learned societies to collate the findings (Brabrook 1893). Throughout this period local scientific societies had enabled members of the newly emergent middle classes, especially in northern industrial areas, to carry out local research, particularly in natural history. From 1885 on, members of corresponding societies met at the Association to discuss work, and to receive proposals from various sections for help in scientific investigations within their local areas (Macleod, Friday, & Gregor 1975). Noting that local societies had already assisted in valuable anthropological research, Brabrook felt that if suitably encouraged they could prove invaluable in gathering information for the Survey.

Brabrook's proposal was impelled by the characteristic sense of urgency motivating much of nineteenth-century ethnography, which placed great emphasis on collecting "facts" (Gruber 1970). Echoing Beddoe, Brabrook noted that isolated populations and ancient customs were fast being eroded by the spread of industrial society: "The centripetal forces, which impel the country folk towards our great towns, and the rapid means of transit from place to place, of which even the poorest are constantly availing themselves, are fast effacing all special local peculiarities and inextricably mixing the races of which our population is composed" (1893:274). Late-Victorian Britons were keenly aware of the changes industrialization had wrought at home and abroad during their own lifetime. Haddon, addressing members of the corresponding societies, compared the vanishing of cultures in Britain with the demise of Pacific Island cultures (BAAS 1897:33; cf. Haddon 1897a).

The Association agreed to organize the Survey and appointed a Committee to oversee the work, with Galton as chairman, although the initial work was arranged by Brabrook as secretary. Succeeding Galton as chairman in 1894, Brabrook held the position until the end of the Survey, assisted as secretary by E. S. Hartland, a solicitor and noted folklorist from Gloucester. Because folklore, linguistics, and the study of antiquities were considered somewhat peripheral to scientific endeavour in this period, a number of non-Association members had to be co-opted onto the Committee (BAAS 1893: 621), and two subcommittees were established to deal with the crucial Celtic fringe. The Irish Committee consisted of members of the Dublin Anthropometric Laboratory; the Welsh Committee included Rhŷs, Archdeacon David Thomas of Montgomery, historian and antiquary, as well as representatives of the Cambrian Archaeological Association, the foremost Welsh scientific society. Two other societies were invited to join the Committee: the Royal Statistical Society, of which Galton and Brabrook were active members, and the English Dialect Society, which was very active in the 1880s and 1890s collecting material on regional dialects, culminating in the publication of Joseph Wright's massive *English Dialect Dictionary* (Brook 1963:152–56).

With Haddon's initial suggestion thus broadened to include language, the Committee defined five headings under which research was to be carried out: physical types of the inhabitants; currents traditions and beliefs; peculiarities of dialect; monuments and other remains of ancient culture; and historical evidence as to continuity of race (BAAS 1893:621, 1895:509). The headings appear to reflect the relative importance of the types of evidence deemed necessary to produce an ethnographic account at this time. Physical anthropology and the study of customs, including folklore, had pride of place; philology, a key subject in earlier ethnological speculations as to race, was now reduced to third. Furthermore, the study of contemporary populations was now of primary ethnographic importance, with historical material secondary and merely supportive. In the historical sections researchers were encouraged to assist the workers in other fields by collecting evidence of changes in racial type, ancient settlements, signs of invasions, and new migrations (BAAS 1893:652). But contemporary evidence was seen as more comparable, and the first task of the Survey was to collect the surviving features of earlier races before they vanished.

While the Committee was to coordinate research, the actual investigation was to be carried out by amateurs, either members of local societies or interested individuals. General appeals for help were published in newspapers and journals (BAAS 1893:621–22), with no qualifications or skills required; people were simply asked to express interest and to suggest places worthy of investigation. The Committee had decided to concentrate on "typical" communities, rather in the manner of Haddon and Browne's Irish studies, and to synthesize these into a general ethnographic account of Britain. People were therefore requested to suggest communities containing not less than one hundred adults whose "forefathers have lived there so far back as can be traced, and of whom the desired physical measurements, with photographs, might be obtained" (BAAS 1893:621).

Amateur investigators of course required detailed instructions. Experts were appointed to "digest" the information they hoped would flow from investigators, and these same experts drew up the instructions under each of the subject headings. Haddon and R. Garson, a medical man with an interest in physical anthropology, were to deal with the physical evidence; Rhŷs and representatives of the Folk-Lore Society, the folklore; W. Skeat, founder of the Dialect Society and expert on Anglo-Saxon linguistics, the dialect material; H. S. Milman and George Payne, as representatives of the Society of Antiquaries, the archeological and antiquarian information; and Brabrook, the historical evidence. A general schedule to aid research was issued with the *Reports* of the Committee and published separately for distribution to individuals and societies (BAAS 1895:509). The instructions were written in the format of other contemporary questionnaires and research aids, and indeed often reproduced sections of these works (Urry 1972).

The most technical section of the schedule was the physical anthropological. Galton provided photographic advice, particularly concerning portraiture (BAAS 1893:642–43). Since the late 1870s he had been experimenting with photography in his research into physical anthropology, including the construction of composite photographs to establish racial or criminal "types" from a number of specific individuals (Galton 1878; Forrest 1974:138–41), and he hoped the Survey would use his rather complex methods to good effect. The equally complex instructions concerning physical features derived from recent laboratory research in London, Dublin, and Cambridge, and required the use of measuring equipment and a detailed knowledge of anatomy. Although the instructions on recording hair and eye color, based on Beddoe's schema, were easier to follow, it soon became evident that the instructions were too complex for most untrained investigators, and the following year Haddon provided simplified instructions with an additional section on nose shape derived from Topinard (BAAS 1894:426–29; Topinard 1885).

The folklore instructions consisted of a series of questions taken from Gomme's *Handbook of Folklore* (1890) dealing with beliefs in natural features, local customs associated with technology, ceremonies, life-crisis rituals, and children's games. Each question was numbered according to the *Handbook's* notation to allow easy synthesis with material from the Folk-Lore Society's wider survey of British folklore. The instructions regarding ancient monuments provided guidance on how to map and record remains by measurements, drawings, and photography. This section, along with that concerned with historical evidence "as to the Continuity of Race" was very brief (BAAS 1893: 652–53). The section on dialects was both short and complex, and no attempt was made to conceal the difficulty of collecting useful information. Prospective researchers were advised to use the phonetical transcription system in Sweet's *Primer of Phonetics* (1890), to follow Wright's *Dialect of Windhill* (1892) for layout, and to consult Skeat's writings in etymological matters. They were warned that if unable "to record sounds according to the above scheme," they had better "make *no return at all,*" since incorrect returns were "misleading in the highest degree," especially if recorded in the "ordinary spelling of literary English" (BAAS 1893:651).

Although the final schedule must have appeared an austere and forbidding document to amateur researchers, the Committee encouraged local societies to reproduce the instructions in their journals. When the Bristol and Gloucestershire Archaeological Society published the schedule in its *Transactions* in 1895, Hartland contributed an introduction outlining the significance of the Surveys, which the Committee then published with the 1895 Survey Report (Hartland 1895). The following year another account by Gomme (1896), on the value of folklore for ethnological study, was also published. These general accounts, which helped to place the work of the Survey in context, were undoubtedly intended to encourage and sustain interest in the project.

The Fate of the Survey at the Local Level

The response to the initial appeal for suitable places to study was encouraging; by the time the Committee issued its first report in 1893; 264 places had been suggested, and the number rose to 367 the following year (BAAS 1894: 423). While most were contributed by representatives of local societies, private individuals also responded, including a number of clergymen extolling the virtues of their parishes.

The initial instructions as to the selection of places had been extremely vague, and this was reflected in the justifications accompanying each proposed place. It was often stated that a place was distant from "civilisation," or that its inhabitants were "untravelled," or "suspicious of outsiders," or "conservative," or "behind the times," or had been "stationary for generations." Village or local endogamy was also cited, sometimes along with physical anomalies: thus the inhabitants of Sheringham in Norfolk were noted both for "their small feet" and for village endogamy (BAAS 1893:628). Peculiar local customs, beliefs, or dialects attracted attention: Beddoe, who made a number of suggestions based on his considerable experience, suggested the Cheshire village of Flash because it was "formerly the haunt of thieves and gipsies," and because "Flash" language was said to have been coined there (BAAS 1893:626). In contrast to those who stressed the oddness of the local people, others, perhaps more in the spirit of the aims of the Survey, suggested places because their people were "representative" of a region or possessed "good specimens" of the local population. Thus Thomas Huxley recalled that when he had been a Sea Fishery Commissioner he had been "very much struck by the uniformity of type" in the inhabitants of certain Norfolk fishing villages. (BAAS 1893: 628). Other reasons also fitted the spirit of the Committee's intentions: certain villages were recommended for their proximity to ancient monuments; others, because their possession of historical records such as parish registers suggested a long period of continuity of population.

Just as the reasons for inclusion varied, so the geographical distribution of places was uneven. Northern and western England was well represented, particularly those northern areas claiming Norse association, but locations in southeastern England and the Home Counties were barely mentioned at all. Only one Sussex village was included, and that by Beddoe, who also suggested another be selected "near the centre of the Weald" (BAAS 1893:637). None was listed for Kent, Surrey, Berkshire, Oxfordshire, or Buckinghamshire. This lack of interest in the eastern and southern counties was partially a reflection of the fact that their racial history was assumed to be well-known and partially a belief that the people had been transformed by recent events. The Celtic populations of the north and west, with their greater variety due to invasion and isolation, were of greater interest. The first listing of places included seventy Welsh locations, and fourteen more were added the following year. Furthermore, many places in the English border region were selected for their "mixed" populations. If the thirty-five Cornish locations and all the Scottish Gaelic areas are included in the total, well over fifty percent of the 1893 list had Celtic affiliations—and this figure does not include the 250 locations identified, but not listed in detail, by the Irish Sub-Committee (BAAS 1893:641).

The Cornish sample was discussed in detail, and the reasons for selection reflect many Victorian preconceptions concerning the Celts. Local traditions of giants, when associated with the discovery of abnormally large skeletons in churches, were obvious signs of an earlier race. The Meneage, a group of villages in the Lizard Peninsula, contained an isolated population whose Rifle Corps, "when standing shoulder to shoulder," occupied more space than an equal number of men in any other British corps. (BAAS 1893:636). Among features requiring investigation were the survival of witchcraft accusations, the use of the dowsing rod, and the presence of strange dialects. Cornish character was described as "characteristically Celtic: they are not very 'straight,' and are exceedingly suspicious; they fall out easily among themselves, but do not make up again easily; feuds go on from year to year, and last out lifetimes" (BAAS 1893:636). Though the people had been "greatly modified" by Methodism, the account concluded that "the Cornish Celt is prolific and exceedingly prone to sexual irregularity" (BAAS 1893:636).

Brabrook appears to have accepted all the places suggested without critical assessment; he merely organized the suggestions under county headings and hoped that people would collect information once they received their instructions. A number of local societies formed subcommittees to encourage and direct local research. The local societies involved were extremely varied; they included naturalist clubs, as well as archeological and philosophical societies in both urban and rural areas (BAAS 1894:24, 40, 423–24; 1895:50–51, 510; 1896:608; 1897:454. Because the Survey *Reports* provide few details, their achievement is difficult to assess; but information was certainly collected, some of which was published in local journals.

In East Anglia, where Mrs. Nina Layard, a pioneer in local archeology, formed a subcommittee in Ipswich to record archeological sites, measure people, and record local dialects and folklore, material was collected and the fact recorded (BAAS 1894:423; 1895:510; 1897:453), but the Survey Committee did not publish the findings. Haddon, along with Macalister and his assistant, W. L. H. Duckworth, formed a subcommittee for the "Ethnographic Survey of East Anglia" under the auspices of the Royal Society (BAAS 1895: 510), and Cambridge graduates were taught how to make physical anthropological observations. Although most of the material collected was of this kind, Haddon and his family also collected accounts of folklore and children's games in Cambridgeshire and elsewhere in Britain (Haddon 1898a; Gomme 1894). Haddon and his students also studied the village of Barley in Hertfordshire after the local rector had drawn attention to its peculiarities (BAAS 1895:510; Haddon 1897b).

In Pembrokeshire, Edward Laws and Henry Owen, under the auspices of the Cambrian Archaeological Association, conducted research that resulted in the preparation of a bibliography on the county, and volunteers recorded archeological and historical material on Ordinance Survey maps. The editor of a local newspaper also ran a column to collect details of the region's customs and folklore (Laws 1896).

Scotland was an area of intense activity. In 1897 the Committee appointed the Reverend Walter Gregor to conduct a survey of Galloway "with the view to ascertaining the special divergences in dialect, the prehistoric monuments, the old cultivation sites, the folklore, the physical types of the people, and objects of obsolete culture in domestic and agricultural occupation" (BAAS 1895:511). Gregor, a noted folklorist, had published a number of books and articles on Scottish folklore, and was highly regarded by the Folk-Lore Society. Although he included a few physical anthropological measurements, the bulk of his report was concerned with folklore and magical cures, doubtless to the consternation of many Association members, accustomed as they were to accounts of oceanography, chemistry, geology, and zoology rather than the superstitions of Gaelic Highlanders (Gregor 1896). The Committee, however, admired Gregor's work and urged him to commence a similar survey of Ayreshire (BAAS 1896:607)—which after his death was carried on somewhat less diligently by the Reverend H. B. H. Reid (BAAS 1898:713).

In 1895 Macalister gave a series of anthropology lectures at Aberdeen that aroused considerable local interest (BAAS 1897:503), and the Buchan Field Club undertook to survey the local population (BAAS 1896:608). The club was more interested in physical anthropology than in folklore or antiquities, and work began at the annual Mintlaw Gathering, where the local population assembled for dancing and sport. The research strategy was ingenious:

The plan of operations decided upon, was to note the colour of the hair and eyes, and the shape of the nose of all persons as they entered the grounds. A tent was also erected in the grounds where measurements were made of all persons who chose to come. At the gate an enclosure was erected for the accommodation of the Club. It was divided into four compartments, within which were stationed eight members of the Club, two in each compartment, an observer and a recorder. The observers noted the colour of the hair and eyes, and the shape of the nose of adults as they purchased tickets at the entrance and passed the divisions between the compartments. At the gate, 2,309 males and 551 females were observed. In the tent 169 male adults were measured and noted as to pigmentation, etc.

(Gray & Tocher 1900:104; cf. BAAS 1896:41; Gray & Tocher 1895)

The work at Mintlaw was repeated by John Gray and James Tocher at other gatherings (Gray & Tocher 1899) and among local school children; by 1897 statistics on 14,561 children had been collected (Tocher 1897, Gray & Tocher 1900:105). The work of the Buchan Club, however, was apparently the only large-scale survey carried out by a local society, and the final report was published by the Anthropological Institute—although only after the Survey had been abandoned.

In Ireland the subcommittee continued the work of the Anthropometric Laboratory, and Browne published a number of regional studies. Another branch was established under the auspices of the Belfast Naturalists' Field Club (BAAS 1894:430–31). Haddon, who lectured in Belfast, carried out anthropometric work there in 1894 (BAAS 1897:503), but most of the material collected by the local society consisted of folklore.

In spite of this effort by a few local societies, when the Committee reviewed the progress of the Survey in 1897, the results proved, as Haddon said, "meagre" (BAAS 1897:453; Haddon 1898c:3). Members of the Committee had made strenuous efforts to enlist the support of local societies, interested groups, and individuals, but with little success. Brabrook addressed the Royal Archaeological Institute on the relevance of the Survey for the history of Kent (Brabrook 1896), learned institutions carried regular reports on the aims of the Survey, and the Survey's work was discussed in various presidential addresses (Macalister 1894:405–9; Gomme 1894:50). However, the Committee concentrated its efforts on delegates of corresponding societies to the British Association, with Brabrook, Hartland, Garson, and Haddon regularly attending their meetings to offer assistance, to answer queries, and to face criticisms from the delegates.

At such a meeting in 1894, J. Kenwood of the Birmingham Philosophical Society noted that in the Birmingham area "almost all traces of the past has been destroyed" (BAAS 1894:23). The same problem was faced by many other active societies affiliated to the Association, most of which came from the highly industrialized areas of north and central Britain. At this same meeting

Brabrook acknowledged also that people had experienced difficulty with Galton's complicated photographic instructions, and Eli Sowerbutts of the Manchester Geographical Society reported that the old people in his district "objected to being photographed and measured, apparently from a notion that to allow it would be to render themselves subject to witchcraft" (BAAS 1894: 41). Sowerbutts apparently failed to realize that these witchcraft beliefs were themselves of interest to the Committee. Members of the corresponding societies were often rational scientists who, while willing to take physical measurements, would not demean themselves by collecting "mere superstitions." But there were also problems with taking physical measurements. Although the survey purchased a number of sets which could be borrowed, the instruments were often difficult to obtain, and even when obtained they proved difficult to operate. When J. Hopkinson of the Hertfordshire Natural History Society complained of difficulties taking "the very elaborate series of measurements asked for" and objected to the "inquisitorial" nature of many of the questions, Hartland suggested he concentrate on other aspects of the Survey's work (BAAS 1895:51).

It was soon obvious to members of the Committee that the local societies, faced with the complexities of the schedule and the broad demands of the Survey, balked at starting work. In 1897 the Committee accommodated by advising that local societies need not investigate all subjects in depth, but could merely carry out general surveys. They appealed to the societies to "reconsider the position and undertake the essential portion of the work in the respective localities," promising the assistance of "competent individual observers" if required (BAAS 1897:454–55). The same points were emphasized the following year, when observers were advised that they need not complete all aspects of the schedule (BAAS 1898:714). In an effort to enlist more skilled observers, particularly for physical anthropology, a special circular was issued to medical men (BAAS 1895:512–13). But although some doctors provided regular information to the British Medical Association, and in France anthropologists had used doctors to collect anthropological statistics, the response from British doctors was poor (BAAS 1895:511).

By 1897 it was obvious to the Committee that the Survey had not fulfilled its original intentions: too few societies had participated, and the material received, both from individuals and local groups, was unsatisfactory. The most significant material had been collected by the skilled members of the Committee, but their time was restricted. Brabrook, in his presidential address to Section H of the Association, appealed for one final effort from local societies to support the Survey (1898:1008), but to no avail. The following year the Committee announced it was issuing its final *Report*, not because the Survey had been completed, but because "the preparation for that work has been carried as far as the means at their disposal have enabled them to carry it, and because they have arrived at the conviction that the work itself may now properly be left to be completed by other hands possessing the necessary organisation and more adequate means" (BAAS 1899:494). Although the Committee still insisted on the value of the Survey, it admitted defeat. The reports and observations it held were returned to the individuals or societies that had submitted them; the measuring instruments were returned to the Association. The Committee ended on an optimistic note, hoping that a proposed Imperial Bureau of Ethnology for Greater Britain might take over the work of the Survey (BAAS 1899:495; cf. Read 1896); but the Bureau, in spite of many efforts in succeeding years, was never established (Myres 1929).

Specialization, Professionalization, and the Decline of Holistic Anthropology

The failure of the Survey revealed a number of problems in the practice and vision of anthropology as it developed in Great Britain in the later nineteenth century. These included the question of research methodology, the nature of ethnographic "facts," the vision of integrated ethnographic accounts, and the very nature of ethnological explanation.

It long had been believed that amateurs, given the proper guidance, could easily collect "facts" to provide a basis for experts to make informed syntheses. The experience of the Survey reinforced doubts many already had about such assumptions. Amateurs could not cope with the instructions; the "facts" were not like pebbles on the ground lying there to be picked up; the material collected was of such varying standards that it proved nearly impossible to synthesize. As Haddon admitted, the aims of the Survey had been too ambitious (1898c:3). The Committee concluded that the role of amateurs in research needed to be reassessed: "[F]or future conduct of the survey, it will not be sufficient to rely upon such assistance, however generously bestowed." To insure "absolute uniformity in the methods of collecting information, upon which the usefulness of the information for the purposes of comparison almost entirely depends, it is essential that one or more persons should be wholly engaged upon the work" (BAAS 1899:495).

The Survey had been conceived within an holistic vision of anthropology. It was believed that different kinds of information, derived by differing techniques from diverse sources, could easily be integrated into a comprehensive ethnography. But the material on which such an enterprise was to be based, and the ideas on which it was founded, proved more diverse than generally thought. Far from being complementary, the ideas and methods of a total science of man were in practice often in conflict. Folklorists who concentrated on oral traditions and survivals of custom, physical anthropologists who stressed rigorous measurement and observation, and museum people who delighted in cataloguing objects had quite different ideas of the value of their evidence and its importance in the final ethnographic synthesis. The failure of the Anthropological Institute and the Folk-Lore Society to amalgamate in the early 1890s was perhaps symptomatic of these difficulties. Folklorists tended to look with contempt at the tables of numbers and collections of skulls of the physical anthropologists. As Edward Clodd put it in 1895 in his presidential address to the society, "Rows of skulls—brachycephalic, dolichocephalic, mesocephalic—touch us never so keenly as conception of the ideas which once vibrated through their hollow cavities, and which set us moralizing like the gravedigger over the bones of Yorick" (1895:68). For their part, some physical anthropologists believed their evidence more scientific and objective than that of the folklorists. Many of them were professional men, holders of university degrees and academic posts; in contrast to the "men of letters," who were numerous in the Folk-Lore Society (cf. Heyck 1982), they were part of the rising group of "men of science." During the 1890s the physical anthropologists played an important role in the rejuvenation of the Anthropological Institute after a decade of decline. In 1899 a new edition of *Notes and Queries*, edited by R. Garson and C. H. Read of the British Museum, was produced to replace the 1892 edition (Urry 1972:48–49). Read noted that because the years since the previous edition had seen marked advances in the methods of physical anthropology, the instructions for this section had been substantially revised, and he advised that observations in physical anthropology could "only be usefully made by a properly qualified physician or surgeon" (1900:11). A similar point was later made by an expert committee established to standardize anthropometric investigations for a general anthropometric survey of Britain (BAAS 1904:334).

In 1900, physical anthropology was the area of anthropology in which professionalization was most advanced, and Haddon was one of the few "professionals" competent in physical anthropology who showed any great keenness for collecting material on folklore and other customs. Even he was led by his experience with the Survey to reconsider the role of amateurs in research, though he never abandoned the belief that they could be useful (Haddon 1909). When he returned to Torres Strait in 1898, Haddon took with him a team of specialists in particular fields to carry out research (Quiggin 1942; Urry 1982). But although Haddon's expedition in fact marked a watershed in the history of anthropological research in Britain, Haddon himself still conceived of the ethnographic enterprise in holistic terms. Thus the results of the expedition were published in a number of volumes Haddon hoped would provide a "total" ethnographic account of Torres Strait. The limitations of such ethnographic holism were manifest in the fact that the volume on "general ethnography" did not appear until 1935 (Haddon, ed. 1901–35). Long before then anthropologists were writing more focussed ethnographies from their field-work, concentrating on particular subjects and themes to the neglect of others. "An ethnography" came to mean the analysis of the particular customs of a single culture, rather than an holistic description of an ethnographic region covering race, culture, and language.

Equally important were changes in the conception of the goals of ethnographic inquiry. As late as 1908, Marett argued that the real value of accounts of exotic cultures to anthropologists was in providing material to reconstruct the evolution of European society and culture (1908:5). But by the late 1890s this position had already begun to change: increasingly, distant savages seemed worthy of study in themselves, and the focus of anthropological attention shifted away from Europe. Instead of compiling lists of curious ethnographic facts, trained anthropologists began to study individual communities in depth, utilizing new techniques. The professionalization of anthropology began to move beyond physical anthropology, and the subject itself became divided into a number of subdisciplines—as was reflected in academic posts created after 1900 with distinct titles, such as "ethnology" and "social anthropology."

The weakening of the holistic vision of anthropology after 1900 was also associated with a shift in the nature of anthropological interpretation. General ideas on the evolution of cultures, in which "race" played a dominant role, gave way to the study of particular cultural areas in terms of geography and history, in which the idea of race was to play a more restricted role. Haddon, for instance, was less interested in establishing worldwide evolutionary stages than in investigating evolutionary processes within particular cultural contexts (Urry 1982). Cultural patterns were increasingly to be explained as the result of local cultural adaptation and development; racial factors, though still investigated, were given less prominence. Evidence from physical anthropology was often relegated to a separate chapter or appendix in ethnographies, eventually to be omitted altogether.

All these changes in anthropology were to have a profound effect on the research and publication of material on the ethnology of Britain after the Survey folded. The scope of investigation was more modest, and the work was carried out by trained individuals. Gray and Tocher, with the assistance of the Association, continued the work of the Scottish Committee studying the pigmentation of school children (BAAS 1902:352–53; 1903:415). In 1902 the Association established a committee for an Anthropometric Investigation of Great Britain, which spent six years compiling instructions (BAAS 1903–1909). Although the committee intended to include studies of racial variation in its research, they particularly stressed the value of anthropometric data for the study of public health. Little actual research was conducted, however, because despite appeals to the government funds were not forthcoming (Anon. 1907). Haddon was involved in all these ventures of the Association, and still hoped that a survey of British ethnology could be begun. In 1909 he addressed the corresponding societies on the subject of regional surveys, appealing for "anthrogeography," defined as the study of "geographical, ethnographical, archaeological, historical, and sociological" factors (1909:329). But race had vanished as a major concept, and instead of a national survey, Haddon stressed a favorite theme of his: "the intensive study of limited areas" (Stocking 1979; Urry 1984).

The traditional interest in racial history persisted most strongly in the work of H. J. Fleure, whom Haddon in 1905 encouraged to begin a detailed anthropological survey of Wales (Fleure & James 1907; Garnett 1970). Like Haddon, Fleure had trained as a zoologist; but he also taught geology and geography at Aberystwyth University College of Wales, and in 1917 succeeded to a chair in anthropology and geography. Although Fleure conducted detailed physical anthropological research, he tended to interpret his material in historical terms, which for Fleure included the study of race: "In Britain . . . race study leads us back to pre-history and helps to give us a deep meaning to our folk tale and tradition" (1919:32; cf. Fleure & James 1916). Although Fleure published a number of books and articles on the racial history of Britain and mainland Europe (1918a, 1920, 1922, 1923), his career in fact documents the breakup of the earlier anthropological holism, the marginalization of folklore studies, the professionalization of archeology, and the ultimate deemphasis of "race." While he acknowledged that the study of folklore could be of assistance in such studies, he stressed the greater importance of the evidence of physical anthropology, geography, and archeology (1913, 1918b). Increasingly, the study of folklore in Britain after 1914 was seen as a subject of antiquarian interest; unlike anthropology, folklore studies failed to establish a secure place in the British university curricula. In contrast, prehistoric archeology, long under the umbrella of anthropology, emerged during this period as an independent discipline with claims to academic respectability. After 1900 new excavation techniques and a concern with recording British archeological sites stimulated a new generation of prehistorians. O. G. S. Crawford, Cyril Fox, Harold Peake, and Mortimer Wheeler, all of whom worked with Fleure, were concerned with relating the distribution of archeological sites to local landscapes and with reconstructing the chronology of settlements. In their early work, all made use of the idea of successive invasions of different races, which they inherited from nineteenth-century anthropology. By 1930, however, though the idea of invasions remained, the concept of race had begun to give way to that of culture: successive cultures, often associated with different groups of peoples, had been involved in the settlement of Britain.

This shift in emphasis can be most clearly seen in the writings of V. Gordon Childe, perhaps the most influential archeologist of his age (McNairn

1980; Trigger 1980). Although in 1926 Childe had published a work entitled *The Aryans*, by 1933 he wrote that "in the prehistoric past as obviously today, culture was independent of physical race, was not a matter of biological heredity but of social tradition" (1933a:417). Childe suggested that archeologists should concern themselves with "ethnic" rather than "racial" history when interpreting material (1933b:199). The complexity of the material of the new archeology presented great difficulties to anyone making statements about European populations in the past, and this was recognized by Childe (1933b:196). At the same time, the rising tide of political racism in Europe, especially stemming from Nazi Germany, made the concept of race suspect. Childe's own comments on the differences between races and peoples were explicitly directed against such radical doctrines, and even anthropologists who once had used the term "race" in their writings now argued against its political connotations (Fleure 1930; Huxley & Haddon 1935).

There was no attempt between the two world wars to establish a general anthropological survey of Britain in spite of continued professionalization of the discipline. The ranks of the social anthropologists grew, but their attention was focussed on distant areas of the British Empire and on issues other than ethnological speculation. Although archeologists continued detailed research in British prehistory, they did so within their own frames of reference. Since the Second World War, physical and social anthropologists have investigated aspects of the British population (Roberts & Sunderland 1973), utilizing research techniques developed in their respective disciplines and producing quite distinctive accounts. The vision of an ethnographic survey, like the memories of the Association's Survey itself, has long since vanished from British anthropology. Carried on by a motley corps of amateurs, its organizers pulled in several directions by uneven pressures of technical elaboration and academic specialization, the Survey was the late and stunted offspring of an embracive nineteenth-century anthropology, which in both its ethnological and evolutionary forms was largely held together by an ill-defined notion of "race" still reflecting the popular idea of an hereditary community of physical, linguistic, and cultural characteristics. Whether the vision of an holistic anthropology can be reestablished on less problematic grounds still remains to be seen.

Acknowledgments

I would like to thank Dell Hymes, B. J. Kirkpatrick, Isabel McBryde, George W. Stocking, and Michael Young for their assistance and advice during the writing of this essay. Miss A. A. Melvin of the Buchan Field Club kindly supplied details of the club's involvement with the Survey.

References Cited

Allen, G. 1880. Are we Englishmen? *Fort. Rev.* 28:478–87.

Arnold, M. 1867. *On the study of Celtic literature.* London.

BAAS. See under British Association for the Advancement of Science.

Beddoe, J. 1885. *The races of Britain: A contribution to the anthropology of western Europe.* Bristol.

———. 1910. *Memories of eighty years.* Bristol.

Blaas, P. B. M. 1978. *Continuity and anachronism: Parliamentary and constitutional development in Whig historiography and in the anti-Whig reaction between 1890 and 1930.* The Hague.

Bolt, C. 1971. *Victorian attitudes to race.* London.

Brabrook, E. W. 1893. On the organisation of local anthropological research. *J. Anth. Inst.* 22:262–74.

———. 1896. Kent in relation to the Ethnographic Survey. *Arch. J.* 53:215–34.

———. 1898. Presidential address, Section H, Brit. Assn. Adv. Sci. *Nature* 58: 999–1010.

Briggs, A. 1966. *Saxons, Normans and Victorians.* Bexhill-on-Sea, Sussex.

British Association for the Advancement of Science. 1883–. *Reports . . . 53rd [and succeeding] Meeting[s].*

Brook, G. L. 1963. *English dialects.* London.

Burne, C. S. 1890. The collection of English folklore. *Folk-Lore* 1:313–30.

Burrow, J. W. 1981. *A liberal descent: Victorian historians and the English past.* Cambridge.

Childe, V. G. 1926. *The Aryans: A study of Indo-European origins.* London.

———. 1933a. Is prehistory practical? *Antiquity* 7:410–18.

———. 1933b. Races, people and cultures in prehistoric Europe. *History* 18:193–203.

Church, A. J. 1889. *Early Britain.* London.

Clark, G. 1966. The invasion hypothesis in British archaeology. *Antiquity* 40:172–92.

Clodd, E. 1895. Presidential address. *Folk-Lore* 6:54–81.

Cunningham, D. J., & A. C. Haddon. 1891. The anthropometric laboratory of Ireland. *J. Anth. Inst.* 21:35–38.

[Cunningham, D. J., et al.] 1907. Proposed National Anthropometric Survey. *J. Roy. Anth. Inst.* 37:424–32.

Curtis, L. P., Jr. 1968. *Anglo-Saxons and Celts: A study of anti-Irish prejudice in Victorian England.* Bridgeport.

———. 1971. *Apes and angels: The Irishman in Victorian caricature.* Newton Abbot.

Daniel, G. E. 1954. Who are the Welsh? *Proc. Brit. Acad.* 40:145–67.

Davis, J. B., & J. Thurnam. 1865. *Crania Britannica: Delineations and descriptions of the skulls of the early inhabitants of the British Isles.* London.

Dawkins, W. B. 1880. *Early man in Britain and his place in the Tertiary period.* London.

Dorson, R. M. 1968. *The British folklorists: A history.* London.

Evans, J. 1956. *A history of the Society of Antiquaries.* Oxford.

Faverty, F. E. 1951. *Matthew Arnold the ethnologist.* Evanston.

Fleure, H. J. 1913. Welsh archaeology and anthropology. *Arch. Camb.* 68:153–58.

———. 1917. A proposal for local surveys of the British people. *Arch. Camb.* 72:32–62.

————. 1918a. The racial history of Britain. *Geog. Rev.* 5:216–31.

————. 1918b. Anthropology and our older histories. *J. Roy. Anth. Inst.* 48:155–70.

————. 1919. Regional surveys. *Soc. Rev.* 11:28–34.

————. 1920. The early neanthropic types in Europe and their modern representatives. *J. Roy. Anth. Inst.* 50:12–40.

————. 1922. *The peoples of Europe.* Oxford.

————. 1923. *The races of England and Wales: A survey of recent research.* London.

————. 1930. The Nordic myth: A critique of current racial theories. *Eug. Rev.* 22:117–21.

Fleure, H. J., & T. C. James. 1907. A preliminary report on the progress of the University of Wales Ethnographic Survey. *Man* 7:139.

————. 1916. Geographical distribution of anthropological types in Wales. *J. Roy. Anth. Inst.* 46:35–153.

[Folk-Lore.] 1892. News and Notes. *Folk-Lore* 3:270.

Forrest, D. W. 1974. *Francis Galton: The life and work of a Victorian genius.* London.

Galton, F. 1878. Composite portraits made by combining those of many different persons into a single figure. *J. Anth. Inst.* 8:132–48.

————. 1891. Retrospect of work done at my anthropometric laboratory at South Kensington. *J. Anth. Inst.* 21:32–35.

Garnett, A. 1970. Herbert John Fleure, 1877–1969. *Bio. Mem. Roy. Soc.* 16:253–78.

Geison, G. L. 1978. *Michael Foster and the Cambridge school of physiology: The scientific enterprise in late Victorian society.* Princeton.

Gomme, G. L. 1890. *The handbook of folklore.* London.

————. 1892. *Ethnology in folklore.* London.

————. 1894. Presidential address. *Folk-Lore* 5:43–69.

————. 1896. On the method of determining the value of folklore as ethnological data. *Rept. Brit. Assn. Adv. Sci.:* 626–56.

Gray, J. 1895. Paper on the ethnographic survey of Buchan. *Trans. Buchan Field Club* 3:216–25.

————. 1911. John Beddoe. *Man* 11:151–53.

Gray, J., & J. F. Tocher. 1895. Report on 'Preliminary ethnographic observations at the Buchan gathering, Mintlaw.' *Trans. Buchan Field Club* 3:226–40.

————. 1899. On the physical characteristics of the population of Aberdeenshire. *Rept. Brit. Assn. Adv. Sci.:* 913–15.

————. 1900. The physical characteristics of adults and school children in east Aberdeenshire. *J. Anth. Inst.* 30:104–24.

Greenwell, W., & G. Rolleston. 1877. *British barrows: A record of the examination of sepulchral mounds in various parts of England.* Oxford.

Gregor, W. 1896. Preliminary report on folklore in Galloway, Scotland. *Rep. Brit. Assn. Adv. Sci.:* 612–26.

Gruber, J. W. 1965. Brixham Cave and the antiquity of man. In *Context and meaning in cultural anthropology,* ed. M. Spiro, 373–402. New York.

————. 1970. Ethnographic salvage and the shaping of anthropology. *Am. Anth.* 72: 1289–99.

Haddon, A. C. 1890. Manners and customs of the Torres Straits islanders. *Nature* 42:637–42.

———. 1893a. Studies in Irish craniology, pt. 1: Aran Islands, Co. Galway. *Proc. Roy. Irish Acad.* 3:759–67.

———. 1893b. A batch of Irish folklore. *Folk-Lore* 4:349–64.

———. 1894. Studies in Irish craniology, pt. 2: Inishbofin, Co. Galway. *Proc. Roy. Irish Acad.* 3:311–16.

———. 1897a. The saving of vanishing knowledge. *Nature* 55:305–6.

———. 1897b. On the physical characters of the inhabitants of Barley, Herts. *Rep. Brit. Assn. Adv. Sci.*: 503–6.

———. 1898a. *The study of man.* London.

———. 1898b. Studies in Irish craniology, pt. 3: A Neolithic cist burial at Oldbridge, Co. Meath. *Proc. Roy. Irish Acad.* 3:570–85.

———. 1898c. Why we measure people. *Sci. Prog.* 7:1–22.

———. 1909. Regional surveys. *Rep. Brit. Assn. Adv. Sci.*: 327–30.

Haddon, A. C., ed. 1901–35. *Reports of the Cambridge anthropological expedition to Torres Straits.* 6 vols. Cambridge.

Haddon, A. C., & C. R. Browne. 1893. The ethnography of the Aran Islands, Co. Galway. *Proc. Roy. Irish Acad.* 3:768–830.

Hartland, E. S. 1891. *The science of fairy tales: An inquiry into fairy mythology.* London.

———. 1895. Notes explanatory to the schedules. *Rept. Brit. Assn. Adv. Sci.*: 513–18.

Heyck, T. W. 1982. *The transformation of intellectual life in Victorian England.* London.

Hill, C. 1954. The Norman yoke. In *Democracy and the labour movement,* ed. J. Saville. London.

Howarth, O. J. R. 1922. *The British Association for the Advancement of Science: A retrospect, 1831–1921.* London.

Huxley, J., & A. C. Haddon. 1935. *We Europeans: A survey of 'racial' problems.* London.

Huxley, T. H. 1871. On some fixed points in British ethnology. In *Man's place in nature and other anthropological essays.* London (1894).

Jorion, P. 1982. The downfall of the skull. *RAIN* 48:8–11.

Laws, E. 1896. Report of the ethnographic survey of Pembrokeshire. *Rept. Brit. Assn. Adv. Sci.*: 610–12.

Macalister, A. 1894. Anniversary address. *J. Anth. Inst.* 23:400–416.

Mackintosh, A. 1866. The comparative anthropology of England and Wales. *Anth. Rev.* 4:1–21.

Macleod, R. M., J. R. Friday, & C. Gregor. 1975. *The corresponding societies of the British Association for the Advancement of Science, 1883–1929: A survey of historical records, archives and publications.* London.

McNairn, B. 1980. *The method and theory of V. Gordon Childe: Economic, social and cultural interpretations of prehistory.* Edinburgh.

Marett, R. R. 1908. Preface. In *Anthropology and the classics.* London.

Morrell, J. D., & A. Thackray. 1981. *Gentlemen of science: Early years of the British Association for the Advancement of Science.* New York.

Myres, J. L. 1929. The science of man in the service of the state. *J. Roy. Anth. Inst.* 59:19–52.

Palmer, J. F. 1885. The Saxon invasion and its influence on our character as a race. *Trans. Roy. Hist. Soc.* 2:173–96.

Parry-Williams, T. H. 1954. *John Rhŷs, 1840–1915.* Cardiff.

Pearson, K. 1924. *The life, letters and labours of Francis Galton. Vol. II, Researches of middle life.* Cambridge.

Quiggin, A. H. 1942. *Haddon the head hunter: A short sketch of the life of A. C. Haddon.* Cambridge.

Read, C. H. 1896. An Imperial Bureau of Ethnology. *Rept. Brit. Assn. Adv. Sci.*: 928.

———. 1900. Presidential address. *J. Anth. Inst.* 30:6–21.

Rhŷs, J. 1890. The early ethnology of the British Isles. *Scot. Rev.* 15:233–52.

———. 1891a. Traces of a non-Aryan element in the Celtic family. *Scot. Rev.* 17:30–47.

———. 1891b. The mythographical treatment of Celtic ethnology. *Scot. Rev.* 17:240–56.

———. 1892. Certain national names of the Aborigines of the British Isles. *Scot. Rev.* 18:120–43.

———. 1901. *Celtic folklore: Welsh and Manx.* London.

Roberts, D. F., & E. Sunderland. 1973. *Genetic variation in Britain.* London.

Stepan, N. 1982. *The idea of race in science: Great Britain, 1800–1960.* London.

Stocking, G. W. 1971. What's in a name? The origins of the Royal Anthropological Institute: 1837–1871. *Man* 6:369–90.

———. 1973. From chronology to ethnology: James Cowles Prichard and British anthropology. In Prichard, *Researches into the physical history of man.* Chicago.

———. 1979. The intensive study of limited areas: Toward an ethnographic context for the Malinowskian innovation. *Hist. Anth. Newsl.* 7:9–12.

Sweet, H. 1890. *A primer of phonetics.* Oxford.

Tocher, J. R. 1897. Ethnographical survey of school children in Buchan; 1, Introductory paper with summaries. *Trans. Buchan Field Club* 4:137–52.

Topinard, P. 1885. *Élements d' anthropologie générale.* Paris.

Trigger, G. B. 1980. *Gordon Childe: Revolutions in archaeology.* London.

Urry, J. 1972. *Notes and Queries on Anthropology* and the development of field methods in British anthropology, 1870–1920. *Proc. Roy. Anth. Inst.*, 45–57.

———. 1982. From zoology to ethnology: A. C. Haddon's conversion to anthropology, 1890–1900. *Canberra Anth.* 5:58–85.

———. 1984. A history of field methods. In *Ethnographic research,* ed. R. F. Ellen. London.

Wright, J. 1892. *A grammar of the dialect of Windhill in the West Riding of Yorkshire.* London.

DR. DURKHEIM AND MR. BROWN

Comparative Sociology at Cambridge in 1910

Edited by
GEORGE W. STOCKING, JR.

It has been said of A. R. Radcliffe-Brown that the one bit of intellectual baggage he literally carried with him through all his scholarly migrations was his set of *L'Année Sociologique*. Some professional gossip among critics of "structural-functionalism" would have it that he did not really understand Durkheim; one disaffected disciple even remarked to me that Radcliffe-Brown, as a lower-middle-class Birmingham boy, could not *really* be expected to have read French. But until recently, the Durkheimian influence, however "true" to the original, has been generally assumed to have been critical to the formation of Radcliffe-Brown's anthropology. That assumption has recently been challenged, however, in the context of a long-due (but unfortunately somewhat overstated) attempt to resurrect the anthropological contributions of William Rivers. The historian Ian Langham has in fact suggested that Radcliffe-Brown's "endorsement of the Durkheimian school was symptomatic of snobbish Francophilia, rather than of genuine intellectual indebtedness." Having derived the "essence" of his structural-functionalism from Rivers, he turned to the writings of the Durkheimian school simply to reinforce his views, and "as a source of pithy quotations" (1981:282).

Certain themes in Radcliffe-Brown's intellectual life do indeed give this view a prima facie credibility. One who knew him early testified to his tendency to "cultivate" a certain Parisian style (Watson 1946:84–85); some recent scholarship would seem to indicate that perhaps he did not always adequately acknowledge intellectual debts (Needham 1974; cf. White 1981). There is no doubt that Rivers was a strong influence, and given Radcliffe-Brown's clear need to mark off his position sharply, and his tendency to view it in apodictic ahistorical terms, it might be expected that once the two had fallen out, indebtedness would be minimized, differences projected backwards, and alternative sources insisted upon.

Thus Radcliffe-Brown's surviving correspondence contains several versions of his early intellectual development that insist he was already committed to sociology before arriving at Cambridge, that emphasize the intellectual influence—mediated by direct acquaintance—of the anarchist Prince Peter Kropotkin and the sexologist Havelock Ellis, and that (in one instance) indicate that he differed with Rivers on issues of method from the outset (Kelly 1983; Stocking 1976). Written no less than twenty years after the fact, and at a point when he was firmly committed to the advocacy of a distinctive point of view, these must be read with caution. If it seems likely that his early familiarity with Kropotkin's writings may have predisposed him toward his characteristic viewpoint (Kelly 1983; cf. Perry 1975), and if we note with interest his early reading of Marx, or the "structuralist" bias derived from his adolescent natural scientific activities, we must still weigh heavily more contemporary surviving indications of intellectual indebtedness.

In a letter written to Marcel Mauss in August 1912, Radcliffe-Brown proclaimed his "complete agreement" with the Durkheimian "view of sociology," and took credit for being "the first person to expound these views in England"—where they otherwise were "ignored or misunderstood." He had done so in lectures on sociology given at Cambridge in 1910, and in his lectures during the same academic year at the London School of Economics (Testart 1979:4; cf. Peristiany 1960). Although apparently overlooked by Langham, despite his extensive research in manuscript sources, a set of notes for Radcliffe-Brown's Cambridge lectures on "Comparative Sociology" during the Lent Term of 1910 has survived, and they provide strong evidence for reasserting the critical importance of Durkheim's influence in the development of Radcliffe-Brown's anthropological viewpoint. Taken either by or for Alfred Cort Haddon, they indicate an extensive dependence on the Durkheimian literature (as well as on R. R. Marett and William Robertson Smith), in the context of what would seem to be Radcliffe-Brown's first attempt to treat his Andaman materials in the mode of his later-published interpretation. The sources are easily identifiable, and they weigh far more heavily than any influence that might be traced solely to Rivers.

How much further back one may legitimately project this Durkheimian influence is an interesting problem. One might conclude from the fabled travelling set of the *Année* that Radcliffe-Brown had been a subscriber from the beginning. Almost a half century later, he recalled that Ellis (who had in fact reviewed *Suicide* somewhat critically in *Mind* in 1898) had called his attention to Durkheim as early as 1899 (Kelly 1983). But one must also consider other evidence of the role of Durkheim in Radcliffe-Brown's early work, as well as what is known of the reception of Durkheim in England.

On the latter issue, there is reason to qualify the rather casual assertion that Durkheim's work "was well-known in Britain from the publication of *De la division du travail social* onwards" (Collini 1978:7). It is easy to document an awareness of "Professor Durkheim's" work, but the question of influence is rather more complex. True, an early meeting of the Sociological Society (June 1904) was devoted to "The Relation of Sociology to the Social Sciences and Philosophy," and a paper of Durkheim's was discussed (cf. Durkheim & Fauconnet 1905). But the tenor of discussions of general sociological issues here and in the *Sociological Review* would suggest that Durkheim was someone whom British sociological writers pushed against rather than emulated. Indeed, since the central problem of the historiography of British sociology has been to explain why England produced no equivalent of Durkheim or Weber, one may perhaps assume a somewhat inhospitable intellectual milieu (Abrams 1968; Collini 1978).

Among anthropologists, an early interest in Durkheim seems to have been mediated by the folklorist E. Sidney Hartland, who from an early point regularly published in *Folk-Lore* favorable reviews of what he considered the relevant materials in the *Année*. Offering a detailed summary of the "acute and learned" paper on "Primitive Classification" (Durkheim & Mauss 1901) he commended it to his readers as "in one word, excellent" (Hartland 1903:435). However, the early anthropological interest in Durkheim seems for the most part to have focussed on his discussion of Australian ethnographic materials, in relation to the problem of "totemism," which was at the center of anthropological debate in the decade after 1900. Thus Andrew Lang devoted a somewhat critical chapter to "The Theories of Dr. Durkheim" in *The Secret of the Totem*, and in fact was involved in an exchange with Durkheim in the pages of *Folk-Lore* (Lang 1905; Durkheim 1905).

The introduction of Durkheimian thought into British anthropology is associated by some with the trio of "ritualist" classicists who reoriented the study of early Greek religion at about this time: Gilbert Murray, F. M. Cornford, and Jane Harrison (Collini 1978:35). Although two of them were at Cambridge during Radcliffe-Brown's time there, available evidence on the chronology of their intellectual development makes it unlikely that they influenced him, and even suggests an influence in the opposite direction. Durkheim is not evident in their early works (Harrison 1903; Murray 1907), and the earlier anthropological influences on them seem to have come from quite different sources: Frazer's *Golden Bough*, and the work of archeologists such as William Ridgeway and John Myres. Indeed, Durkheim is not manifest in any of the Oxford lectures edited by R. R. Marett in 1908 as *Anthropology and the Classics*. By the time Harrison published *Themis* in 1912, Durkheim was of course very much in evidence. But given what we know about the genesis of that work, which after slow gestation was pushed rapidly to conclusion in 1911 (Stewart 1959:91–97), it seems unlikely that Harrison was an influence on Radcliffe-Brown. Quite the contrary, a footnote in *Themis* indicates her debt for the idea of pretotemistic societies to "views expressed by Mr. A. R. Brown in a course of lectures delivered in 1909 [*sic*] at Trinity College, Cambridge" (1912:125).

What led Harrison from Bergson to Durkheim after 1907 is not clear; but it may well have been the work of Marett, which is cited at several critical points in *Themis*. Surely one of the most underestimated figures in the history of modern British anthropology, Marett was the author of several very important essays criticizing Tylorian and Frazerian interpretations of primitive religion, which appeared as *The Threshold of Religion* in 1908. Perhaps because his Channel Island origins gave him a special sensitivity to French thought (Marett 1941), Marett seems to have been the first British anthropologist to appreciate the importance of the theoretical differences between the French "sociological" and the English "anthropological" schools—although remaining himself poised between the two (1908b).

At whatever point he purchased the early volumes of the *Année*, we may assume that Radcliffe-Brown was familiar with the more ethnographically oriented materials at least as early as 1905, when he spent his first postgraduate year reading anthropology at Cambridge. On the other hand, it seems clear that his Andaman research was originally neither conceived nor written up in Durkheimian terms: what survives of the fellowship thesis he wrote upon his return is very Haddonian, or even Boasian, in its historical orientation (cf. pp. 144–46, this volume). While it is impossible to be sure, it seems likely that he became reinvolved in the Durkheimian literature while teaching Australian ethnography at the London School of Economics in the fall of 1909—when he was making plans for a second fieldwork expedition, this time to Western Australia—and that, perhaps stimulated by Marett or the sociological milieu of the School, he moved beyond the ethnographic materials to some of the general sociological work.

It is not clear that he had yet fully assimilated all the implications he was to derive from the *Rules of the Sociological Method* (1895); but he had read *Suicide* (1897), and the role of *The Division of Labor* (1893) in his interpretation of "primitive" social forms is absolutely critical. Furthermore, there is an interesting discrepancy between the printed program announcing the lectures, and the sequence of topics actually preserved in the notes. While one addendum sheet was obviously out of place when the materials were first consulted in 1969, and the differing length of the topical units suggests some slippage in the original note-taking process, there are nevertheless grounds for arguing that the sequence preserved represents the sequence of topics as actually given. The fact that in the one case, where a break between lectures occurs in mid-page in the notes, the order preserved inverts the sequence originally announced, suggests at least that the printed order was departed from. More to the point, however, is an obvious division in the notes between the first six lecture topics and the last two, which occupy a disproportionate number of pages. The former are heavily derivative from specific materials in the Durkheimian literature—above all, *The Division of Labor*. But in the latter, there is much more of Radcliffe-Brown's own Andaman material, in the context of a general consideration of the problem of totemism and the evolution of religion. These discrepancies assume greater significance in view of his later suggestion in the first edition of *The Andaman Islanders* that he had first worked out his analysis of their myth and ceremony in 1910 "as an attempt to develop a new method in the interpretation of the institutions of a primitive people" (1922:ix).

Any academic who recalls his early lecturing experience—when courses are often composed in process, with particular topics "worked up," often in a heavily derivative manner, as one goes along, and ideas develop in response to immediate intellectual stimuli—has an experiential basis for interpreting the discrepancy between the printed program of the lectures and the sequence and substance that are actually preserved. Having decided, or been asked, to give a course on "Comparative Sociology," Radcliffe-Brown created a generalized topical outline, which is reflected in the printed program. In actually preparing the lectures, however, he began by relying rather heavily on one book, bringing in other materials from the Durkheimian literature as he moved along. With the appearance of Frazer's *Totemism and Exogamy* (which was published shortly after the series began), he shifted direction, and in the context of what may have been his first systematic working through of the Durkheimian corpus, he was inspired to use the lectures as the occasion for reanalysis of his Andaman fieldwork data.

While there are strong grounds for doubting that the two interpretive chapters of *The Andaman Islanders* were actually put into final form at this time, we do find here an early version of what Lévi-Strauss called Radcliffe-Brown's "first theory" of totemism (1962:58–59), and there is an evident continuity (as well as significant further development) between these lectures and those that have been preserved from the 1920s and 1930s (cf. Schapera n.d.; Tax 1932). In this context, it would seem, then, that the earliest extant formulation of Radcliffe-Brown's lifelong project for a "Comparative Sociology" was, as both his memory and conventional interpretation have insisted, already very much in a Durkheimian mode—although as some would have surmised, it is strongly that of "early" Durkheim. In view of his tremendous later influence (cf. pp. 131–91, this volume), it would seem that it is to these lectures that we may most appropriately trace "the beginning of British anthropology's long affair with Durkheimianism" (cf. Collini 1978:35).

As preserved in Folder 4058 of the Alfred Cort Haddon Papers, the notes are in typed form, with a small number of handwritten corrections and additions. While several of these (annotated here A. C. H.) are by Haddon, most are in a quite distinct hand. The latter bears a superficial similarity to that of Radcliffe-Brown, but there are some important differences, particularly in the initial letters "f" and "t"; and I assume therefore that it is that of the person who transcribed the notes—probably Mrs. A. Hingston Quiggin, who long served as Haddon's secretary and was his eventual biographer. Because the interest here is in approximating the originally delivered text, rather than in preserving the results of the note-taking process, these latter emendations have simply been quietly incorporated without annotation—except in one or two cases where the emendations themselves offer insight into the reaction of more conventional anthropologists. So also, abbreviations frequently used in the typed text ("indiv." for "individual," etc.) have been similarly augmented. On the same grounds I have felt free to convert the somewhat unsystematic outline structure of the preserved notes into a more compact and readable paragraph form. This has involved inserting bracketed words—mostly articles and verbs—all along the way, as well as some unbracketed modifications of punctuation. To mark the major breaks in the text as preserved, numbered lecture headings have been inserted in accordance with the justification indicated above.

Given the differing length of the topical units, we may assume that a good bit of the substance of the lectures has not been preserved. This is especially the case in regard to the fourth topic, "Society and the Individual." Such fluctuation in the attentiveness of the note-taker might easily be overinterpreted. Nonetheless, the fact that totemism and religion occupy such a large proportion of the notes may perhaps say something about the way a traditional English anthropologist—whose French connections were to LePlay— responded to all this new-fangled Durkheimian sociology. Although I have not attempted to document all of Radcliffe-Brown's French connections, I have added a few bracketed references to some of the relevant Durkheimian literature.

A. R. Brown, Birmingham, 1909 (courtesy of Cynthia Pike).

Mr. A. R. BROWN, Fellow of Trinity College, will give a course of twelve lectures on Comparative Sociology in the Lent Term of 1910. The lectures will be delivered in the Archaeological Museum on Thursdays and Saturdays at 5:30, beginning on Jan. 22. No previous reading in the subject will be required.

LECTURES

I.	The Aims and Methods of Sociology.
II.	The Classification of Social Types.
III.	General Laws of Social Evolution.
IV.	The Evolution of Social Structure.
V. and VI.	The Origin, Development, and Function of Religion.
VII. and VIII.	The Origin, Development, and Function of Law and Morals.
IX.	Economic Institutions.
X.	Society and the Individual.
XI.	The Social Origin of General Ideas.
XII.	Sociology and Contemporary Social Problems.

COMPARATIVE SOCIOLOGY

A. R. Brown, lectures in
Trinity College [sic]:
Cambridge Lent Term 1910

[Lecture Topic One: cf. printed schedule II & III]

[The] evolution of societies [is] not unilinear, but arranged in branches like [a] tree [cf. Durkheim 1893:141]. [The] direction of the line of evolution [is] determined by natural selection, if the science of sociology is similar to those of zoology and biology. Changes of structure [are] accompanied by changes in institutions and beliefs—religious and otherwise. *[The] connection between social structure and religious and economic institutions [is] very close. As structure changes, [the] whole life changes.*

Note Robertson Smith on [the] structure of tribes: division into clans, each with a totem. Where there is division into clans, there the religion is totemism —religion [is] parallel to social structure. Totemism changes when people change descent from matri- to patrilineal. Brown says *structure is primary*, and not religion, which is parallel with it.

[The] breakdown of totemism is due to the breaking up of the clans. Totemism may develop into the belief in [a] guardian animal for each individual, and also to worship of ancestors. [The sequence in] Australia [is]: (1) simple totemism, (2) matrilineal totemism, (3) change from line of mother to line of father. These are progressive stages. Totemism disappears with [the] breakdown of [clan] social structure.

What produces [a] change in social structure [cf. Durkheim 1893:257]:

1. *Change in population,* affecting [the] density of society. [The] most complex societies are those in which volume and density are greatest. When [the] clan increases beyond a certain number, *either* (a) [the] relation of individuals changes (intimate at first) *or* (b) [the] clan splits up. [The] causes of increase of population are largely accidental. Note [the] difference between town and country in this respect. Migration may lead to a decrease. [The] geographical cause [is the] means of subsistence. [The] outline of the way in which society has changed in historic times [is]:

a. Tribal: progressive change—simply increase in population.

b. Tribe broken up into local divisions or clan divisions.

c. Town and country: collected and scattered. [The] change from country life to town life is one of the most important of all.

2. *Change in economic structure* [cf. Durkheim 1893:260]. [There is] no distinction of labour at first, no division of labour except that of man and woman —[the] minimum division. [This is] not [the] division of labour in [a] strict economic sense (note priests). Note [the] importance of [the] introduction of agricultural life. Note [the] extreme specialisation in labour and science today. Division of labour becomes [a] matter of necessity with [the] increase of society. Economic differentiation [is] due primarily to increase in population.

Three stages of society:

1. Primitive state of society.

2. Clan-system.

3. Clan superseded.

Is [the] clan-system universal? Lewis Morgan [is] affirmative. Note [the] division of tribes of Hebrews into families (clans), [and the] Numeri.

Generations:

		grandmother
father's sister,	father	mother, mother's brother
wife's brother,	wife	brother
	children	sister's children

This fits in perfectly with clan [class–A.C.H.] [classificatory?] system.

Various institutions in society are functions in the social structure. This occurs in every case where there is any social organisation. [The] question of patriarchy comes in in the matter of descent: (1) family, (2) matrilineal clan, (3) patrilineal clan, (4) break-down of clan. These four are progressive.

1. The clan is religious as well as social. [In] totemism, each clan has its animal. Religion consists in ceremonies connected with the animal, [and] con-

stitutes a bond which holds the clan together, [as in] initiation ceremonies.

2. The clan has [an] economic function. At [the] beginning, [there is a] long-house for each clan: house-mates shared meal, so that proceeds of [the] hunt belonged not to [the] individual member but to [the] clan. On marriage [a] man must leave his own house and go to his wife's. [The] clan here [is] determined by mother's line. [The] next step is when clan [is] determined by [the] father's line.

3. Moral and juridical function. [An] offence against members of clan [is] quite different from [an] offence [against] members of another clan. Religious institutions pass very gradually from the clan—perhaps [a] church [is] formed which takes them over. In some cases [the] clan retains religious ceremonies, etc.

4. Political function. Cf. [the] organisation of [the] Iroquois Confederation formed by the bringing together of several tribes, each clan retaining [an] independent council-house and organisation.

Change in structure [is] due to change in population. [There are] two possibilities: either (1) two clans formed, or (2) change in structure. In the first case the newly formed clan has [the] same nature as [the] first clan; in [the] second case, [the] clan changes its nature and organisation. With ancestor-worship (probably the disintegrating factor) we get male line, that is to say patrilineal descent as regards religion. But [a] man may belong to another tribe through his mother. [A] change of function in society in this way produces [a] change of structure.

[Lecture Topic Two: cf. printed schedule VII & VIII]

Origin of Moral Ideas:

1. Certain actions are forbidden—if performed [they] bring [the] individual into conflict with [the] state; others [are] disapproved of by society.

2. [A] different set of actions have religious plus social sanction [and] breaches are "sins."

3. Crimes [also] have, as well as [the] rest, a punishment.

4. [Certain] actions [are] adjusted by civil process—[the] readjustive [sic] sanction.

Crime produces disapproval in society by offending strong definite sentiments of [the] collective conscience. [A] crime must be very definite [cf. Durkheim 1893:80].

Immorality offends less intensive sentiments; produces disapproval in society, and [the] individual who does not share disapproval is himself disapproved of by society. Moral law is very different in [a] complicated society from what it is in simpler societies, where there is [a] definite common conscience.

As regards crime, [an] offence against [the] state [is] more heavily punished than one against [an] individual. Punishment varies directly with [the] intensity of [the] collective sentiments offended [cf. Durkheim 1893:85, 96]. If punishment arose as vengeance it would be [an] individual matter, whereas in fact it is social. In primitive society death is avenged, but always from one society to another—not on [a] fellow-tribesman (cf. [the] compensation of [the] dead man's *genos* in Ancient Greece). In primitive society punishment is for [a] ritual offense, and is death (e.g., [a] woman [is] killed if accidentally she sees [the] bullroarer among some Australian tribes)—i.e., religious sentiment, very intense, is offended.

Evolution of punishment [cf. Durkheim 1893:96ff.]:

1. At first no one does offend, [because the] sentiment [is] too strong; so that murder of [a] fellow-tribesman [is] unpunished (Nandi) because vengeance on [the] offender is [an] equal offence. For [a] breach of ritual prohibition, offender or community are expected [automatically] to draw [the] vengeance of [the] offended power.

2. Fear of these evil consequences leads society to punish or kill [an] offender—[but this is] not organised in [a] primitive community.

[The] first offences are those against religion. Vendetta ceases when two societies draw closer together and form [a] whole; then compensations [are] arranged—i.e., [the] wrong is to be righted or else [the] murderer must die to make things even. Punishment [is] really expiation, not deterrent, because it varies with [the] intensity of [the] eclectic sentiment outraged; it is [a] reaction of society against [the] offence. [The] coherence of society [is] increased by collective indignation against offence, and so [the] social conscience [is] stimulated—to that extent punishment [is a] deterrent.

As society evolves, actions affecting religious sentiments become less important than those against [the] individual. [The] cause of this [is] obscure. [The] relation of morality to religion persists—[the] divergence of [the] good and [the] *sacer* arises later. [The] dissociation of religion and morality develops with more complicated society.

Every type of society has [a] special type of collective conscience [cf. Durkheim 1893:105ff.]. In primitive society, morality and religion [are] closely bound together; then individual offence grows up and preponderates over ritual [offence]. In [the] most highly developed societies ritual offences [are] hardly considered. Vendetta [is] a religious matter—supernatural calamity [is] expected if it is neglected. With weakening of [the] clan, offense against [the] individual comes to fore. Individual responsibilities arise collaterally with individual rights. As simple society becomes more complex, tradition weakens and [the] individual [is] freer. Intense conservatism of primitive society; hence [the] great part of religion in daily life. [The] progressive nature of offence [is] exemplified from Ancient Greece and Rome (ritual offence); also in Deuteronomy and Leviticus [cf. Durkheim 1893:138].

Why does tradition weaken? It first changes from concrete to more general—due to increase in size of [the] community. With [the] growth of society, man travels longer distances and learns other individual variations. In modern times with [the] increase of population and density [in] towns, [the] weakening of tradition [is] manifest as compared with country. Contact with others produces liberty of [the] individual; and so arises [the] importance of [an] offence against [the] individual. Morality [is] thus freed of [its] religious element [cf. Durkheim 1893:159].

Crimes—things considered as such at various stages of development of society:

1. Violation of sacredness [and] offences against ritual [are the] greatest crimes at first—[there are] extremely few such today.

2. Strict regulations of family relations in older codes—filial obedience, etc., [is] insisted on.

3. Growth of civil law—i.e., restitution, payment of damages—[is a] result of [the] complexity of interrelation of individuals.

[An] instance of [this] development [is the] condemnation of incest in all societies. In [the] first stage, exogamy in [a] community of two sections [is] very strict. [With the] later development of kinship more as we regard it, [it is] consanguinity which regulates marriage after [the] clan has broken down—e.g., cousin-marriage among Todas. Forbidden degrees vary diametrically in different societies.

Growth of crime: [the] sociological view [is] that it is due to [a] crisis of society—e.g., sectarian, political, economic crises always produce [an] increase of crime. (Prof. Lombroso attributes crime solely to physiological causes—[the] criminal [is] born of [a] degenerate type.) In primitive society [there is] no crime because [there are] no moral crises—[the] social conscience [is] in stable equilibrium.

[Lecture Topic Three: cf. printed schedule XI]

Representation: a way of thinking and feeling about objects or classes of objects which is peculiar to [an] individual. There must be something in common between our representations for us to understand each other. Actions [are] determined by representations in individuals.

Collective representations: consensus of individual representations due to social not physiological causes: e.g., sun and moon in collective representations in England as compared with that of savage—[though the] disc of light [is] common to all. [Compare] also [the] collective representations of God, death, women, animals (totemic and non). Definition: Collective representations are ways of thinking and feeling imposed on [the] individual from without by society. [The] conflict between religion and science is [a] conflict between social concepts and individual concepts.

In primitive society collective representations play [a] greater part, and are much fuller and more complex (e.g., concept of totemism). [The] same thing [is] true of modern small sects like theosophists, etc. That is to say, [a] small isolated group has strong traditions—i.e., [the] strength of tradition varies inversely with [the] density of society. In complex society several different circles impress different collective concepts on the individual. In [a] very small society [a] small circle of individual objects [is] common to all and thought is concrete—each rock has individuality. In larger societies, [there are] local variations and less concreteness. Religious ideas [are] also concrete in [a] very small society. [The] idea of species instead of individual develops with larger society. Objects of worship become generalized—finally divinity [is] put right outside [the] concrete world.

Relation of mental life of society to its structure: classification [is] not by similarity but into two phratries with savages, and [the] world [is] divided in same way. All animals belong to one or [the] other phratry—so too winds, constellations in certain totemic societies in Australia, [and this is] probably universal [cf. Durkheim & Mauss 1901:10–11]. With Pueblo Indians [there are] seven groups with animal totems; all colours [are] so classified, [the] points of [the] compass, and every conceivable object. Probably [there were] originally two—parrot for South and raven for North—i.e., [the] universe [is] modelled on [the] village where clans [are] allocated [cf. Durkheim & Mauss 1901:42–43]. In West Africa [we find the] same idea of dividing up [the] universe (cf. Dennett, *Black Man's Mind*). Thus concepts [are] based on social structure. [The] individual, apart from psycho-physical conditions, is [a] result of social conditions. With increased density of society, liberation from traditions and differentiation of individuals [occurs].

Evolution of general ideas: mind [is] best studied through language—which is [a] way of thinking, and is imposed on [the] individual by society. Causes [are] to be sought for changes in language. Institutions [are] dependent on social structure. Vocabulary varies [in] different groups or sets of individuals (cf. slang, medieval and modern). Language also varies with sexual solidarity—cf. different language for men and women, or common language for both and special one for men in addition. Extreme concreteness of primitive languages: e.g., Torres Straits; Ponka Indian; Australian languages have verb varying for number of [the] direct object, whether done for first time, in morning, midday, or evening. Often [there is] no generic term for tree (special names for each species) nor for animal, fish (Andamanese). [There is a] tendency to pictorial character: e.g., Klamath Indians express motion for all directions, not simply moving. [A] large vocabulary [is] therefore necessary: e.g., [the] Andamanese [have] different verbs to express binding one thing to another. Thought [is] more concrete, [there are] less general ideas—[as] exemplified by gesture language. Hence [there is] difficulty of expressing emotions in language, and therefore [a] difficulty to find out about savages' feelings.

But art is fundamentally [an] expression of emotion, so that [the] evolution of art should be studied. Art [is] very conventional in simple societies: e.g., Andamanese dancing and singing [is] always exactly [the] same in form—three beats in songs (two short, one long) or maybe four beats followed by three. [There is] gradual evolution till we get to art which is [an] individual expression of emotion. At [the] primitive stage every man is poet, artist, etc.

[Lecture Topic Four: cf. printed schedule X]

Relation of Individual to Society:
1. Progress in division of labour, differentiation of social function.
2. Same thing in language and thought—development from concrete [to] general.
3. Religion [is] more concrete and [the] individual [is] bound. In latest development, when national culture has broken down, individual variations arise.
4. Morals—in primitive society [there are] very strict and detailed laws, [and] no individuality. Freedom [comes] with progress, and regulations survive only to protect individual.

Sociology is [the] study of collective concepts or representations, psychology that of individual concepts; but psychology of religion is also [an] application of sociology, so too is psychology of art.

[Lecture Topic Five: cf. printed schedule IX]

Economic Institutions. Economic institutions of primitive peoples [are] little studied. Sociology tries by finding a series of phenomena to establish definite causal laws; whereas the political economist starts from a priori theory, from which he tries to deduce all the economic institutions around him, at the same time separating them from all the other institutions found in any social group. Moral, juridical and technical institutions [are] to be taken into account to understand economic institutions.

In primitive societies economic institutions [are] more closely bound up with other institutions than in more developed societies. In Australia economic life [is a] function of totemic beliefs. [A] clan does not eat [its] totem but must perform ceremonies for its increase. With [the] change of structure of society to more complex [forms, the] means of obtaining livelihood change.

[It is] therefore convenient to speak of economic systems which have followed one another, e.g.,

1. In lowest society, [there is] communism in production and consumption —[e.g., the] Andamanese, so too Eskimo in winter (less communistic in summer).

2. Communism within the clan. In these cases society [is] divided into bodies larger than [a] family. In North Australia [the] clan produces and consumes wealth—[this is] found only where [there is] no division of labour other than [the] sexual one, which exists all over the world:

Men: hunting pig, turtle, dugong, fish, use canoes mostly, travel through jungle, make canoes, bows and arrows; communal cooking by bachelors.

Women: collecting roots, firewood, shellfish, catch fish in hand nets, carry water for family, cooking, basket-making, make nets and all ornaments.

3. Hunting and agriculture—harder time for women. In primitive society women [are] signified by digging stick, [and] in third stage [they are] still so represented. Agriculture may develop while still in [stage two], but [as] a rule not till individual production and consumption by [the] family have arisen.

[Here the] division of labour begins. Making of implements [is] separated from [the] general life of community—e.g., in Polynesia canoe-making is [the] work of definite people. [The] causes of this [are] difficult to understand:

1. Before Adam Smith it was thought division [is] due to desire to exchange —[this is] scarcely true, though division presupposes exchange.

2. Division of labour [is] due to pressure of population on means of subsistence. Division produces more wealth.

3. [It is] impossible to make [a] general law without studying special cases; in Polynesia [it is] said to be due to development of special ability, but [this is] not proved.

Against [cause number] (2) we have [the] fact that we do not live at [the] same level as primitive societies, and we can trace [a] greater need in higher [ones]; therefore, [the] individual needs higher level of subsistence. [The] greater needs of [the] same population could not be supplied with [the] same amount of labour that would be required if [the] needs were those of savages. [The] chief feature in economic institutions has been [the] fact of [the] division of labour. Hence institutions have gradually changed.

[Economic] systems [are] not yet properly classified, e.g.:

1. Economy of Greece with slave labour. Family was [the] unit of consumption and production, but with [the] adjunct of slaves.

2. Economy of German tribe when first known. Various communities carried on trade in [their] own country. [This] developed into mediaeval system of guilds (bodies performing special tasks).

3. From guilds came [the] establishment of factories, [and the] economic institutions of the nineteenth century.

[The] first general idea in [the] evolution of mankind is [the] production of wealth; from this, specific problems can be solved (cf. *L'Année Sociologique I*).

[Lecture Topic Six: cf. printed schedule XII]

Laws, though [the] heritage of society, [are the] work of individuals—mechanical causes working through individuals (according to sociologist). Sociology deals with what is, not with what should be. [The] distinction [is] between normal and abnormal developments: cohesion [is] necessary to all society—what makes for cohesion is normal; contrary tendency [is] abnormal. Desires to change institutions, ethical movements are [the] results of certain sets of conditions. Development [is] slow in primitive society, crises rare. In highly developed society [there are] constant crises, always movement towards change. In present day movements like socialism and feminism, [the] sociologist seeks causes. [The] chief difficulty is [the] complexity of society.

Theory: Institutions of society depend on its social structure. [There are] five sorts of cohesion: local solidarity; national solidarity; religious solidarity; domestic or family solidarity; professional solidarity (of people performing same functions).

1. [The] diminution of local solidarity during last centuries in Europe [was] caused by (a) increased density of population, concentration into towns; (b) development of means of communication in nineteenth century. This is [a] normal development—increase in population [is] quite normal.

2. National solidarities have developed unevenly, [with the] breakdown of barriers by increased communication and commerce, [the] increase of social and moral intercourse. [This is a] normal development, [and] has gone on all through history. But [there is] perpetual recurrence to national ideals, especially in [the] nineteenth century: e.g., Protection—normal or abnormal? Tendency to break down solidarity [is] stronger at present.

3. Religious solidarity [shows] diminution. Growth of free thought shows this. Double wave: [at] first, [the] universal church splits up into smaller bodies, but these have strong tradition and greater solidarity. [The] normal development [is that] tradition steadily gives place to individual as society develops.

4. Domestic solidarity [is] weakening mostly in Europe—[e.g., the] facility of divorce—but [it is] impossible to say whether [this is a] permanent development.

5. Professional solidarity regulates [the] relations of people where division of labour [is] very fully worked out. At first [it] increased proportionally: Colleges of Ancient Greece and Rome, Guilds of mediaeval Europe, continuous development till [the] end of [the] eighteenth century. Then [the] guilds dis-

appeared just when machinery set up new conditions and further specialised labour. Guilds could not be adapted to fit new conditions. [This was an] abnormal change, because this form of organisation [is a] necessary development with division of labour.

Thus [the] cohesion of society has tended to diminish in modern times—to this [are] due [the] movements of [the] nineteenth century. (Cf. Durkheim on Suicide—[which is] greater where religious and domestic solidarity [are] less.) Mostly [this] movement has its countermovement: [the] counter to socialism is individualism (Ibsen, Nietzsche), but individualism brings out [the] very cause of socialism, viz. detachment of [the] individual. [The] same causes lead to both movements.

[Lecture Topic Seven:
No counterpart on printed schedule]

Totemism and Exogamy. Exogamy: two or more divisions of tribe which must marry outside. Where two divisions [are] again subdivided, these [are] called phratries, and [the] subdivisions of phratries [are] clans. [They are] supposed to be descended from [a] common ancestor. [Their] social structure [is a] segmentary organisation assuming kinship. There may be a stage prior to exogamy, but exogamy appears [to be] universal at one stage, [though the] evidence [is] less clear for us and Semitic peoples.

Totemism: true totemism only exists where clans [are] exogamous, but not always there. [The] relations between individual and totem animal vary—killing, food-tabu, reproduction ceremonies. In some parts [a] man [is] said to work magic with help of totem. [There are] other religious institutions distinct from totemism: e.g., [the] Guardian Animals most developed in North West America, Salish, etc. This is not [the] origin of totemism because [it is] found where totemism is declining: e.g., [the] series in North West America from totemism of Thlingits shading off to guardian animals of Salish, parallel with change from matri- to patrilineal descent. Breaking down of totemism [is] due to change from matri- to patrilineal descent (cf. series in Southeast Australia).

Typical totemism [is] found only where matrilineal exogamous clan [exists]. Among [the] Arunta, [the] totem of [a] child [is] taken from [the] place where [the] mother [is] supposed to conceive it. Patrilineal eight-class structure [has] arisen out of matrilineal four-class. Change from condition A to condition B: if B [is the] generalised type of totemism we must ascertain general type of pre-totemic exogamic society if we are to determine cause of change from A to B. [The] only pre-exogamous society known as yet is [the] Andamanese (possibly also Malay and Philippine Negritoes, Eskimo, Bushmen].

Andamanese: [The] small group [is] divided into families, food [is] largely communal, society [is] domestic. [There is] no question of matri- or patrilineal descent; no matri- or patripotestas. [The] individual simply belongs to territory where [he is] born. [There is] no rule about living with man's or wife's people after marriage. Control of bachelors [is] vested in old men, of spinsters in old women. [To have] no descent at all seems characteristic of general type of pre-totemic pre-exogamous society. [Their] kinship [is] also unique. [There is] no word for uncle or aunt; [their terminology is] more limited than anywhere else. [It is] not classificatory; [the] name for father [is] applied to one man only.

The general type of exogamous society is

1. matrilineal—[there are] very many instances of change from matri- to patrilineal descent.

2. exogamous division into two phratries. Exogamy occurs with three, four, five divisions, but in many cases [there is] evidence that this organisation [was] preceded by two divisions—e.g., Zuni, [where] other divisions arose out of original raven and parrot dual division. (Frazer thinks patrilineal and matrilineal [are] separate and non-successive—[he] argues from Arunta. But [the whole] series for Australia seems to disprove this—they are [the] final stage with patrilineal descent & individual totems.)

How did pre-exogamous society change to exogamy? [There are] two possibilities: (1) segmentation, (2) fusion. Segmentation can be seen going on in several instances—[it is] sudden; fusion [is] a slow process brought about by economic relations. [The] fundamental change is one of social structure, and if [a] theory for this [is] found, exogamy and totemism [will be] accounted for.

[The] great cause is increase of population. Supposing [there is a] great increase of pre-exogamous society, [then] solidarity must change or segmentation take place. [There is a] homogeneous mass about [a] centre, [a] sudden increase, then two centres of cohesion (purely mechanical), and [a] certain tendency for opposition between the two. Structure tends to become organised in primitive societies, therefore [there is a] drawing apart of two groups. At first [the] domestic organisation in [the new] group [is] as in [the] old one, but [a] new expression of solidarity would arise, and this new expression of [the] two-division society is found in exogamy and totemism. [The] veiled hostility between [the] two [is] expressed in exogamy; totemism also is [the] expression of [the] solidarity of [a] single phratry and hostility to [the] other division. [The] religion of [the] Andamanese regards animals as related in [a] certain sense to themselves, so [the] animal world [is] divided when society splits into two groups. [The] change is merely [the] expression of solidarity and hostility between two [phratries—A.C.H.]

[Lecture Topic Eight: cf. printed schedule V & VI]

Religion: ways of thinking, feeling and acting in close connection with [the] functions of society, in accordance with institutions which are concerned with objects termed sacred. In defining religion, [the] usual custom is to take some particular belief, but a definition is required which covers all [the] various kinds [of manifestations]:

1. thinking–myths, beliefs,
2. feeling–sentiment, reverence, awe,
3. acting–ritual, etc. prohibitions.

N.B.: Belief [is] not to be taken as chief or only element. It is through ways of thinking that [the] idea of [the] *sacred* comes in. Sacred [is] to be taken in [its] broader meaning like Latin *sacer*, cf. French *sacre*, applied to powers of evil. Profane [is] that which is not sacred; now it has come to mean contradiction to sacredness. *Sacred originally meant that which is divided off*, whether by reason of purity or impurity. *Taboo* also means something which is set apart, to be dealt with care, approached in a different way from ordinary objects. The object becomes possessed of a power. Religion [is thus] sentiments and ways of acting connected with sacred.

Robertson Smith (*Religion of the Semites*) says originally purity and impurity [were the] same thing. Sacred and unclean [things] both are taboo—in each case to be avoided. At first [they are] avoided for exactly [the] same reason, viz. [a] power residing in the object. With [the] differentiation of this power into good and bad we get ideas of clean and unclean. Religion may be again defined as thoughts, feelings and actions which are connected with a certain idea called sacred. This definition will cover all stages from lowest to highest.

Religion is imposed on [the] individual from without by society—even in [the] latest societies. [In primitive society there is] no case where disbelief in a particular doctrine has been punished. With savages it is difficult to conceive what would happen if a person disbelieved. [Religious beliefs are traditions handed down by society.–A.C.H.]

Religious beliefs and actions are social institutions. But in advanced society religion becomes more individual; such individual religion comes under [the] head of psychology and not of sociology [i.e., individual religion is a psychological phenomenon of quite recent origin–A.C.H.]. Sacred–best illustration is sabbath, [when] certain actions [are] prohibited, others recommended. Sacred actions and profane [are] distinguished–[the] distinction runs through modern society.

Origin of Religion: Among lowest savages we know we have religion as well as language. We cannot get back to [the] very beginning. [There are] two schools of thought: Anthropological (Tylor, Frazer, etc.); Sociological (Durkheim and

French sociologists). [The] anthropological school hold that religion arises as a sort of mistaken science. [The] savage had scientific curiosity, and religion is [an] accidental result of his philosophising. [The] sociological school say religion [is] not [a] result of accident, mistake, etc., but in intimate relation to social life. [It is] a social function, not an individual function, not so much thinking as feeling, not accidental but essential, without which society could not exist [cf. Marett 1908b].

Religion is represented in the mythology, ritual, legends of social life of the people: e.g., with *Andamanese*.

Social Relations:

1. The relation of [a] body of men to food supply and objects used is essential to society, and finds representation in religion.

2. Phenomena of wind, sun, moon, stars, etc. [are] not useful so much, [but] this is another relation which may also be called social.

3. Also changes which take place in relation of individual to society: marriage, death, etc.

1. [*Prohibitions:* There are a] large number of prohibitions with regard to eating of food; e.g., after eating turtle, [the Andamanese] cover [the] body with wet clay. [There are] certain periods at which you may not eat the food, because these are regarded as critical periods in life; such are [the] several years after puberty, before marriage, before [the] birth of [a] child, when [a] relative dies. Prohibitions [are] simply due to belief in a certain power connected with these objects. How does [this] connection of ideas arise? [The] life of [the] Andamanese [is] quite taken up with [the] food question. When not hunting they are dancing or telling stories connected with hunting. [Their] whole religious life [is] set on one object—namely food. [The] social feelings of [the] Andamanese in connection with food find expression in connection with food. [The] sense of the struggle of hunting [them] creates [the] notion that it is not quite safe to eat the animals, therefore [they] abstain at dangerous periods or cover themselves with clay afterwards.

2. *Mythology:* Myths [are] connected with two monsoons, also with natural landmarks (e.g., two blocks supposed to be frogs), and with creatures of [the] forest. [These are] perpetually spoken of as though they were human beings: [they are] said to be ancestors. [There are] stories of how a man became a bird, and how a bird became a man by having [its] wings and tail cut off. [Their] whole surroundings—sun and moon, rocks, animals—all [are] taken into [the] body of myths, and these are almost exclusively religious.

3. *Institutions*—connected with initiation, marriage and death. At puberty [the] change of [the] relation of [the] individual to society is regarded as a change in his religious life. [They have] no chiefs, but intelligent people become wizards. [Their] power came from the dead. This is [the] whole social life of [the] Andamanese.

Ceremonies connected with death [cf. Radcliffe Brown 1922:285ff.]: Death is [a] social change, since individual leaves society to which he belongs, and [a] gap remains:

Readjustment [is] necessary. Relatives mourn for three months (till [the] bones [are] exhumed and made into ornaments), during which time they must abstain from dancing and certain foods, [and are] smeared with clay. At [the] conclusion of [this] period of mourning, [the] mourners dance while all the rest weep to ward off danger of [a] magical-religious nature. During period of mourning, mourners have been in [a] dangerous condition. After death [a] man does not entirely leave society, [but is] still there more or less, and [the] place where death occurred is abandoned. [His] relatives and friends share in his condition, and so [it is] dangerous to come in contact with them. While [the] man is still hovering between [the] land of [the] dead and [the] land of [the] living, his people are to some extent separated from both worlds. When [the] flesh has come off [his] bones, mourners are free to come back to ordinary social life. [The] man has then finished his journey to [the] land of dead (sometimes [this] takes even two years). N.B.: Little notice [is] taken of [the] death of [an] uninitiated child, [who is] not yet a full member of society.

[At this point there are instructions to insert the "next" page marked A; although in fact four pages farther on in the preserved sequence, it is incorporated here.]

In Australia [there are] elaborate ceremonies connected with death. Each man occupies [a] certain religious position in society. [A] kangaroo man will perform certain ceremonies to make his totem animal increase. If he gets old and useless and his successor has taken his place, [then] when he dies very little account [is] taken of him. The belief in [the] continued existence of [a] man may be connected with this idea of his absence from society. [The] concrete form of the idea is found in the idea that the man has gone away to another world. Again, any natural phenomena which can be placed over against society as strongly affecting it come to be religious. Death comes to have [a] religious quality. [The] society of [the] dead is [a] society cut off from [the] society of [the] living, but [a] certain relation [is] thus established between [the] two worlds. With [the] savage, death [is] not due to natural causation but to [the] intervention of [the] dead, if not [the] result of violence. [He] does not explain how [the] influence of [the] dead works. Death may be due again to influence of magician. [end of insert]

Similarly, in initiation there is a social change, a passing from [the] condition of [a] child to that of [a] grown-up person. Marriage also [is] a change in social relation. All these changes become religious.

[The] anthropological school [say] animism [is a] certain mistaken philosophy about dead men, etc., [a] belief in a soul, arising from (a) dreams, (b) death, which seems [a] curious change (dead body left, soul must have gone, so every man is double).

Objection: Savages are just ordinary people and do not theorise about dreams. Nowhere do we find this belief in a soul among savages, but [there are] enormous complications, myths, etc. Tylor's theory [is] really too simple—if a theory at all, it must be simple.

[The] sociological school say [the] origin of all these beliefs is found in social structure. *The soul is representative of [the] social relation of [the] individual.* [The] individuality of man [is] made up of social relations; he realises [this] emotional and social relation. He pictures this, hence [there arise] myths concerning the soul.

[The] change[s] in social relation[s] of [the] individual at initiation and death are parallel. At initiation ceremonies there is a suggestion that there is a giving of a soul to a man. [The] outward sign may be [a] bullroarer, etc. [But] what you really give the initiate is a new set of social relations—a new soul. In some tribes a man can keep on being initiated into further stages, continually getting a new name with each step (North American tribes).

As regards *Magic*, Frazer says [it is a] sort of mistaken science; [the] sociological school explains magic as [a] social relation. [There is a] belief in [a] certain power. [A] person has supernatural power—is a magician (cf. essay on magic by [Hubert & Mauss 1902]). Anything which is a man's property has some sort of religious relation to him; [the] thing participates in [the] nature of [the] individual. You buy something from him and so get power over him; therefore in selling he goes to [the] trouble of getting rid of this power. [The] sociological school explain most features of magic according to this belief.

Function of Religion—to organise as a definite social institution the main feelings which are connected with [the] relation of [the] individual to society, and so to intensify those feelings and bring them into a sort of order. Feelings are changeable and therefore they require organising, and this religion does. When emotions become associated with definite belief (as with death) they can be handled, talked about, and customs and myths arise.

In all primitive societies the first sanctions are religious sanctions—disapproval and approval. [The] origin of moral ideas is religious—e.g., homicide [is a] religious sin rather than [a] crime. Religious offences are actions prohibited, such as incest, etc., many of which seem to us to have no meaning. These are always associated with religious sanction. This or that thing has been made sacred. Morality [is] not dependent on law but on religious customs.

[There are] various emotions, but they may be classed together under sacredness and religion. No descriptive terms exist for many of the emotions. Emotions of different societies and different individuals vary, for instance what Romans placed under *sacer*—hence [the] difficulty of defining religion in savages.

Mana—defined. All ghosts of dead people [are] supposed to possess it to some extent; a man who possessed it in life is much more powerful when dead. Among [the] Andamanese [there is] no specific word for mana, sacred, etc., but they called rainy season "hot" (Kimil) and [also] those passing through initiation ceremonies. No one will name initiates at the time. [A] magician can remove hotness or coldness from the wind.

[The] whole problem of religion resolves itself into two questions: (1) to what different things the notion of sacredness is applied; (2) and how the notion has changed from time to time. What is found in religion therefore is a notion of the kind which we cannot precisely define. The whole of religion is not for instance found in totemism. What we must do is to endeavour to class certain beliefs connected with definite objects, such as those connected with initiation. Another class of phenomena are those connected with death. We can class the notions together and trace their evolution through various societies.

Distinction between Magic and Religion: Frazer says in magic [a] ceremony [is] efficacious per se, in religion [the] intervention of [a] higher being [is] necessary. Objections to Frazer's theory: religion and magic have this much in common—both [are] derived from society; both start with [the] same set of ideas and beliefs—as, e.g., [the] idea of mana [is] found in both. Many religious ceremonies are immediately efficacious, and many magical ones require spirits. [The] distinction lies in another direction—religion [is] essentially [a] matter of [the] whole society; magic [is] essentially [a] matter of the individual. (Hubert & Maus) [*sic.*] [The] distinction [is] sociological, [and] not concerned with [the] nature of the rites. E.g., [the] rain-making rite [is] gone through for [the] advantage of [the] whole society by [the] whole society—therefore [it is] religion. (Brown saw [an] Andamanese magician trying to stop [a] cyclone. Frazer would say if [it were] magic, it would not involve prayer.) [The] fundamental notions of mana, etc., [are] common to both religion and magic; therefore [the] definition of religion includes magic. In India exactly [the] same ritual [occurs] in magic and religion (Brahman's sacrifice).

Acknowledgments

I would like to thank Mark Francillon for suggestions regarding the early Durkheimian literature in England, as well as Robert Ackerman, Stefan Collini, and Robert Alun Jones for responding to inquiries. My research assistant Timothy Van Housen helped track down references, and my colleague Raymond Fogelson was, as usual, forthcoming with helpful comments on a draft of the introduction. I would like to thank the Syndics of Cambridge University Library for permission to reproduce the lecture notes, and to express my special gratitude to Mrs. Cynthia Pike, Radcliffe-Brown's daughter, for so graciously providing the accompanying photograph.

References Cited

Abrams, P. 1968. *The origins of British sociology: 1834–1914.* Chicago.

Collini, S. 1978. Sociology and idealism in Britain, 1880–1920. *Archives Européennes de Sociologie* 18:3–50.

Durkheim, E. 1893. *The division of labor in society.* Trans. G. Simpson. Reprint ed. New York (1966).

———. 1895. *The rules of the sociological method.* Trans. S. Soloway & J. Mueller. Reprint ed. New York (1964).

———. 1897. *Suicide: A study in sociology.* Trans. J. Spaulding & G. Simpson. Reprint ed. New York (1966).

———. 1905. Rèponse à Monsieur Lang. *Folk-Lore* 16:215.

Durkheim, E., & M. Fauconnet. 1905. Sociology and the social sciences. *Soc. Papers* 1:258–82.

Durkheim, E., & M. Mauss. 1901. *Primitive classification.* Trans. R. Needham. Chicago (1963).

Ellis, H. 1898. Review of E. Durkheim, *Le suicide. Mind* 8:249–55.

Frazer, J. G. 1900. *The golden bough: A study in magic and religion.* 2d ed., 3 vols. London.

———. 1910. *Totemism and exogamy.* 4 vols. London.

Harrison, J. E. 1903. *Prolegomena to the study of Greek religion.* Cambridge.

———. 1912. *Themis: A study of the social origins of Greek religion.* Cambridge.

Hartland, E. S. 1903. Émile Durkheim's *L'Année Sociologique,* 1901–02. *Folk-Lore* 14:426–35.

Hubert, H., & M. Mauss. 1902. Esquisse d'une théorie générale de la magie. *L'Année Sociologique.* 7:1–146.

Kelly, L. 1983. Structure, function and anarchy in Radcliffe-Brown. Annual Meeting of the Central States Anthropological Society, April 8.

Lang, A. 1905. *The secret of the totem.* London.

Langham, I. 1981. *The building of British social anthropology: W. H. R. Rivers and his Cambridge disciples in the development of kinship studies, 1898–1931.* Dordrecht, Holland.

Lévi-Strauss, C. 1962. *Totemism*. Trans. R. Needham. Boston (1963).

Marett, R. R. 1908a. *The threshold of religion*. London.

―――. 1908b. A sociological view of comparative religion. *Soc. Rev.* 1:48–60.

―――. 1941. *A Jerseyman at Oxford*. London.

Marett, R. R., ed. 1908. *Anthropology and the classics*. New York (1966).

Murray, G. 1907. *The rise of the Greek epic*. Oxford.

Needham, R. 1974. Surmise, discovery, and rhetoric. In *Remarks and inventions: Skeptical essays about kinship*, 109–72. London.

Persistiany, J. 1960. Durkheim's letter to Radcliffe-Brown. In *Essays on sociology and philosophy*, ed. K. H. Wolff, 317–24. New York (1964).

Perry, R. J. 1975. Radcliffe-Brown and Kropotkin: The heritage of anarchism in British social anthropology. *Kroeber Anth. Soc. Papers* 51/52:61–65.

Radcliffe-Brown, A. R. 1922. *The Andaman islanders*. Cambridge.

Schapera, I. n.d. Social anthropology. [Notes on the lectures of Radcliffe-Brown at Capetown University, 1924?] in the library of the Institute of Social Anthropology, Oxford.

Stewart, Jessie. 1959. *Jane Ellen Harrison: A portrait from letters*. London.

Stocking, G. W., Jr. 1976. Radcliffe-Brown, Lowie, and *The history of ethnological theory*. *Hist. Anth. Newsl.* 3(2):5–8.

Tax, S. 1932. Primitive religion: Notes on the lectures of A. R. Radcliffe-Brown, winter 1932. *Anth. Tomorrow* 4(2) (1956):3–41.

Testart, A., ed. 1979. Lettres de Radcliffe-Brown à Mauss. *Études durkheimiennes* 4:2–7.

Watson, E. G. 1946. *But to what purpose: The autobiography of a contemporary*. London.

White, I. 1981. Mrs. Bates and Mr. Brown: An examination of Rodney Needham's allegations. *Oceania* 51:193–210.

RADCLIFFE-BROWN AND BRITISH SOCIAL ANTHROPOLOGY

GEORGE W. STOCKING, JR.

Two Views of British Social Anthropology at Midcentury

Late in 1951, an exchange took place in the pages of the *American Anthropologist* between George Murdock of Yale University and Raymond Firth of the London School of Economics. The immediate occasion was the appearance the preceding year of *African Systems of Kinship and Marriage* (Radcliffe-Brown & Forde, eds. 1950), in which exemplary products of two decades of empirical research were analyzed in the context of a theoretical orientation there given its final formulation after four decades of elaboration and refinement. The volume's contributors included most of the leading figures of the elite Association of Social Anthropologists, which five years previously had sorted itself out from the motley assemblage of the Royal Anthropological Institute (ASAM: 7/23–4/46). As the contributors' institutional identifications in the table of contents testified, they by then occupied professorial positions from which they were to dominate academic anthropology in the British sphere over the next two decades. Looking back from that later vantage point, their epigonal historian described them as "an exceptionally tightly-knit professional group, with a revolutionary methodology, shared standards of training and evaluation, and a fairly coherent theoretical framework" (Kuper 1973:9–10). From the perspective of their transatlantic critic in 1951, they seemed to have all of "the characteristic earmarks of a 'school'"–which Murdock regarded as per se grounds for questioning their membership in an international scientific community of "anthropologists" (1951:470).

Although granting them an "average level of ethnographic competence and theoretical suggestiveness probably unequalled by any comparable group elsewhere in the world," Murdock felt that their work was characterized by "offsetting limitations" further justifying their exclusion from the anthropological community: narrowness of substantive and ethnographic interests, theoretical parochialism, "disinterest" in general ethnography, "neglect" of history and the processes of cultural change in time, and a "widespread indifference to psychology." Not only did their narrow focus on kinship and social structure lead to a "fractionating tendency inconsistent with functional theory" and greatly increase "the dangers of reification," it also implied the abandonment of "the special province of anthropology in relation to its sister disciplines": "Alone among the anthropologists of the world the British make no use of the culture concept." They were, in fact, not anthropologists at all, but "professionals of another category," and like "many other sociologists," they tried "to discover valid laws by the intensive study . . . of a very small and non-random sample of all societies," without adequate "comparative or cross-cultural validation." Having resolved his totemic "ambivalence and uneasiness" by defining them as sociological fowl rather than anthropological fish, Murdock was willing to let the British do their own thing—even if it was, as sociology, outdated by a generation (1951:467–72).

Murdock's posture was more than a bit paradoxical. He was himself somewhat marginal to the characteristically Boasian perspective from which he criticized the British; charging them with abandoning history for social typology, he was nonetheless, as a critic and outsider, himself impelled toward intellectual typology. Perhaps because Firth was a non-Africanist insider "not afraid to be called eclectic," he viewed "Contemporary British Social Anthropology" in somewhat less monolithic and more historical terms—as the qualifying temporal adjective implicitly suggests. Although granting the strong influence of "their personal ethnographic experience," Firth suggested that the alleged narrowness of British social anthropologists was more apparent than real. More ethnography was "read than cited," and transatlantic movements of staff and students had "spread knowledge of the more important contributions to American social anthropology." But it was in fact by isolating a particular sphere of inquiry and developing a "more precise framework of ideas and substantial propositions" that British social anthropology had "got its character." However, that character was not peculiarly British, and it was oriented toward a broader scientific community. That this community was not primarily composed of human biologists, students of primitive technology, and archeologists was of small moment. What was important was not to maintain "an old fashioned—and spurious—unified science of man," but rather to strengthen meaningful interdisciplinary connections with other social sciences: "sociology in the narrow sense," psychology, economics, political science, jurisprudence, and "such history as is problem oriented" (1951: 475–80).

But if he insisted that it was by being sociological that British social anthropology had achieved its "unequalled" ethnographic competence and theoretical suggestiveness, Firth was nonetheless willing to grant that "much of what Murdock has said is just and calls more for reflection than reply." Responding to the serious scientific issue underlying Murdock's specific charges, Firth treated various aspects of "the central problem of allowance for variation." In general, his approach was, first, to insist on the legitimacy of a scientific strategy ("generalizations in the natural sciences are assumed to be valid for a wide field of phenomena without the need of testing every instance"); then, to grant in effect certain limitations in its actual implementation ("the unwillingness or inability of the theorist to state clearly how far he was describing the behavior of an abstract model created by himself, and how far he intended his analysis to describe the behavior of people in an actual named society at a given period of time"); and then, to suggest either that not all British were guilty of such failings, or that recent practice showed signs of taking them into consideration ("this view, however, is ceasing to be an effective British position"). After twenty-five years in which it had "done much to establish a more significant typology," British social anthropology now appeared to be "moving slowly and unevenly toward a more systematic study of variation, including variation over time" (1951:478-88).

Because it so neatly juxtaposes the perspectives of the outsider and the insider, the Murdock/Firth exchange would seem to provide a good standpoint from which to view British social anthropology as an historical phenomenon. But it also highlights certain methodological issues in intellectual history—which, like anthropology, faces problems of abstraction and variation. This is the case even when an intellectual phenomenon bears a label (e.g., "Freudian" or "Durkheimian") that protagonists, critics, and historians are all inclined to employ unquestioningly; it is much more so when a unifying label or concept raises hotly debated epistemological issues (as in the case of "paradigm"), or lends itself to a derogatory interpretation (as in the case of "school"). In the present instance, there are so many qualifications, not only in Firth's historicizing defense of British social anthropology, but even in Murdock's typologizing critique, that the historian is hard put to specify just when and in which actors the phenomenon under attack was actually realized. Murdock in fact exempted almost every major British social anthropologist from some aspect of his criticism, and various passages suggest that he, too, saw the "school" as a rather recently emergent historical phenomenon. Postulating a declension from Firth to Fortes to Evans-Pritchard (whose recent rehistoricization he seemed unaware of), Murdock in fact allowed that Richards, Schapera, Forde, Nadel, and Firth all showed "definite intimations" of the "possible emergence" of "a group of anthropologists in the strict sense." He also recognized a considerable distinction between Malinowski—who had still studied culture and who "continued to expand and revise his theories to the last year of his life"—and Radcliffe-Brown—who "seems never to have

corrected a mistake nor to have modified his theoretical position in any significant respect since its earliest formulation decades ago" (1951:466, 472). Murdock's "school" thus threatens to collapse into a single individual.

From this perspective, then, the 1951 exchange suggests that historical inquiry concerning modern British social anthropology might well start with
the career of A. R. Radcliffe-Brown. There, if anywhere, we might expect to
find a proximate source for the distinctive typological features that Murdock
characterized so negatively. But taking a clue from Firth's historicizing response,
and from a concern all would accept as characteristic of British social anthropology, we may perhaps place the problem in a slightly larger framework—one
that may also help in approaching issues of variation and abstraction elsewhere in intellectual history.

Insofar as intellectual movements may be compared to "unilineal descent
groups," one would expect their fission or segmentation to produce groupings
with a distinctly relative or situational character—groupings that would be
both construed and evaluated differently by insiders and outsiders, depending on the context in which group definition was at issue (Beattie 1964:99–
101; Fortes 1953). Although Murdock was not a member of the traditionally
dominant lineage in American anthropology, in confronting the tribe from
across the sea, he tended to view it from a traditionally Boasian standpoint,
and to minimize its internal differentiation. Although Firth was not a member of the currently dominant lineage in British anthropology, and therefore
saw it in much more differentiated fashion, he nevertheless felt it necessary
to defend his tribe against attack from without.

The modern study of segmentary lineages emerged from the work of
Radcliffe-Brown, and it seems appropriate that his own career followed a
definite pattern of oppositional self-definition. As any dominant clan leader
might, he himself tended retrospectively to construe such episodes so as to
emphasize the purity of his descent from earlier ancestral figures. These self-
validating ancestral claims are not without basis; Radcliffe-Brown did, indeed,
derive much of his thinking from Emile Durkheim. However, contemporary
historical evidence suggests that his characteristic anthropological viewpoint
was first developed in opposition to that of a more immediate mentor, W. H. R.
Rivers, during the years between 1910 and 1914; and that its final elaboration
was only accomplished in the 1930s, in opposition first to the dominant orientation within American anthropology, and then to the views of Bronislaw
Malinowski, his competitor for lineage leadership within the British anthropological tribe. While it will not be possible here to treat Radcliffe-Brown's
career in an exhaustively historical fashion,[1] close examination of these criti-

1. Although some gossipy oral history circulates among anthropologists, the career of Radcliffe-
Brown has elicited so far relatively little in the way of serious intellectual historiography. There

cal oppositional episodes may cast light on the historical roots of the viewpoint at issue in the 1951 exchange.

Radcliffe-Brown and the Sequence of Paradigms in Anthropology

Rather early in his career, fifteen years before he augmented his name to distinguish himself from the "many Browns in the world" (ACHP: RB/ACH 11/12/21), A. R. Radcliffe-Brown became possessed of a set of ideas which, as applied to the particular national disciplinary tradition in which he worked, were significantly innovative. Their elaboration, systematization, and refinement became the preoccupation of his somewhat nomadic professional career. Shedding books and papers as he moved from place to place around the intellectual periphery, he deliberately carried little intellectual baggage. Although he acknowledged certain large intellectual debts that placed him in legitimating relation to major traditions in social theory, he was reluctant to see his own viewpoint as an historical phenomenon. Much given to retrospective systematization, he later bridled at Robert Lowie's suggestion that he had "shifted his position" on significant theoretical issues (Stocking 1976b), and

---

are several important obituary essays and appreciations (e.g., Eggan 1956; Elkin 1956; Firth 1956; Fortes 1956a; Fortes, ed. 1949; Stanner 1956, 1968) as well as chapters based on published sources in various histories of anthropology, either general or specifically British (e.g., Kuper 1973; Harris 1968; Hatch 1973). He is discussed in works of an historical-theoretical character (Fortes 1969a; Jarvie 1964; Leach 1961, 1976), and there is by now a body of what might be called historical-critical writing largely devoted to the question of the originality or derivative character of his work on Australian social organization (e.g., Needham 1974; White 1981). The only extended historical treatment, a chapter in Ian Langham's history of the Rivers school (1981:244–300), shares the strengths and weaknesses of that volume, which is indeed characteristically Riversian in its combination of systematic empirical research and questionable interpretation. Although based on extensive archival research, and a commendable concern with the technical details of kinship analysis, it is marred by the overinflation of Rivers' theoretical influence on Radcliffe-Brown, and rather uncritically accepts the recent attacks on him. A satisfactory historical understanding of Radcliffe-Brown's contribution to the development of British Social Anthropology will have somehow to transcend not only the myth-history generated by some of his followers, but also the debunking efforts of his critics. While it is of course necessary to dispose of certain exaggerated claims of originality, the attempt to reduce Radcliffe-Brown to an entirely derivative figure does not help us understand the great impact he had on anthropology on both sides of the Atlantic in the 1930s, 1940s, and 1950s. It should be, but probably is not, needless to assert that to focus on episodes in the career of a single anthropologist is not to commit oneself to a "great man" theory of the history of anthropology, nor to deny the importance of many other factors, including the funding and the colonial context of anthropological inquiry. I have approached the funding question in an unpublished manuscript drawn upon herein (Stocking 1978c); the latter merits more systematically historical treatment than that initiated in Asad (1973).

perhaps tended to push back the dates by which he formulated his character-istic positions. But however cavalierly he may have treated the ideas or the empirical data of those he regarded as amateurs, and however much his olym-pian posture may have alienated some of those with whom he came in con-tact, his devotion to the refinement and propagation of his viewpoint was a critical factor in a major intellectual reorientation in British anthropology.

To place that reorientation in the broadest perspective, it will help to keep in mind that anthropological speculation prior to 1900 had always been car-ried on in an essentially diachronic framework, in the British as in all other European anthropological traditions. In somewhat simplified schematic terms, the history of anthropology from its earliest origins may be viewed as the al-ternate dominance of two paradigms: on the one hand, a progressive develop-mental paradigm, deriving ultimately from Greek speculation on the origin of human civilization, which was expressed in sixteenth-century humanist, eighteenth-century progressivist, and nineteenth-century evolutionist specu-lations on the same topic; on the other, a migrational or diffusionary para-digm, deriving ultimately from biblical assumptions about the genealogy of nations, which was expressed in medieval and again in seventeenth-century speculation, and was reasserted in the early nineteenth century as the "ethno-logical" tradition (Stocking 1973, 1978a, 1981a, 1983b). While it is impossible here to offer a detailed comparison, it is important to emphasize that although the assumptions of their inquiry differed in many respects, both paradigms focussed on processes of change in time, which given the nature of the evi-dence they dealt with, could only be approached by indirect means. Both paradigms compared forms coexisting in the present in order to reconstruct the past, whether in terms of hypothetical developmental sequences or pre-sumed historical connections.

In this context, Radcliffe-Brown's work may be seen as an important con-tributing factor to the first major break in the alternation of diachronic paradigms, and the reorientation of an important current of anthropological inquiry toward the investigation of synchronic sociological problems. This dehistoricization—which was never complete (cf. Lewis 1984), and arguably was never intended to be, which would surely be derogated by many anthro-pologists today, and seems likely now to be reversed—is by no means to be attributed solely to the influence of Radcliffe-Brown. In a somewhat different way, Malinowski also contributed to it; and the fact that a similar change occurred in American anthropology suggests that more general influences may have been at work (cf. Stocking 1976a). Nevertheless, it is in this context that Radcliffe-Brown's anthropological career takes on its maximal historical significance.[2]

2. These two paragraphs take for granted an orientation to the general history of anthropol-ogy that cannot be fully elaborated here, and has been developed so far largely in my lectures,

At the time Radcliffe-Brown came upon the scene, the evolutionary embodiment of the developmental paradigm was entering a state of crisis. Although this crisis has yet to be studied systematically, it is abundantly evident in contemporary historical materials. E. B. Tylor's long-awaited magnum opus on the evolution of religion, already partially in galleys, lay gathering dust in his files, in part at least because of intellectual developments that had called into question some basic Tylorian assumptions (Stocking 1981b). Andrew Lang had just fallen from evolutionary orthodoxy to embrace a degenerationist hypothesis of primitive monotheism (1901). R. R. Marett had just postulated the existence of preanimistic religious phenomena (1900). More generally, there was a growing discomfort with the way in which evolutionary categories articulated with what Marett now preferred to call "magico-religious" phenomena (Stocking 1983a:91). Anthropological debate swirled particularly around the problem of totemism, with special reference to the striking new ethnographic data Baldwin Spencer and Frank Gillen had published on the Arunta of Central Australia (1899). McLennan's original socioreligious conception, in which matrilineal exogamous clans were held together by respect for a single animal emblem (1869), did not fit too easily with the complexities of the section systems regulating Australian Aboriginal marriage. Indeed, by 1906 one observer felt the new Australian data threatened to "overthrow all recognized principles . . . [of] the totemic regulation of marriage" (Thomas 1906:37).

At the center of the turmoil stood James G. Frazer. Despite tension that had arisen with his intellectual master Tylor by the time of its second edition, *The Golden Bough* (1900) is a fine instance of the almost parodic reduction

---

seminars, and certain unpublished manuscripts (though cf. Stocking 1973 and 1978a). Although I use "paradigm" in a way that departs significantly from Kuhn's original usage (cf. Kuhn 1962, 1974), I nevertheless find it a nicely resonant term for recurrent alternative frameworks of anthropological speculation that have some of the characteristics Kuhn attributes to "paradigms." In addition to the developmental and the diffusionary paradigms, one can distinguish a third major traditional anthropological orientation: the polygenist, which is in fact essentially atemporal, since it assumed the existence of distinct types or races of mankind unchanged since their creation. However, its denial of human unity made it fundamentally heterodox to the European anthropological tradition, and it surfaced as a legitimate anthropological alternative only in the mid-nineteenth century, when it was a factor in the crisis of the ethnological paradigm and the emergence of "classical" evolutionism. In viewing Radcliffe-Brown as part of an even more fundamental paradigm discontinuity, I do not wish to imply that a synchronic sociological orientation was without precedent—which he himself appropriately found in Montesquieu (R-B 1958:147). But within the empirical sphere that historically has distinguished "anthropology" as a realm of inquiry and speculation—the comparative study of non-European peoples—the Montesquieuan tradition previously manifested itself always in a diachronic guise, so that it does not seem appropriate to distinguish a synchronic sociological paradigm in the history of anthropology prior to the twentieth century (cf. Stocking 1978a and 1981b).

of the basic assumptions of an intellectual viewpoint that may occur in the work of epigones arriving on the scene after the impulse of originally generative problems has been spent. Its opening pages display all the fundamental assumptions of social evolutionary thought: the uniformity of nature, the psychic unity of mankind, the comparative method, regular stages of development, and the doctrine of survivals (cf. Carneiro 1973). But what is most striking in Frazer are those assumptions that especially characterize what Evans-Pritchard (1933) later called the "English Intellectualist School": the classical principles of associationist psychology (similarity and contiguity) embodied in the two forms of sympathetic magic, and the overriding preoccupation with the problem of the motives behind bizarre customs—notably of course those that "gave birth to the priesthood of Nemi" (1900:I, 4). The same preoccupation motivated the three "theories" of totemism Frazer incorporated into his encyclopedic compilation of data on *Totemism and Exogamy* of 1910, by which time the presumed unity of the diagnostic features that McLennan had linked together back in 1869 was in radical danger of unravelling. Whatever may be the evaluation of his status by more recent anthropologists (cf. Jarvie 1966, and Leach 1966), there is no doubt that in the first decade of the century, Frazer was the figure who more than any other exemplified the evolutionary paradigm, now after four decades in a state of increasing disarray.

Rivers' Conversion from Evolution to Ethnology

Although Frazer was ensconced in his evolutionary armchair in Trinity College when Radcliffe-Brown came up from Birmingham in 1902, Brown's anthropological training came largely from W. H. R. Rivers; he was in fact Rivers' first (and best known) student in that field. Because he later took what proved to be the "wrong" road out of the early twentieth-century paradigm crisis, it has been difficult to gain an adequate understanding of Rivers' historical influence; even the recent effort to resurrect it suffers a bit from compensatory overestimation (Langham 1981; Slobodin 1978). But if the leaders of the next generation reacted sharply against the rather extreme conjectural history of Rivers' later years, it is nonetheless the case that for two decades he was the most influential figure in British anthropology. His electric intellect and striking presence had great impact on all with whom he worked, and his ideas, even when later rejected, helped define the framework of anthropological debate.

Trained originally in medicine, Rivers moved to neurology and psychology in the early 1890s, becoming the first Lecturer in Physiological and Experimental Psychology at Cambridge in 1897. When Haddon organized the Cambridge Anthropological Expedition to Torres Straits, he chose Rivers to carry out the first systematic attempt to apply the "new" experimental psychology to a "primitive" population. To a psychologist familiar with the work of Francis Galton on the inheritance of mental ability in family lines, it seemed only natural to collect genealogies to "discover whether or not those who were closely related resembled one another in their reactions to the various psychological and physiological tests" (Rivers 1908:65). Rivers quickly perceived that the "genealogical method" he used in the Torres Strait had sociological potential as well (1900:75); it in fact articulated admirably with the approach to the study of kinship elaborated thirty years previously by the American evolutionary anthropologist Lewis Henry Morgan in *Systems of Consanguinity and Affinity* (1870). Although Rivers continued to carry out important psychological researches, he devoted much of his energy in the decade after his return from Torres Strait to further ethnographic fieldwork, and to the explication, defense, and revision of Morgan's theories—or, as Rivers put it, to "sifting out the chaff from the wheat of his argument" (1914a:95; cf. 1907).

Although some of Morgan's assumptions had been sharply criticized by the leading British evolutionary theorist of primitive social institutions (McLennan 1876), Morgan's disciple Lorimer Fison early on introduced them into the Australian ethnographic tradition (Fison & Howitt 1880). Subsequently taking the deceased Morgan's place as Fison's armchair mentor-by-correspondence, Tylor was able to suggest an integration of McLennan's conception of exogamy with Morgan's classificatory system (Tylor 1888:265). Via this Australian connection Morganian assumption was also very much a part of Frazer's speculation. If to speak of Rivers' "rediscovery" of Morgan is thus to overstate the novelty of the matter, it is nonetheless true that Rivers' "insistence on Morgan's principle that kinship terminologies and customs depend on social causes, have social functions, [and] reflect socially ordained rights and duties" marked a stage in the development of British social anthropology (Fortes 1969a: 17, 26). As Rivers himself saw it in 1914, the special significance of "the body of facts which Morgan was the first to collect and study" lay in the fact that it provided the basis for a "rigorously deterministic" science of sociology. "We have here a case in which the principle of determinism applies with a rigour and definiteness equal to that of any of the exact sciences, since according to my scheme not only has the general character of systems of relationship been strictly determined by social conditions, but every detail of these systems has also been so determined" (Rivers 1914a:95). Although subsequent exponents (and in some of his moods, Rivers) were not always so naively positivistic, the point of view and tone are authentically those of the later social anthropological tradition: social anthropology was to be the natural science of society, not simply on the basis of a generalized reductionist analogy, but because certain characteristic social phenomena were asserted to be analyzable by a rigorously scientific method.

But if Rivers helped to define the tradition, he himself remained on the other side of a major theoretical divide, insofar as his analysis of social organization was still carried on within a diachronic interpretive framework. In this respect he accepted without question the traditional assumptions of the discipline to which he came rather late in life. Although his scientific training made him quite sensitive to certain issues of method, he seems to have started out in anthropology by rather self-consciously relating himself to the evolutionary viewpoint which, despite evident signs of paradigm strain, still dominated British anthropological theory. One gets a sense of this in his first full-length ethnographic monograph: *The Todas* (1906), based on fieldwork that he did in 1902. Like some of his later work, *The Todas* is a paradoxical amalgam of methodological self-consciousness and uninhibited explanatory imagination—which manifested itself in the context of difficulties Rivers had presenting his somewhat recalcitrant ethnographic data within an evolutionary framework (cf. Mandelbaum 1980; Rooksby 1971; Stocking 1983:89).

To have selected the Todas for ethnographic study in the first place was of course to engage evolutionary theory at a critical point, since their polyandry illustrated a problematic stage in McLennan's sequence of marriage forms (McLennan 1865:73). That Rivers' initial overall explanatory strategy was, however, still evolutionary is variously manifest. He often referred to aspects of Toda culture as representing a certain "stage" of evolution—frequently, a transitional one: thus they had reached "a stage of mental development in which it seems that they are no longer satisfied with the nomenclature of a purely classificatory system, and have begun to make distinctions in their terminology for near and distant relatives" (1906:493 cf. 541). Beyond this, there is a kind of general checking of categories of Toda culture against those of evolutionary theory—often with negative results. Thus the Toda data offered "little to support the idea that the gods are personifications of forces of nature" and "no definite evidence towards the solution of the vexed question of the relation between polyandry and infanticide"—issues that derived respectively from the work of Tylor and McLennan, although Rivers mentioned neither by name (447, 520). Finally, there is Rivers' fundamental idea of what constituted "explanation" in anthropology. Following the English intellectualist tradition, he saw explanation in terms of origin and motive—of discovering or reconstructing what utilitarian purpose people have (or once had) in their minds when they perform a particular customary act. Thus Rivers argued that some features of Toda childbirth ceremonies "had their origin in the motive" of promoting lactation by imitating the flow of milk (329).

It is in this context, as well as the conjunction of ill-starred occurrences that dried up his sources of information toward the end of his fieldwork, that one must view Rivers' often frankly acknowledged difficulties of explanation. Although it ran counter to the assumptions underlying the notion of survival, the most direct way for the field ethnographer to explain a cultural practice in terms of motive was to ask people why they did it. But in most cases, "the Todas were quite unable to give explanations of their customs, the answer to nearly every inquiry being that the custom in question was ordained by the goddess Teikirzi" (1906:14); and Rivers had to make his own inferences about Toda motives. In some cases he simply confessed his inability "to satisfy myself as to what people really had in their minds" (356); in others we can see him retreating toward the doctrine of survivals: "Possibly the Todas may have some clear ideas about the connexion between their bells, gods and dairies, but I could not discover them, and am inclined to believe that the people are now very hazy about the exact place of the bell and the god in their theology" (427). At a more general level, however, there was a recurring problem of evolutionary fit, or the failure of evolutionary expectation: the combination, for instance, of strict regulation of marriage choice with what to Rivers seemed almost total sexual promiscuity (529–32, 549), or the "highly developed" idea of a god and the complete indifference to the desecration of the hilltop cairns associated with Toda gods (453–55). In the end, Rivers was forced to conclude that Toda customs, many of which had "no exact parallels in other places," ran counter to "perhaps the most definite result which modern research in anthropology has brought out": "the extraordinary similarity of customs" among "widely separated races"—which was of course a basic assumption underlying the notion of parallel evolutionary development (4).

It is therefore not surprising that Rivers' specifically generalizing chapters disappoint or otherwise abuse our expectations. After seventeen chapters describing the ceremonies of the Todas, his chapter on Toda religion in general is conceived in residual rather than integrative terms (1906:442)—a fact especially illuminating in contrast to Radcliffe-Brown's *Andaman Islanders* (1922), where the two explanatory chapters take up half the book. The structural equivalent in *The Todas* is a concluding chapter on their "origin and history." Here, after seven hundred pages in an evolutionary key, Rivers suddenly struck a "highly conjectural" diffusionary chord, using his recalcitrant data on Toda religion to suggest that they had come to the Nilghiri hills a thousand years before from the Malabar region, where they had been influenced by Christian and Jewish settlements (693–715). Given the failure of evolutionary assumption to explain so much of the Toda data, Rivers turned instead to another approach to the problem of origins: the diffusionary historical approach characteristic of the alternative diachronic paradigm, which in its "ethnological" incarnation had not disappeared entirely from British anthropology during the era of evolutionary dominance, and was still reflected in many of the interests of Rivers' colleague Haddon (Urry 1982).

Although Rivers' difficulties with his Toda data document some of the stresses a more systematic ethnography helped create in the evolutionary para-

digm around 1900 (cf. Stocking 1983a), and in fact foreshadow his later theoretical development, it was not until the 1911 meeting of the British Association for the Advancement of Science that he announced his "conversion" to
an "Ethnological Analysis of Culture." Rather than interpret cultural phenomena in terms of "independent processes of evolution based on psychological tendencies common to mankind," Rivers now joined the German ethnologists Graebner and Schmidt in explaining them in terms of "the mixture of
cultures and peoples" (1911:125). Elaborating his argument in the context of
difficulties he had with Melanesian data he had collected in 1908, Rivers applied it to Australian Aboriginal culture, which since the work of Spencer
and Gillen had, according to Andrew Lang, become lost "in a wilderness of
difficulties" (1907:209), largely due to problems in relating the section systems
and the totemic clans—ethnographic manifestations, respectively, of Morgan's
and McLennan's evolutionary viewpoints. While for evolutionists Australia
provided a "homogeneous example of primitive human society," Rivers was
troubled by the "coexistence" there of two forms of social organization. So
long as he had been "obsessed" by "a crude evolutionary point of view," this
fact "seemed an absolute mystery" to him. Viewing them now as the result
of a mixture of two peoples similar to that which he had found in Melanesia,
everything was clarified: one had possessed "the dual organisation and matrilineal descent"; the other was "organized in totemic clans possessing either
patrilineal descent, or at any rate clear recognition of the relation between
father and child." Generalizing his argument, Rivers insisted that "evolutionary speculations can have no firm basis unless there has been a preceding
analysis of the cultures and civilizations now spread over the earth's surface."
Otherwise, it was "impossible to say whether an institution or belief possessed
by a people who seem simple and primitive may not really be the product
of a relatively advanced culture forming but one element of a complexity which
at first sight seems simple and homogeneous" (1911:130–32).

Rivers' conversion to ethnological analysis implied neither the abandonment of the Morganian focus on social structure nor the total rejection of
evolutionary assumptions. Precisely because social structure was so "fundamentally important" and resistant to change "except as the result of the intimate blending of peoples," it furnished "by far the firmest foundation" on which
to base ethnological analysis. If one could determine the sequence of changes
in social structure, one could use this to establish "the order in time of the
[other] different elements into which it is possible to analyse a given [culture]
complex" (1911:134, 138). Although Rivers' diffusionary hypotheses required
him in many cases to assume the degeneration of culture in order to account
for "advanced" cultural elements in peoples of otherwise "low" culture, his historical analysis of social structure was at least as dependent on the doctrine

of survivals as evolutionism had been. Without it, he could not use present kinship terminology to reason back to prior marriage practices. Thus to buttress his new theoretical possession, he felt it necessary to argue, successively, *both* "The Disappearance of Useful Arts" (1912a) and "the persistence of the useless" (1913:293).

Viewed in terms of his relation to subsequent social anthropology rather than to evolutionism, there are several further aspects of Rivers' conversion that merit comment. Although Rivers (like many evolutionists) had an incipient notion of "function," it was to be, in the language of Macbeth, "smothered in surmise"; and if he helped transmit the Morganian conception of system, his later diffusionism in fact tended to fragment cultures into their "component elements," which were related to each other not in synchronic systemic terms, but rather in stratified diachronic terms as the layered residues of different episodes of culture contact (1914b:II, 2). Beyond this, there is the problem of Rivers' attitude to "psychology." His stated position, even after his "conversion" to ethnology, was to insist on the continuing validity of a psychological analysis of "the modes of thought of different peoples" as a parallel enterprise (1911:132), and within a few years he in fact moved toward an integration of psychology and ethnology (1917), under the influence of another of his intellectual enthusiasms—psychoanalysis, which he encountered while treating shell-shocked soldiers during the Great War. But for a period after his "conversion," in the context also of his failure to explain Toda culture in psychologistic terms, he seems to have put aside the psychological analysis of culture, because his current psychological viewpoint seemed inadequate to the task. As we shall see, all of these issues were implicated in his relationship to Radcliffe-Brown.

"Anarchy" Brown and the Andaman Islands

Brown first came in contact with Rivers as an undergraduate enrolled in the Moral Science Tripos, which at that time consisted of philosophy, political economy, and psychology (Stocking 1977). He later recalled that as a result of his youthful acquaintance with the British avant-garde intellectual Havelock Ellis and (apparently through Ellis) the exiled Russian anarchist, Prince Peter Kropotkin, he had come up to Cambridge already a "sociologist," intent on devoting his life to "the scientific study of culture" (BMPL:R-B/BM 12/31/29; R-B/Kroeber, as cited in Kelly 1983; cf. Perry 1975). After taking his degree in 1905, he stayed on for a year of work with the newly established Board of Anthropological Studies (Gathercole n.d.), reading physical anthropology with Duckworth, archeology with Ridgeway, ethnology with Haddon, and kinship with Rivers—with whom he had already studied psychology. Retrospectively, he insisted that "from the outset" he and Rivers disagreed "on the subject of method" (R-B 1941:50), and recalled having undertaken in 1905 a "long essay on the concept of function in science" as part of a general work on scientific method (Stocking 1976b). Surviving evidence from the period, however, suggests that his disagreements with his mentor emerged more gradually, and did not fully crystallize until 1913.

Certainly Brown's Andaman fieldwork was undertaken within a framework of diachronic assumption. Although at one point he later said that he had gone out to study a "primitive people who had no totemism" (R-B 1923:22), contemporary evidence and subsequent retrospection both confirm that he was interested in reconstructing the "primitive culture" of the Negrito race, which was presumed to have been the lowest of four population strata in Southeast Asia (R-B 1932:407; cf. ACHP: Temple/ACH 3/16/06). Modelled on that of the Torres Straits expedition, his fieldwork encompassed every aspect of anthropological research, including material culture, physical anthropology, and psychological testing (Stocking 1983a:83). Insofar as social anthropological data were concerned, his work seems not to have been so successful as he and Rivers may have hoped. He had difficulty collecting genealogies, admitting in print that "this branch of my investigation was a failure" (1932:72). Even so, his attempt at what might be called "social paleontology" was—by retrospective systematization in another theoretical context—to provide the underlying empirical basis for the "social physiology" later associated with his name (cf. Kochar 1968).

In 1908, however, that development still lay in the future. Judging by the one long surviving published fragment (which may even *be* the missing Trinity Fellowship thesis?) the first version of Brown's Andaman ethnography was influenced more by Haddon than by Rivers, and showed not a trace of Durkheim (despite his later recollection that he had been introduced to Durkheim's work by Ellis in 1899 [Kelly 1983]). Indeed it seems to have been an almost Boasian attempt at historical reconstruction on the basis of a comparative analysis of culture elements (R-B 1932:407–94). Similarly, articles he published in 1909 and 1910 reflect little of his mature theoretical viewpoint—though in defending himself against the criticisms of the German diffusionist Schmidt he did offer certain strictures on historical arguments based on the doctrine of survivals (R-B 1910a:36). One suspects that it was during the same academic year, when he lectured on Australian ethnology and the Kwakiutl potlatch at the London School of Economics, that he had his first systematic encounter with the Durkheimian literature.

A record of that encounter survives in notes of the series of lectures he gave on "Comparative Sociology" at Cambridge early in 1910 (cf. pp. 113–28, this volume). Brown later said that he had "all his life accepted the hypothesis of social evolution as formulated by Spencer as a useful working hypothesis in the study of society" (R-B 1958:189). Whether derived from Spencer (whom he would have read in large doses for the Moral Science Tripos) or from Kropotkin (whose *Mutual Aid* is, among other things, a melange of social evolutionary assumptions [Perry 1975]), evolutionism provided the underlying framework of the lectures. And though he began by rejecting the principle of unilinearity, he in fact tended to treat institutions in terms of a series of progressive stages. One must immediately add, however, that his evolutionary orientation was heavily Durkheimian. Characteristically, it was the "origin, development, and function" of particular social institutions that he discussed. And indeed, one can pretty well relate particular segments of the lecture series to particular Durkheimian sources.

What is most interesting, from the point of view of the development of Brown's thought, are the two concluding topics, which together occupy close to half of the notes. They consist of reflections on "Totemism and Exogamy" (which may well have been provoked by the appearance, while the series was in progress, of Frazer's compendium), followed by a treatment of the evolution of religion, in which Brown drew on Robertson Smith and Hertz, as well as on Durkheim. It is here that he made the most extensive use of his Andaman data. It is almost as if suddenly, in the course of explicating Durkheim, the Andaman material took on a new significance. If he had found no classificatory system among the Andamanese, it was because they were the type case of the preexogamous society—indeed, the only one yet encountered. Drawing heavily on early Durkheim—the Durkheim of *The Division of Labor*—Brown offered a hypothesis as to how under the pressure of population increase such a society might divide and become exogamous, with a sharing out of the animal world in the process (cf. R-B 1923:20–21).

Contrasting two schools of the interpretation of religion—the British "anthropological" and the French "sociological"—Brown clearly inclined toward the latter as he called on his Andaman data for material to illustrate "The Origin, Development, and Function of Religion." He later suggested that the last two chapters of *The Andaman Islanders* had been written in 1910 "as an attempt to develop a new method in the interpretation of the institutions of a primitive people" (R-B 1922:ix), and some of the lecture material in fact roughly parallels certain portions of the book. But it seems clear that he had not yet fully developed that analysis, if only because certain later theoretical catch-phrases (such as "social value") are absent from the notes. More important, from the point of view of his overall theoretical development, Brown had not yet made the crucial shift from a diachronic evolutionary viewpoint to that of synchronic analysis. This critical shift seems not to have taken place

until several years later, in the context of debate with Rivers over the interpretation of data Brown collected during his second fieldwork expedition to
Western Australia.

The Problem of Totemism in Australia

Brown's original proposal for a field trip to Western Australia was simply for
a general survey, with subsequent concentration on whatever tribe promised "the most valuable results" (ACHP: R-B/Cambridge Board of Anthropology 11/4/09). By the time he arrived in Perth in September 1910, his goals
were more definite. Despite his later much-debated recollection that he had
gone there to find a kinship system he had previously hypothesized to exist,
the interview he gave to The West Australian (R-B 1910b) suggests rather that
he hoped to provide evidence for the hypothesis advanced at Cambridge on
the origin of totemism—on which his views were in critical respects still
rather traditional. Thus although Frazer had been forced to the conclusion
that totemism and exogamy were institutions "fundamentally distinct in origin and nature" (1910:I, xii), Brown still saw them as intimately related. He
proposed nothing less than to "settle" the issues of the totemism debate. The
Australian Aboriginals "personified" a "stage" that "probably every race"—
including "our own ancestors"—had passed through. By studying all the variations of Australian marriage regulations, his expedition would cast light on
"the origin of the system," and on its "progressive development" from "two
to four and from four to eight" exogamous classes (cf. JSBL: R-B/D. Bates
n.d.).

The various accounts of Brown's Australian fieldwork suggest that it, too,
was at best a mixed success (Watson 1946:105–25; cf. Watson 1968 and Salter
1972). Once again, however, mediocre ethnography was to be transformed
by theoretical reflection. Rather than recount what is known of his fieldwork,
first among the syphilitic Aboriginals incarcerated on Bernier Island and later
among mainland groups, or enter the debate about his debt to Daisy Bates,
the devoted ethnographic amateur who for a time accompanied the expedition (Needham 1974; White 1981), it will be more worthwhile to turn to the
surviving contemporary evidence of his developing theoretical viewpoint in
correspondence he carried on with his mentor Rivers while living in Birmingham after his return to England early in 1912.[3]

3. Broken off late in 1912, the Brown/Rivers correspondence resumed the summer of the
following year and continued into the early part of 1914. This correspondence provides the source
material for this and the following section. Because the letters are almost all undated, I have
offered no parenthetical citations to the Brown/Rivers correspondence. Langham (1981:373–74)
offers more specific citations to envelopes 12027, 12039, 12058, and 12062 of the Haddon Collec-

The first letter affirmed a not-yet-disrupted discipleship: Brown was pleased that a manuscript on childbirth customs fitted with Rivers' Melanesian work; he asked for a copy of Rivers' British Association address, which he had missed while in Australia. Discussing his own plans for further Australian research, he suggested that he now had "a good working hypothesis of the origin of the Australian social organisation, and indeed of the origin of totemism in general." The key was the dual division, and he was "more wedded than ever" to his theory that it was "essentially a mode of organising the 'oppositions' that arise in savage societies in connection with marriage, initiation, etc." For the present, however, he proposed to publish only factual data, leaving "questions of origin" until after further field research. Although he expected the intermediate forms of the Lake Eyre tribes to provide the ultimate key, he hoped first to go to north Queensland to study "the local and relationship organisations in their relationship to the totemic clans" among a tribe whose "maternal descent of the totem" would contrast to the male descent he found in Western Australia.

Responding subsequently to Rivers' "conversion" address, Brown at this point defined their differences in minimal terms. "Fully" accepting the proposition that "analysis of a mixed culture must precede sociological explanation," he simply insisted that Australian culture was unmixed. Rivers' argument to the contrary depended on treating the system of marriage classes and the system of totem clans as separate institutions (a la Frazer), and associating each with a different population stratum. Brown insisted that both classes and clans were "inseparably bound up with the relationship system," and that the form totemism took in any group was a reflection of its particular social organization. "Social structure" was "fundamental," and "the specialisation of religious functions [was] the result of the specialisation of social functions." Although further correspondence revealed that basic matters of conceptualization and definition were at issue, Brown concluded by reiterating his "full agreement" with "the main point" of Rivers' address.

Rivers' unpreserved answer apparently suggested the two disagreed "quite fundamentally about Australia." In response, Brown further explicated his view of the "two essential features of the relationship system" on that continent: "the existence of clans due to the distinction of nearer and more distant relatives of the same kind," and "the classification of the world of natural objects" of religious or mythic significance into two divisions "according to the divi-

---

tion (here cited as WHRP), in which most of the correspondence is contained. Langham's reading of this material differs quite substantially from my own, perhaps because he did not have access to Brown's critically important letter responding to Rivers' article on survivals (1913), a copy of which was made available to me by Fred Eggan prior to its subsequent publication by Meyer Fortes (R-B 1913b).

sions of the human society." Although both together constituted "the totemic organisation of the Australians," the former was more fundamental, since "a society might possess the social organisation without the classification, but [not] . . . the classification without some sort of social divisions." But until he carried out his proposed field study of the "connection of the local organisation, the relationship system and the totemic clans in tribes with female descent," he could not rebut Rivers' argument that the "intimate connection" of the latter two was "the result of blending."

In this context, Brown introduced new ethnographic data that were to bring matters more sharply into focus: the case of the Dieri of Central Australia, who had recently been discovered to have a double system of totems, one with male descent similar to those in Western Australia, and one with female descent similar to eastern tribes. In the next several letters he advanced a "working hypothesis" of the origin of the Dieri system: assuming a single developmental sequence of Australian totemism, he argued that the Dieri represented a special transitional state in which the newer western paternal form had been superimposed by borrowing in a tribe that still retained the older eastern maternal totems. Although he was able to justify this "imitation" by a lengthy conjectural argument, in evolutionary terms his position was, to say the least, incongruous, and it left Rivers with an obvious diffusionary alternative. In the meantime, however, Brown went on to react to Durkheim's recently published *Elementary Forms of the Religious Life* (1912), in which the interpretation of the totemism of another Central Australian tribe had even further complicated "the whole question of the evolution of totemism in Australia."

Brown had of course already accepted Durkheim's general thesis of the "sociological origin of religion," and he agreed with "almost everything" Durkheim said about the Arunta system per se. But on certain more general issues, he was critical. Durkheim had not explained why totem objects were selected from "the practical economic life of everyday," and he was wrong about the evolutionary position of Arunta totemism. Reaffirming the hypothesis of his Cambridge lectures, Brown argued that the Andamanese "pre-totemic" social organization had developed into the "classificatory system of Australia" with its "dual divisions" and its originally matrilineal clans. The Arunta, rather than being primitive, were a late stage. Beyond this, Brown disagreed with Durkheim's definition of totemism as "above all" a name or emblem; and this led him to pose explicitly certain definitional issues in an unpreserved note (or notes) on the concepts "totemism" and "clan." The former apparently emphasized the presence of "a specific magico-religious relation between the clan and some species . . . of natural object"; the latter was apparently that used in a subsequent letter, emphasizing the "distinction, within the classificatory system of kinship, between near and distant kindred" (cf. R-B 1913a:159).

Rivers' only extant letter in this first series was brief, pointed, and a bit condescending. Accusing Brown of basing his definitions too narrowly on Australian materials, he suggested this was justifiable only if one adopted the Frazerian view "that the Australians represent a stage in the evolution of human society in general." Arguing that Brown's definition of clan was too narrowly genealogical, Rivers offered his own somewhat overlapping definitions of the contested concepts: a clan was an exogamous group within a tribe, whose members were bound together *either* by "a belief in common descent" *or* by "the common possession of a totem" (cf. Rivers 1914b:I, 7); totemism was simply the term he used for "a form of social organisation . . . in which the totemic link forms an essential element of social structure." Having chosen his definitional ground, Rivers had no objection to Brown's explanation of the Dieri case "except that it assumes at the outset" what had to be explained. If the Dieri already had two kinds of social grouping, Rivers saw easily "how one of them may have taken on the magico-religious ideas and practices of western totemism." But it was their presence in the first place that required explanation, and by implication Rivers had an explanation even if Brown did not: they were a type case of the blending that characterized Australian culture.

Brown responded to the definitional issues by appealing to his fieldwork. In Australia there were "two different sorts of social groups that may be totemic"; he used the term "clan" only for those based on the distinction between near and distant kin. Exogamy was not their defining characteristic, but simply the consequence of the fact that their members were nearly related. These groups were sometimes totemic and sometimes not, sometimes constituted by male descent and sometimes by female, sometimes localized and sometimes not. Although he did not wish to "define terms in sociology on the basis of Australian facts only," these groups seemed to "correspond fairly closely" to what were elsewhere called clans; but what was important was "not the name but the facts." On the question of Dieri totemic groupings, Brown felt that he could not deal with this adequately without offering "a theory of Australian social organisation in general." In view of Rivers' criticisms, and many things in Durkheim's book, he was postponing the paper in which he would offer it; and for the present it seemed best to abandon the correspondence.

Viewing the first exchange as a whole, it seems clear that Brown had begun to move out of the relationship of student-to-mentor. Despite the failure of his Andaman kinship work, he had by this time published articles on Australian kinship whose excellence Rivers himself was to acknowledge (Rivers 1924:194–201). The exchange also heightened his sensitivity to certain definitional problems, which he insisted on approaching in terms of his empirical data rather than in terms of traditional evolutionary categories. On the other hand, his continuing underlying commitment to a diachronic evolutionary viewpoint, and his simultaneous unwillingness to insist on that viewpoint when pushed on questions of "origin," compromised his position. When Rivers threatened to force him into a corner on an issue of conjectural history, Brown backed off from the battle.

Survivals and Causal Relations in the Present

By the time the correspondence was resumed in the summer of 1913, Brown seems to have resolved the ambiguities of his position. One can only specu-late as to the catalyst. Perhaps it is to this period that we may date the read-ing of Russell's mathematical philosophy, which several writers have suggested was critical to Brown's development (cf. Singer 1973; Stanner 1968). It seems more likely, however, that he went back to Durkheim, and to the *Rules of the Sociological Method*—the fifth chapter of which argues for an essentially synchronic approach to the explanation of social facts (Durkheim 1895:89–124). But it may simply be that he realized that his position would be much stronger if he put aside the diachronic framework in which he had previously been operating.

Be that as it may, the exchange opened on July 12, with Rivers comment-ing on the last chapters of *The Andaman Islanders*, which Brown had men-tioned as soon to be forwarded when the previous exchange broke off the preceding August, and which by now were already in proof form. Brown's whole interpretation of Andaman myth as an expression of their "system of social values" ran quite counter to a thesis Rivers had developed to the effect that myth ordinarily dealt with the rare and exceptional in native life (Rivers 1912b). Rivers nevertheless found Brown's argument compelling, and it was now he who minimized the differences between them. At the same time, he called attention to the contrast between "psychological" and "what I should call sociological or historical interpretation," suggesting that the history of Andaman culture might not be "so hopeless" as Brown seemed to feel.

In response to further unpreserved comments, Brown granted he had not got "to the bottom" of Andaman kinship, and decided therefore to back off from his argument that it was "really a pre-classificatory system"—although he continued privately to believe it was. Having thus withdrawn from the battlefield of conjectural history, he was now finally free to disentangle him-self from issues of origin Rivers had apparently continued to press by pointing out that there were customs similar to those of the Andamanese elsewhere in the world. To this Brown now simply responded, "I am afraid you will be sorry to hear that I feel quite comfortable with this"—that is to say, he had decided the issue of origin was no longer to the point, that from his point of view it was a nonproblem. It did not really matter whether the Andamanese customs were invented or borrowed, or adopted "from their own early ancestors," which "seems to me to be much the same thing." Whatever their origin, they must be "adapted to some need of the Andaman collective conscience (to speak teleologically, and not meaning a conscious need)." Historical questions were no doubt interesting and important, but they did not "affect the questions of causal relations in the present." As Durkheim argued, these had to do with how "the customs of a society" served "to maintain a certain system of ideas and emotions which in its turn is what maintains the society in existence with its given structure and its given degree of cohesion." Drawing analogies to the study of language and examples from Andaman technology, Brown distinguished between "dynamical" and "statical" problems. Although the latter did not depend on the former, he was prepared to argue that "in many cases the dynamic (historical problems) must depend on the static (psychological) problems."

With this letter, the separation of the two points of view was accomplished. The critical passages are those referring to "causal relations in the present" and "the needs of the Andaman collective conscience." The former rejected both the problem and the concept of diachronic causation; the latter redefined the framework of psychological interpretation from that of individual motivation to that of the functional needs of the whole culture. But there were still other issues to be dealt with, and it is significant that they came together in relation to the problem of "survivals"—which was a critical assumption to both the evolutionist and the Riversian historical approaches, and which Brown admitted would, if accepted, compromise his position.

Responding to an article on "Survival in Sociology" Rivers published in October, Brown sent him the draft of an essay elaborating his view "of the methods to be adopted in the study of social institutions" (R-B 1913b). He began by rejecting Rivers' antithesis of the "psychological" and the "historical" methods. Following McDougall (1905:1), Brown defined "psychology" as "the science of human behaviour," of which sociology was simply that branch dealing with "those modes of behaviour that are determined in the individual by the society." Sociology in turn encompassed both static and dynamic (or as Rivers would have it, "psychological" and "historical") problems. Assuming that there were "only a limited number of ways in which a human society can be constituted," social statics sought the laws governing "the causal relations subsisting between different elements of the same social organisation." Social dynamics dealt with "the causes that produce changes of social organisation, and therefore with the origins of social institutions." Where he and Rivers disagreed was on the order in which these two sets of problems should be approached (R-B 1913b:35–36).

In this context, Brown turned to the problem of survival, which Rivers had defined as a custom "whose nature cannot be explained by its present

utility but only . . . through its past history." Arguing that the notion of "utility" was ethnocentric (or, as he put it, "subjective"), Brown suggested that
calling the customs connected with the mother's brother in the Torres Strait
"useless" depended on a prior conception of "the fundamental purpose or
end of society." Proposing that society be regarded as "a condition of equilibrium or balance of forces of cohesion and disruption," Brown suggested
that its purpose was "its own continued existence in a state of equilibrium,"
and that the "utility"—or better, the "social function"—of any social institution was the way it contributed to this end. Here, then, was an *objective* crite-
rion of survival: "In any given instance the hypothesis that a custom or institution is a survival must depend on some hypothesis as to the function
that such a custom fulfils (or on the nature of the necessary connections between such customs and the other institutions of the society)"—which was
in effect to say that "any argument about survivals must necessarily rest on
hypothetical solutions of problems of social statics." It was not enough to appeal to "the mental disposition which we call conservatism." Calling into question what in fact had been an unexamined methodological assumption of
anthropology for at least fifty years, Brown suggested that conservatism itself
needed explanation: "We must know what is the social function of conservatism in general and what is the cause of the variation of its intensity in
different conditions" (R-B 1913b:35–41).

Pushing his attack, Brown argued, on the basis of an analysis of the "logical" structure of arguments from survivals, that their use to reason from "the
present condition of a society back to its past" depended on a general knowledge of the principles of social statics. Since in the present state of sociological
knowledge, "almost nothing was known of the functions of social institutions
and of the laws that regulate their relations one to another," arguments from
survival were only of value "when we have independent historical evidence
(not based on survival hypotheses) as to the process of historical change." In
short, the idea of survival had only limited utility for sociology; its main function was as a foil: "It is of extreme interest in social statics to determine which
customs in a society are really survivals, if there be any such" (R-B 1913b:43–45).

In drawing his argument together, Brown shifted back to the general question of the psychological explanation of social phenomena, which (following
Durkheim's *Rules*), he defined as "modes of thinking, feeling and acting common to all or to a great number of the members of a society and imposed
upon them by the society itself." If Rivers would accept that definition, they
might agree on the "proper task of the sociologist"; but Brown suspected that
he would exclude thinking and feeling, on the grounds that as "purely mental
processes" they could not be "directly observed." Against this, Brown argued
that since actions were determined by thoughts and feelings, any explanation
would be incomplete that did not take them into consideration. But he felt

he could not proceed without having from Rivers an explicit definition of social phenomena—and awaiting that, the manuscript broke off, in midparagraph (R-B 1913b:45–46).[4]

Rivers' answer was brief. Without apparently considering the implications for his theoretical position, he "very largely" accepted Brown's comments on the issue of "utility." But he disagreed "absolutely" with his definitions of psychology and of social phenomena, and therefore felt that "as regards the main question," his position was "wholly untouched." Refusing to go into the matter by letter, he said that he planned to give a talk at Oxford the next summer on "the relations between sociology and psychology," and that meanwhile Brown might like to "defer rewriting" the paper until he had a chance to read Rivers' "little book on social organisation," which would appear shortly (R-B 1913b:33–34).

Although Brown professed to find "hardly anything in it with which I do not agree," and to look forward "still more eagerly" to Rivers' forthcoming *History of Melanesian Society* (1914b), the appearance of *Kinship and Social Organisation* (1914a) did not so much resolve matters as make explicit the fact that the two were talking past one another. While in 1912 Brown had taken the stance of the empiricist appealing to his data against a priori assumption, now that he had finally achieved his own mature theoretical stance, he saw their roles reversed: whereas Rivers insisted that sociologists must confine themselves "to concrete or objective phenomena such as are capable of exact observation," Brown insisted that this could only produce "empirical generalisations," never "explanations," and that social institutions were dependent on fundamental laws of psychology. Brown felt that he got along "much better and ever so much more rapidly" when he had "a working hypothesis of the fundamental nature of human society, such as I have now." But this hypothesis "would be quite useless" unless he "worked out the psychological explanations" as he went along. The advantage of this "conscious psychological method" was that it protected one from unconsciously accepting the "unscientific" assumptions of "popular psychology," or of "the associationist intellectualist psychology of thirty years ago." Rivers' empiricism in fact concealed such assumptions, and therefore they could neither reach agreement "nor even properly argue with one another" about specific issues.

Shortly thereafter, Brown offered some final comments in the course of remarks on manuscripts each man had written for the journal *Anthropos* on the issue that more than any other had given focus to the anthropological discussion since 1900: the definition of totemism (Rivers 1914c; R-B 1914a). In opposition to Rivers' continuing insistence on defining totemism as a

---

4. The version of this article-draft published by Meyer Fortes omits a parenthesis inserted by Brown explaining the reason for its unfinished state (R-B 1913b:46).

"form of social organisation," Brown proposed to cut through the empirical and theoretical confusion surrounding the concept by using totemism to refer only to a "special magico-religious relation between each social division" and "some species of natural object." On this basis, he suggested that there were "five different forms of totemism in Australia which *may* have originated entirely independently of one another," but between which there was "a close relation of *psychological* dependence." Admitting that "his theoretical and methodological bias" largely determined his choice of definition, Brown still insisted his was better, since it was more adaptable to historical problems than Rivers' was to psychological problems, and because Rivers' in fact presupposed a specific theory of "clan totemism." But in the end he appealed simply to his "prejudices": "What makes me cling so much to my own is that I do so strongly feel the necessity of dealing with many psychological problems before attempting to attack the historical problems."

In view of the fact that Rivers was for most of his career well-known as a psychologist, and Radcliffe-Brown was for much of his known to oppose psychological interpretations, it seems more than a bit paradoxical that their parting of theoretical ways should have ended on this note. One way of resolving the paradox is to place both men once again in relation to nineteenth-century evolution, which (as Radcliffe-Brown was later fond of pointing out) had a dual character. On the one hand, the basic problem of evolution was one of historical reconstruction, broadly conceived, and causation was conceived in diachronic terms. On the other, this historical reconstruction was undertaken on the basis of a set of assumptions about the basic laws of human psychology, which was conceived in essentially individualistic, utilitarian, and intellectualist terms. Up to a point, one can interpret the intellectual development of Rivers and of Radcliffe-Brown as alternate responses to the crisis in evolutionism in the context of this basic duality. Rivers retained an historical orientation to the definition of problem and causation, but abandoned (for the moment) the psychological approach, rejecting the problem of "motive," because he was unable at this point to conceive it in other than intellectualistic, individualistic terms (1916). In contrast, Radcliffe-Brown rejected the historical problem, but retained (for the moment) the psychological approach—but on the basis of a redefinition of psychological assumption. "Motive," construed in individualistic, intellectualist terms, became "function," construed in unconscious collective terms.

But however apt, this formulation of their opposition has nonetheless a somewhat fleeting situational character. Rivers was in fact shortly to turn again to psychology, when in the course of his wartime work with shell-shocked soldiers he discovered Freud, who seemed to promise another route out of the crisis (Rivers 1917). And Radcliffe-Brown did not in fact immediately abandon diachronic problems entirely; nor did he ever abandon an underlying

W. H. R. Rivers in his Cambridge study, 1919. Photograph by Sarah Neill Chinnery (courtesy of Sheila M. Waters).

commitment to evolutionism. Furthermore, once Rivers no longer stood in his path, he cast off the psychological idiom in which his own Durkheimian alternative was initially phrased.

The brief definitional opposition in *Anthropos* was the only occasion during Rivers' lifetime that the two men confronted each other in print. No doubt this was due in part to the fact that Brown returned to Australia later in 1914, remaining in the antipodes until well after the war was over. But it seems clear also that the power of his still-living mentor's personality may have reinforced Brown's natural reticence to publish his theoretical formulations. It was not until after Rivers' death in early June 1922 (when Brown had begun to adopt his mother's maiden and elder brother's middle name) that he finally offered in print a strong programmatic statement of the differences between "The Methods of Ethnology and Social Anthropology" (R-B 1932). With Rivers no longer preempting the framework of definition, it was possible for Brown

to redefine their relationship, claiming for himself the field of a now dehistori-
cized "sociology"—whose relationship to psychology he now in fact argued in
terms not dissimilar to those Rivers had argued in 1916.

The Romantic and Classical Modes
in British Social Anthropology

Radcliffe-Brown was not the only contributor to the dehistoricizing process
that helped to form modern British social anthropology. The same shift from
a diachronic to a synchronic emphasis may be followed in the early work
of Bronislaw Malinowski—who in 1913 also found reason to criticize Rivers'
essay on survivals (BMPY: 1913 n.d.). For Malinowski, however, the dehistoricizing process was perhaps less a reflection of theoretical reconsideration than
a by-product of a new mode of ethnographic inquiry. For if Radcliffe-Brown's
recension of Durkheim provided the major portion of the theoretical ground-
work of modern British social anthropology, Malinowski's self-consciously
wrought creation-myth provided the charter for the modern British fieldwork
tradition (cf. Stocking 1983a).

These contributions reflect the respective intellectual temperaments of the
two men, which Firth described in aesthetic terms as representing the "romantic" and the "classical" modes. For Malinowski, "imaginative insight" had
priority over scientific generalization, if the "formal expression" of observed
regularity meant forcing "the diversities of the human creature into an artificial mold." For Radcliffe-Brown, who valued precision, proportion, and re-
straint, the notion of "system" had priority, sometimes "to the neglect of the
full content of phenomenal reality." In contrast to Malinowski's need to "test
postulates of group action in terms of individual action," Radcliffe-Brown always emphasized the "formal qualities inherent in the structure of groups as
systems" (Firth 1951:480).

The anthropological consequences of these differences in intellectual tem-
perament—their respective attitudes toward what Malinowski sometimes called
"kinship algebra," their contrasting interpretations of the relation of individual
anxiety and social ritual, or their different conceptions of a social "institution"
—are well-known, and need not be rehearsed here (cf. Parsons 1957; Homans
1941). But if Firth's formulation deftly epitomizes the contrast between the
two lineage elders, it is also true that the differences between them only gradually became matters of intellectual controversy, and that the later elaboration
of Radcliffe-Brown's theoretical viewpoint can only be understood in this
context.

After Malinowski had passed from the scene, Radcliffe-Brown offered an
account of their intellectual relationship (R-B 1946). Focussing on their con-

trasting uses of the concept "function," he implied that Malinowski had turned from the strict Durkheimian path, while he had remained constant. Retrospectively, he felt that Malinowski's article on "Culture" for the *Encyclopedia of the Social Sciences* (1931) marked a distinct break in his thought—the beginning of a final phase in which it was dominated by the individualistic biologizing functionalism ultimately systematized in the posthumous *Scientific Theory of Culture* (1944).

While this account does indeed describe the movement of Malinowski's anthropology, which at one point he spoke of as an attempt to reduce Durkheim to the terms of "behaviouristic psychology" (1935b:II, 236), the historical process is somewhat more complex. Just as Radcliffe-Brown tended retrospectively to rationalize the development of his own anthropology, so did he tend to view Malinowski's development more discontinuously than was actually the case. Even before he went into the field, Malinowski had expressed serious reservations about Durkheimian theory; and the position he later articulated in the article on "culture" had in fact been developing from the first time he encountered Freud in the context of his Trobriand experiences (cf. Stocking 1984).

On the other hand, Radcliffe-Brown's structural interests took some time to come sharply to the forefront of his own anthropology. That he spoke of his early work as "psychology" was not merely a function of Rivers' preemption of "sociology" for diachronic inquiry. He had studied psychology with Rivers, and had evidently been influenced also by the *Social Psychology* of William McDougall (1908)—which in turn reflected the influence of the then highly respected Alexander Shand, who between 1890 and 1914 had attempted to realize John Stuart Mill's long-neglected project for a science of "ethology" (Shand 1914; Leary 1982). Shand's influence is in fact manifest in the early work of both Malinowski and Radcliffe-Brown. Shand's conception of "sentiment" was integral to the "working hypothesis" in terms of which Radcliffe-Brown interpreted the customs of *The Andaman Islanders* (1922:233–34); indeed in its Andaman phase, his anthropology was a study of the social formation of sentiments, and might appropriately be described as a "functional psychology of culture." It was only later that the social structural interests associated with this Australian fieldwork came to the fore. And even as late as 1931, when he first read Malinowski's article on "culture," he spoke of it as a "fine" piece, and regularly assigned it in the course on "The Comparative Science of Culture [sic]" that he continued to give throughout his stay at Chicago (Paul 1934; Rosenfels 1932).

In short, the theoretical falling out between the two lineage elders was an interactive rather than an asymmetrical process. Although implicit in their respective intellectual temperaments and in their respective responses to Durkheim and Rivers, it also depended on the gradual development of certain themes in each man's thought, and the repression of others. Furthermore, the process took place not simply in an abstract intellectual realm, but in the context of their changing positions within evolving institutional structures, which around 1930 brought them into direct competition for the control of resources and personnel.

Supermen United from Afar for Functional Anthropology

By the time Malinowski arrived in London to seek training in anthropology in 1910, Radcliffe-Brown seems already to have left for Australia. Although both men were in England from 1912 to 1914, and Malinowski actually followed in Brown's footsteps as lecturer at the London School of Economics in 1913–14 (Firth 1957), Brown seems to have spent his time in Birmingham, and the two did not actually meet until August 1914 at the Australian meetings of the British Association. By that time Brown had praised Malinowski's first monograph (1913) as "a model of method" and an "overwhelming argument" against the evolutionary hypothesis of "group marriage"—although he was critical of the treatment of Australian kinship without reference to the system of clans and marriage classes (R-B 1914b). Nevertheless, he subsequently recalled that their "lengthy discussions" at this time had ended in "fairly complete agreement" (1946:38).

Both men were in the southwest Pacific during World War I, but the next direct intellectual contact between them seems not to have taken place until after the publication of their two landmark monographs of 1922. Malinowski had apparently written to Radcliffe-Brown praising *The Andaman Islanders*— although his marginalia in a copy that later came into his possession ("not 'the society,' but every bloody man and woman") reflect the characteristic contrast between their viewpoints (BMSC, R-B 1922:253). Although a copy of *Argonauts* had not yet reached him in South Africa, Radcliffe-Brown nevertheless responded on a similar note of mutual intellectual identification: Malinowski's *Baloma* said things he wished he had included in his own book. Expressing the hope that Malinowski might join him on the Cape Town faculty, he responded to a query about the extreme diffusionism of Elliot Smith and William Perry by recalling his debate with Rivers in 1913–14. Frobenius and the Americans were more reliable, but the general methodological approach was as "unsound" as the "old comparative method" of framing an hypothesis, scouting the world for confirmatory data, and simply neglecting the evidence that did not fit (BMPY: R-B/BM 11/6/22).

Malinowski of course shared an antipathy to the "heliolithic" diffusionists; his copy of one of Rivers' works includes the doggerel, "It gives me the shivers / To think of poor Rivers / Being made a megalith / For our Lord Elliot Smith"

Bronislaw Malinowski, ca. 1925 (courtesy of Helena Wayne Malinowska and the Department of Anthropology, London School of Economics).

(BMSC, Rivers 1924:174). But it is interesting that at this time both men still entertained the possibility that distribution studies might cast light on the history of culture. Radcliffe-Brown had in mind a complete study of the distribution of Australian cultural elements—although he insisted that any historical hypothesis must be based also on a consideration of each element "in relation to the cultural system in which it occurs" (BMPY: R-B/BM 11/6/22; cf. BM 1922:232).

A year later, the note of mutual identification was again struck. Congratulating Malinowski on his recent appointment at the London School of Economics, Radcliffe-Brown commented on the fact that both suffered from recurrent respiratory illnesses—which in his own case made it likely that he would spend most of his life in the antipodes, despite his longing for the amenities of European civilization. And he was struck by a singular similarity in their anthropological interests: Malinowski's essay on "The Problem of Meaning in Primitive Languages" (1923) recalled an unpublished draft on Andaman languages in which he, too, had sketched a new linguistic method (cf. R-B 1932:495–504). The rest of the letter, however, is in a retrospectively more expected mode. His teaching was now "almost entirely from the sociological point of view": "pouring out" the "accumulation of twelve years thinking," he was giving his students "a theory of social structure, a theory of kinship, of law, of religion, and a theory of art." Given five lives, he might write on them all, but for the present he proposed to concentrate on Australian kinship and totemism, and on African law (BMPL: R-B/BM 5/22/23; cf. Schapera n.d.).

When plans began to be developed about this time to establish a chair at Sydney as the focus for anthropological work in Oceania, both Malinowski and Radcliffe-Brown were obvious prospects. Malinowski, now on the way to establishment at the intellectual center, felt that his primary commitment was to the London School of Economics, and he wrote to Haddon (one of the electors) that Radcliffe-Brown was "as alike in his outlook to me as is possible in such an unsettled science as ours" (BMPL: BM/ACH n.d.). Radcliffe-Brown's eventual selection (over A. M. Hocart) provided the occasion for a second face-to-face meeting, when both men were brought to the United States in 1926 under the auspices of the Rockefeller philanthropies. Radcliffe-Brown visited several American universities on his way to take up the Rockefeller-funded chair in Sydney, and Malinowski conducted a survey of American anthropology for the Laura Spelman Rockefeller Memorial (Stocking 1978c). This was the year in which Malinowski published his functionalist manifesto as the article on "Anthropology" in the *Encyclopedia Britannica* (1926a); and Radcliffe-Brown later recalled that, staying together at the Yale Club in New York City, they had disagreed over "the most convenient and profitable way to use the word 'function' in social anthropology" (1946:39). Although this was indeed the issue on which later theoretical confrontation was to hinge,

A. R. Radcliffe-Brown, Sydney, Australia, ca. 1930. Photograph by Sarah Neill Chinnery (courtesy of Sheila M. Waters).

contemporary documentary evidence does not yet convey a sharply focussed sense of opposition.

In May of 1927, Malinowski apologized to Radcliffe-Brown for not having answered some unpreserved communication: "But surely we supermen need not stick to any conventions, and I always feel that my towering spirit and yours touch above the highest levels of microcosmic nebulas and there gaze in silence at one another." Pleased that Radcliffe-Brown was "taking over" his "best pupil," Raymond Firth, who would appreciate Radcliffe-Brown's "point of view in theory," Malinowski suggested that he might also like to consider Firth as lecturer (BMPL: BM/R-B 5/11/27). Replying that he already had Firth in mind as successor, Radcliffe-Brown congratulated Malinowski on his recent promotion to professor, and wondered if perhaps Malinowski might help get him a job in Europe that would allow more time to write (BMPY: R-B/BM 8/29/27).

In the same letter, Radcliffe-Brown raised several points of theoretical difference suggested by his reading of the first half of *Sex and Repression in Savage Society* (1927). Commenting on Malinowski's presentation of the Trobriands as a social order based on "mother-right," he insisted that all kinship was inherently bilateral. It was now thirty years since Durkheim had distinguished *parenté* and *consanguinité* (cf. Maybury-Lewis 1965), and in these terms the Trobriand father and son were consanguineous kin, even if they failed to recognize the relationship. Beyond this, he felt that in general Malinowski had conceded entirely too much to the Freudian viewpoint. Noting that he himself had read everything the Freudians had written on the topic of mythology, he insisted that it was valueless.

The first two essays on *Sex and Repression* had been Malinowski's contribution to the general upsurge of anthropological interest in psychoanalytic theory in the early 1920s—an interest pioneered of course by Rivers (cf. Stocking 1984). But when Ernest Jones rejected out of hand any attempt to revise Freudian orthodoxy in the light of comparative ethnographic data, Malinowski had countered with a sharply critical attack on *Totem and Taboo*, in which he drew on Shand's concept of "sentiment" to develop the idea of culture as creating a "secondary environment" that modified the instinctual endowment of man. In retrospect, Malinowski's argument on these issues seems clearly an early formulation of his later psycho-biological functionalism (1927:204–8; cf. 1944). If Radcliffe-Brown in 1927 evinced no trace of his later criticism, it is perhaps because he was himself in this period still speaking of the "biological function" of "culture" in imposing the common "sentiments" that united human beings into social groups (1930:269). Indeed, after reading the second half of Malinowski's book, he sent a brief note withdrawing all of his objections. In the end, Malinowski had granted the Freudians no more than he himself would (BMPY: R-B/BM 9/5/27).

Raymond Firth, Sydney, Australia, 1932. Photograph by Sarah Neill Chinnery (courtesy of Sheila M. Waters).

The matter of bilaterality of kinship was subsequently pursued by Radcliffe-Brown in the context of debate with Rivers' follower Brenda Seligman over the interpretation of the Ambrym data collected by Bernard Deacon before he died of blackwater fever in 1927 (cf. Langham 1981:200–243; Larcom 1983). Radcliffe-Brown attributed Rivers' earlier difficulties with the Ambrym material to his inability to allow for the coexistence of matrilineal and patrilineal institutions—remarking in a footnote that even so "acute" a thinker as Malinowski had been similarly misled. Kinship—the recognition of genealogical relations as the basis for the regulation of social relations—was always "necessarily bilateral." In contrast, descent—the entrance of an individual into a social group as the child of one of its members—was always necessarily "unilateral." If anthropologists would give up the old evolutionary (and the new diffusionist) attempt to classify whole societies as either "matrilineal" or "patrilineal," and instead apply those terms to the specific institutions of descent, inheritance, succession, etc., they would think "much more clearly." In this context, Radcliffe-Brown offered a general plea for a "functionalist" anthropology, and (despite his footnote) pointed to Malinowski as its best exemplar in England (R-B 1926, 1929a, 1929b).

Malinowski was of course gratified, and early in 1929 responded with the hope that Radcliffe-Brown would indeed soon return to Europe, where there was plenty of room for two upholders of the functionalist method (BMPL: BM/R-B 3/25/29). He did, however, later respond in print to the issues that Radcliffe-Brown had raised, in a general treatment of what he called "the impasse on kinship." That impasse would never have arisen "if the study of kinship ties had been carried in the field along with the life history of the individual, if terminologies, legal systems, tribal and household arrangements had been studied in process of development and not merely as fixed products." But although he spoke of clan relationships as "one-sided distortions" of the original parental relationship and promised subsequently to return to the issue, he seems in effect to have accepted the point about the unilaterality of descent (1930:156, 161). Despite derisive comments about the "vast gulf between the pseudo-mathematical treatment of the too-learned anthropologist and the real facts of savage life" (151), he was in general quite laudatory of Radcliffe-Brown's application of "the functional method." Indeed, he seems in effect to have abandoned the whole problem to Radcliffe-Brown from that point on, leaving the many chapter drafts of his promised book on kinship to gather dust in his office files (cf. Fortes 1957; Stocking 1981b).

By this time, the interchange of students previously initiated by Firth was beginning to develop into a regular traffic between Malinowski's London seminar and Radcliffe-Brown's rooms in Sydney. Malinowski wrote that he was sending Hortense Powdermaker along, inquired about possibilities for Audrey Richards, and even wondered if something might be done for his diffusionist rival William Perry—with whom he had got "chummy" lately, and who with fieldwork experience might even become interested in the "right" kind of anthropology (BMPL: BM/R-B 3/25/29). Radcliffe-Brown responded that he was leaving the selection of Powdermaker's site to E. P. Chinnery and Gregory Bateson, that a year's research money was available for Richards, that Ian Hogbin would be coming to London for a year when he finished his Ontong Java fieldwork, and that while there was a shortage of funds, he would see what he could do for Perry (BMPL: R-B/BM 7/9/29; cf. Stocking 1982).

Despite some hints of the lineage segmentation yet to come, the 1920s ended with the leaders of functionalist anthropology still maintaining between themselves and to the world at large a theoretical and methodological united front. Writing to Malinowski on the last day of the decade, Radcliffe-Brown recalled his youthful decision to devote his life to "the scientific study of culture." The trouble with anthropology was its name, which by tradition included such studies as physical anthropology and prehistoric archeology—which he hoped he would never again have to teach. He was now planning to leave Sydney in 1931 to get a job in America or, preferably, Europe. Despite his respiratory problems, he was ready to try even Cambridge or Oxford, just as long as he did not have to teach courses on "The Races of Man." In this context, he was much in favor of a scheme Malinowski had for establishing a "Colonial Institute," and offered himself as the only man "in the British Empire who has been lecturing regularly on the principles of Native Administration." Once back in England, "you and I and anybody else who will help us" could join in building up "the new sociology or anthropology that is needed" (BMPL: R-B/BM 12/31/29).

Rivalry for Influence in the Rockefeller Foundation

In fact, Radcliffe-Brown's return from the anthropological periphery, in the context of competition for influence with major sources of institutional support at the center, was to lead to the first serious rifts in the united front for functionalist anthropology.[5] Malinowski's "Colonial Institute" was part of a developing plan to win major support for anthropological field research in the functionalist mode. Involved in competition with the diffusionists at University College, where Perry's seminars for a time attracted more students than his own, Malinowski could not afford to rely on indirect access to the field research on which the "revolution in anthropology" was to be grounded. With Rockefeller support in Oceania organized since 1926 under Radcliffe-Brown's

---

5. The argument in this section draws from a yet unpublished paper (Stocking 1978c), where fuller documentation will be provided.

aegis, Malinowski began to explore possibilities for African research. By 1929 he had joined forces with Dr. J. H. Oldham, a leading figure in the recently established International Institute of African Languages and Cultures, in a campaign to win support for a "practical anthropology" oriented toward problems of African colonial development. Faced with a competing initiative from the politically influential Rhodes House at Oxford, the African Institute forwarded to the Rockefeller Foundation in March of 1930 a printed appeal for £100,000 over a ten-year period.

That fall, while both these proposals were under consideration, Radcliffe-Brown suggested to the Foundation that they be included, along with the renewal of the Sydney grant and a proposal he offered for research at Cape Town, within a "concerted plan" for a series of "functional" studies of all "surviving native peoples." He had been invited to serve as president of the anthropology section at the centenary meeting of the British Association in London, and he proposed to make his visit the occasion for "doing all in my power to bring about a world-wide cooperation in the systematic scientific investigation of the backward cultures" (RA: R-B/M. Mason 11/17/30). Although the Foundation voted in April 1931 to make a $250,000 five-year grant to the African Institute, when Radcliffe-Brown stopped off in New York that summer, Foundation officers were quite receptive to the idea of a general reconsideration of their anthropological commitments.

In September 1931 Radcliffe-Brown made his long-delayed reentrance upon the metropolitan anthropological scene. During the 1920s, Malinowski, holding high the banner of "functional anthropology," had been able to push himself through a motley crowd of aging evolutionists, retired colonial ethnographers, and diffusionist children of the sun to win the central place upon the stage of British anthropology as writer, teacher, and chief informal advisor to both the Rockefeller Foundation and the Colonial Office (cf. Kuklick 1978). But at the moment when his role as leading man of functionalist anthropology seemed guaranteed, back upon the stage from the colonial wings came Radcliffe-Brown, as the featured speaker "On the Present State of Anthropological Studies" at a major scientific gathering (R-B 1931a). Granted it was only a "cameo" appearance during a stopover on his way to a new appointment at the University of Chicago, the reports Malinowski received while on sabbatical leave in the south of France were such as to cause second thoughts about close collaboration with his fellow anthropological "superman."

Radcliffe-Brown was undertaking to advise Oldham on the implementation of the African Institute's "five year plan" of research. Worse yet, Oldham was taking seriously his advice that research be carried on in strictly scientific nonevaluative terms, focussing on economic life in its relation to social structure and "social cohesion" (BMPL: Oldham/BM 9/9/31). From the standpoint of Malinowski's more loosely integrative functionalism, the study of economic life implied "the study of all the other essential aspects of culture," and theory must be constantly cross-fertilized by practice: any investigation carried on without regard to "whether certain changes would be ruinous to a society or benefit it" would not help to forward the practical administrative goals by which the grant had originally been justified (BMPL: BM/Oldham 9/12/31). Although a compromise was worked out by Malinowski's "lieutenants" Gordon Brown and Audrey Richards (BMPL:BM/Oldham 9/13/31), they were both concerned lest Radcliffe-Brown would somehow "snaffle" the money when he arrived back in the United States (BMPL: Richards/BM [9/24/31]).

The situation was further complicated because Radcliffe-Brown's actual presence in London was having some influence on certain members of the Malinowskian circle—notably, Evans-Pritchard. Two years previously, Evans-Pritchard had written to Malinowski suggesting a correlation between his field-work experience and his theoretical orientation: "no fieldwork/Durkheim's views"; "limited fieldwork/Radcliffe-Brown's views"; "exhaustive fieldwork/ Malinowski's views"—which Malinowski had blue pencilled to indicate only a "very short distance" from "God's view" (BMPL: E-P/BM 11/25/28). Now, however, in the context of personal friction with Malinowski, Evans-Pritchard was moving back toward Radcliffe-Brown. Meyer Fortes spoke of his "particularly vivid recollection" of the evening in Evans-Prichard's "sumptuous Blooms-bury flat" when Radcliffe-Brown, "with characteristic self-assurance," gave "a whole lecture on lineage systems, ending with the recommendation to look up Gifford on this subject" (Fortes 1978:2, 6–7; cf. BLUA: R-B/E. W. Gifford correspondence 1922–23). As perceived by Malinowski's lieutenants at the time, the encounter portended "possibilities of yet future strife!" (BMPL: Richards/BM [9/24/31]; cf. BMPY: E. Clarke/BM 9/24/31).

Such fears must have seemed confirmed when Radcliffe-Brown wrote to Malinowski suggesting that the School of Oriental Studies, which at this point also had an application before the Rockefeller Foundation for massive support, was the logical center in England for the future development of anthropology (BMPL: R-B/BM 9/27/31). Pursuing the matter in a letter from Chicago, he asked Malinowski's cooperation in winning from the Foundation £50,000 a year for his worldwide ethnographic salvage plan (BMPL: R-B/BM n.d.). Malinowski forwarded the correspondence to Oldham and to his colleague Seligman at the London School of Economics with comments of dire foreboding: if "Radcliffe-Brown got into England, it would be a damn bad job for our [African] Institute," and would "probably mean that our department at the School would have to be scrapped" (BMPL: BM/Oldham 12/20/31; BM/Seligman 12/15/31).

Toward Radcliffe-Brown, Malinowski adopted a delaying policy. He drafted but did not send a letter suggesting that Radcliffe-Brown, who was even more sociological than himself, should of all people see the importance of keeping anthropology in a social science context at the London School of Economics (BMPL: BM/R-B 12/15/31). Nor did he quickly answer the letter Radcliffe-Brown wrote early in 1932 telling of his efforts to organize American anthropologists in support of the "vanishing cultures" scheme, and once more pushing the School of Oriental Studies as the single best center for cooperation between all British anthropologists and a similar American center he expected would emerge at Yale. Emphasizing the delicacy of the negotiations, he suggested that the only alternative to a plan that all in England could agree on was one centered in the United States, and that he had to hear from Malinowski soon in order to decide which to work for (BMPL: R-B/BM 1/30/32).

It was not until April, when he had a better sense of how winds were blowing in the Rockefeller Foundation, that Malinowski finally responded. By that time, Malinowski's influence had been a factor in redefining a scaled-down grant to the School of Oriental Studies in terms complementary rather than competitive to the African Institute (BMPY: BM/Sir E. D. Ross 2/14/33). Furthermore, the Foundation had decided to conduct a survey of anthropological institutions throughout the world before coming to a decision in regard to the "vanishing cultures" scheme. In this context, Radcliffe-Brown's continued arguments for the School of Oriental Studies as a center for "functional" anthropology—which he would be willing to direct if no one else could be found (BMPL: R-B/BM 5/25/32)—were less threatening, and Malinowski resumed a cooperative stance. He even suggested that the real key to the English situation was to "get people like yourself or Raymond Firth to occupy the chairs in Cambridge and Oxford," proposing that they discuss the whole matter when he came to lecture in the United States (BMPL: BM/R-B 8/21/32)—although by this time Radcliffe-Brown had decided he should stay in the United States so that "our mode of thinking" would help mold the worldwide ethnographic salvage scheme (BMPL: R-B/BM 9/1/32, 10/22/32). However, when the two finally met again in Chicago in April 1933, that plan had suffered setbacks from which it never recovered. After a drastic reevaluation of its funding policies, the Rockefeller Foundation initiated a year's moratorium on all funding of research in anthropology, which was in fact followed by a phased withdrawal from existing commitments in the field.

The Opening of Theoretical Fissures in Functional Anthropology

Although the issues of institutional influence that exacerbated relations between Malinowski and Radcliffe-Brown in the early 1930s thus receded for a time into the background, the sense of opposition they had engendered continued to affect their relationship, and it is in this context that their underlying theoretical differences began to come to the fore. Malinowski by this time had second thoughts about the advantages of interchanging students. Although at one point he was willing to have Meyer Fortes go to Chicago for advanced study, he decided that Fortes had better stay in London (BMPL: BM/Oldham 3/7/32); thenceforth, all the African Institute's Rockefeller fellows were pushed in the same direction. It was also at about this time that Malinowski began to take to himself the credit for founding the "Functionalist School of Anthropology," although in a characteristically joking manner: it was a title he had "bestowed by myself, in a way on myself, and to a large extent out of my own sense of irresponsibility" (R-B 1946:39).

In 1934 it was he rather than Radcliffe-Brown who first publicly threw down the theoretical gauntlet by insisting strenuously on a fundamental difference between their points of view in his introduction to Ian Hogbin's *Law and Order in Polynesia*. Offering an extended critique of Radcliffe-Brown's article on "Primitive Law" in the *Encyclopedia of the Social Sciences* (R-B 1933)—which he took as an implied criticism of his own *Crime and Custom* (1926b)—Malinowski appealed to his article on "Culture" (1931) as the basis for a "functional theory of custom" that would start from the "living, palpitating flesh and blood organism of man which remains somewhere at the heart of every institution." Although he suggested that the "only point of theoretical dissension between Professor Radcliffe-Brown and myself, and the only respect in which the Durkheimian conception of primitive society has to be supplemented" was the "tendency to ignore completely the individual and eliminate the biological element from the functional analysis of culture," he made it clear that this tendency "must in my opinion be overcome" (1934:xxxiii, xxxviii).

Radcliffe-Brown's rather acerbic response disclaimed association with "the figment of an automatically law-abiding native," and suggested that the variegated nature of social sanctions was an "elementary truth" that required the construction of strawmen-opponents so that it could be "claimed as a discovery made by him in the Trobriand Islands." Denying that he ignored the individual and eliminated the biological in the functional analysis of culture, he suggested that their really important differences were in "the uses of words." The "slow and laborious process of establishing a scientific terminology" in the social sciences required exact definitions that had the same sense in all societies and did not conflict with current usage. So far as he could tell "without the aid of a definition," it seemed that Malinowski meant by "law" any "socially sanctioned rule of behaviour." If he would only stick to that meaning in his writings, "he would find that not only do I not disagree with him, but neither does anyone else, since the greater part of his statements are commonplaces of social science, only made to appear novel and profound by a novel and obscure use of words" (1935a).

Obviously chagrined, Malinowski ironically pled guilty to creating a straw man by having described Radcliffe-Brown as one of social anthropology's "theoretically most acute thinkers." Promising fully to document his criticism elsewhere, he preferred for the moment to defend himself against charges of truism by noting that when he had advanced his "theory of primitive sanctions" *before* he went to the Trobriands, authorities such as E. S. Hartland had rejected it. Like Radcliffe-Brown, however, he still minimized the differences between them; it was only regarding primitive law and economics that he had "ventured" disagreement on "certain specific points" (1935a). That careful circumscription of difference seems still to have been manifest when Malinowski came to Chicago in April 1935, and students arranged a formal debate with Radcliffe-Brown. Although a "bloody" confrontation was apparently expected, the chairman, Harold Lasswell, described it as a "love fest"—to which Malinowski is said to have responded: "The function of old age is tolerance" (McAllister 1978).

Privately, too, relations between them remained cordial, and Malinowski was in fact to play a role in realizing Radcliffe-Brown's hope of capping his career with a major English professorial chair. With the failure of his rival's attempt to enlarge the institutional framework in which Rockefeller support was dispensed, and the declining fortunes of the diffusionist enclave at University College, Malinowski was left in a very strong position in British anthropology. The first academic generation represented by Rivers, Haddon, Marett, and Seligman was passing, and among their offspring only Malinowski had achieved a British professorial chair. When it came to filling such chairs, his opinion was very likely to carry weight. Declining himself to be a candidate for the chair at Oxford, he proposed Radcliffe-Brown instead, testifying to his "genius" at organizing departments in South Africa and Australia (BMPL: BM/R. Coupland 7/6/36). Although one of the electors expressed disappointment that they "must be content with second-best," Radcliffe-Brown was indeed chosen—although apparently by a close vote over Evans-Pritchard (BMPL: RC/BM 7/31/36; Evans-Pritchard 1973). Later that year, Radcliffe-Brown wrote Malinowski a note (now, in the more informal 1930s, addressed "Dear Bronio" and signed "Rex") thanking Malinowski for his efforts, looking forward to a continuing close association, and indicating that in formulating plans for Oxford anthropology, he would first seek Malinowski's advice (BMPL: R-B/BM 12/10/36).

Toward a Natural Science of Society

By the time he returned to England in 1937, however, Radcliffe-Brown's theoretical orientation had undergone changes that brought more sharply into focus his differences with Malinowski. No doubt the matter may be regarded

merely as the highlighting of tendencies present in his work from the beginning, as he left the Andaman materials behind and became more and more
involved in problems of Australian social structure—a view we may assume
he himself would have taken, insofar as he acknowledged change in his intellectual viewpoint. But the changes also reflect the oppositional contexts
in which he found himself: not only his incipient opposition to Malinowski,
but also his debates in the 1920s with the diffusionist heirs to Rivers' study
of kinship, and later with American social scientists, who sometimes accommodated to the functionalist revolution by reducing functionalism to the psychological integrationist view of culture that had emerged in this period in
American anthropology (Stocking 1976a).

In this context, some of the changes do seem to some extent to be simply
renamings—as when in lieu of extensive rewriting, Radcliffe-Brown proposed
that the word "sociology" be used in the second edition of *The Andaman Islanders* where the word "psychology" had appeared in the first (CUPA: R-B/
Roberts 9/14/32). But in addition to this terminological suppression of certain conceptual motifs—which might not be a trivial matter for someone who
came to weigh so heavily the problem of precise terminology in the social
sciences—there is evidence of a certain receptivity to new influences as well.
The net result of all this was that by 1937, Radcliffe-Brown's anthropology
could no longer appropriately be described as a "functionalist psychology of
culture."

The matter goes perhaps somewhat deeper than the development noted
by Meyer Fortes, who emphasized a vacillation (eventually resolved in favor
of the latter) between a Durkheimian "functionalist" and a more strictly "structuralist" approach—the one seeing the systemic character of social institutions
in "external" terms as an adaptation to particular environments, the other
seeing it in "internal" or "genotypical" terms as the reflection of particular factors inherent in each system (Fortes 1969a:45). However, Radcliffe-Brown's early
involvement in the "dyadic paradigm" and the reflections of "extensionist" assumption in his paper on "The Mother's Brother in South Africa" (1924) were,
at the time, more than simply intellectual "survivals"; the extant notes from
his Cape Town lectures indicate that he did indeed see social organization
based on kinship as an extension outward of the principles of behavior governing the various dyadic units in the nuclear family (Schapera n.d.). It would
seem to be in the context of his movement away from Rivers, his rejection of
Freud, his increasing differentiation from Malinowski—who assailed "kinship
algebra" from an ontogenetic, extensionist perspective—and not merely as an
internal development governed by the requirements of his Australian data,
or the logic of his thought, that he dropped his extensionist vocabulary for
that of "structural principle" by the time he published "The Social Organisation
of Australian Tribes" (1931b; cf. Evans-Pritchard 1929; Needham 1962:30–37).

And as Fortes' argument in fact suggests, the movement from a more Durk-heimian functionalism, which was still alive and well in the centenary address of 1931, to the more characteristically Radcliffe-Brownian "social structuralism" of the later 1930s, seems to have taken place during his Chicago years. It seems likely that it was there, in the somewhat more Germanic intellectual milieu of Chicago sociology and the close proximity of the Law School, that Radcliffe-Brown first felt the direct intellectual influence of Sir Henry Maine in a significant way. Maine's concept of "corporation" provided the basis for a view of the individual in more clearly structural terms (R-B 1935b:37); one suspects that it is in this context that his emphasis shifted from "sentiment" to "sanction" as the primary reinforcement of social cohesion. And while the exact timing of the influences of Russellian mathematical philosophy is perhaps a moot issue, it seems likely that his exchanges with Mortimer Adler, the Aristotelian philosopher for whom President Hutchins had found refuge in the Law School, heightened its salience (cf. Singer 1973; Stanner 1968; Stocking 1979).

It was, in any case, Mortimer Adler's suggestion—in a Dean's Seminar in the Social Science Division, in which they both participated—that psychology was the only human science which apparently provoked Radcliffe-Brown to elaborate his own theoretical views in a philosophical context in his famous seminar of 1937. Although he continued to be interested in the processes of "social cooptation" by which individual behavior, thought, and emotion were standardized within a given social group, he was now at some pains to argue that there was "only one theoretical natural science of society," and that it was "in no sense" a psychology (1937:110). And although he continued to assert the analytic utility of a Durkheimian conception of function, he now felt it necessary—after having debated American anthropologists on the concept both in person and in print—to insist that he had "never claimed" the appellation "functionalist" (R-B 1935c:394; cf. 1949; Stocking 1978b). Furthermore—apparently at the urging of his Chicago student Fred Eggan, who suggested that his persistence in talking of a "Comparative Science of Culture" simply obscured the differences between him and American cultural anthropologists—he now insisted that there could be no "science of culture," because there was no bounded phenomenal entity to which culture corresponded, in the way that the system of mind was contained within the human body and the system of society was contained within a territorially bounded community (1937:106–7; cf. Eggan 1971; Tax 1978).

Having completed the long refinement of his "natural science of society," Radcliffe-Brown was now brought for the first time into what promised to be fairly close permanent relationship with his long-time collaborator in the "revolution in anthropology" (Jarvie 1964). Given the fact that he now occupied an independent and potentially competitive position in the same general institutional framework, it is not surprising that intellectual controversy between the two quickly flared up again.

From "Pure" to "Hyphenated" Functionalism

In January 1938, Radcliffe-Brown attacked a book for which Malinowski had written a laudatory preface, calling it "another of those monuments of muddled thinking that are occasionally but still too frequently erected in the name of anthropology" (1938). Malinowski indicated that he was drafting a reply "all in the same Blood and Thunder manner in which we conduct our printed correspondence," and that this time he was going to "make a real villain" of Radcliffe-Brown (BMPL: BM/R-B 1/29/38). Instead, however, he proposed (through a third party, in the manner of a duel) that they hold a public discussion of the issues between them. As challenged party, Radcliffe-Brown chose the topic "the use of the concept 'function' in sociology"; and at Malinowski's suggestion, he opened the discussion on June 17, 1938, at Le Play House with a formal statement of his position (BMPL: H. Clark/BM 4/22/38; BM/HC 5/5/38). Although its substance survives only in Radcliffe-Brown's typed summary of the thirteen propositions he would defend and in extensive notes Malinowski prepared for his rejoinder, it seems clear that this time the outcome was not a "love-fest."[6]

Radcliffe-Brown began by arguing that cooperative work in science depended on acceptance of a common terminology, which made it "essential to give precise unambiguous definitions of all technical terms." In scientific usage, the term function had two precise but distinct meanings: physiological function referred to the contribution an organ made "by its activity to the persistence of the organic structure"; mathematical function, to expressions in which the substitution of a specific value for a variable term would give a value for the expression as a whole. By a process of degradation, each scientific usage had in popular speech a corresponding "imprecise" meaning: one equivalent to "activity" or "effect"; the other, to "any relation of covariation." Radcliffe-Brown proposed to use the term "social function" in a sense analogous to the scientific conception of physiological function, as the contribution any usage or belief made "to the persistence of the total complex of social reactions [sic—relations?] which constitute the social structure of that society." Appealing to Hsun Tze, Montesquieu, Saint-Simon, and Durkheim, he made a point of "deprecating" the recent usage referring to "any and every relation of interdependence," or simply to the idea of "use" and "purpose."

6. This account of the debate between Malinowski and Radcliffe-Brown is based primarily on materials preserved in BMPY, Series II, Box 12, folder 34.

Responding in a "semi-serious, semi-jocular vein," Malinowski cast himself as the "humble craftsman" of functionalism, against Radcliffe-Brown's black-caped "High Priest" exorcising demons with black magic formuli. In truth, both of them were functionalists with minor divergencies, sharing a belief in the "scientific analysis of actual reality" as opposed to speculation on origins or history; both of them were committed to the search for "general laws of cultural process"; both were convinced that "human society and culture [were] one integral subject of study." The trouble was that Radcliffe-Brown insisted on embellishing his fine empirical work with a "window dressing" of "verbal or scholastic" definitions. He spoke of science as if all science were one, whereas the essence of scientific definition was that concepts should be derived from the reality a particular science studies empirically.

Ridiculing the derivation of sociological concepts by analogy from physiology, Malinowski suggested there was a sense in which the debate itself was an organism, with MG [Morris Ginsberg?] its head, R-B its brain, he himself its liver, and the audience its bowels. But whatever their short-run utility, "no science can live permanently on analogies"; and the organic analogy (along with the "collective soul") had long since been found wanting in sociology. Deriding Radcliffe-Brown's "puritanism of prim precision," polishing words for a "dictionary of homophones," Malinowski insisted that true precision required "turning to facts and developing your concepts always in touch with bedrock reality." For him, that reality was revealed in fieldwork, which had shown that culture was not a "scrap-heap," not an "evolving or still less a 'persisting' organism," but an active, integrative, adaptive, and instrumental process.

In this context, Malinowski defiantly embraced the looseness of usage Radcliffe-Brown had condemned, arguing that fieldwork had in fact revealed four different levels of meaning for the concept function, correlating roughly with Radcliffe-Brown's four usages: use and utility, mutual dependence ("or if you like, co-variation"), the satisfaction of "the biological needs of the human organism," and the satisfaction of "derived needs" or "cultural imperatives." All things considered, the difference between them was really "not very much," if in Radcliffe-Brown's definition one glossed "contribution" as "use" or "purpose" and replaced "persistence" by "integral working" (on the grounds that persistence was "a moral issue"). All that Malinowski did was add "flesh and blood human beings to the shadow of 'purely social system.'"

This "small" difference was perhaps more consequential than Malinowski would allow. Although they came by it in rather different ways, both men shared the bias toward concrete experience that is commonly associated with the British anthropological tradition (cf. Lombard 1972:113). With Malinowski, this concretism expressed itself at a level closer to that of actual observation. Although for him abstraction entered the process by which data were constituted out of the undifferentiated experience of the field observer, it was contained within a circuit that began and ended in the behavior of living human beings he had experienced in the field.

The same empiricist heritage was manifest in Radcliffe-Brown's insistence that social (in contrast to cultural) systems were "real," "concrete" phenomena (1940a:190; cf. Tax et al., eds. 1953:153). However, converted early on to Durkheim and touched at some point by the philosophical notions of Whitehead and Russell, Radcliffe-Brown insisted on the methodological necessity of abstracting typical relationships of structure from the phenomenal reality in which they were embedded, and of distinguishing between different kinds of abstraction from reality. And for him, abstraction moved always away from observation toward the formulation of general social laws. From this point of view, the most revealing passage of the debate is perhaps a marginal annotation Malinowski offered to the tenth point of Radcliffe-Brown's outline. There, Radcliffe-Brown had suggested that "the social function of a usage or belief is to be discovered by examining its effects." While these were in the first instance effects upon individuals, it was "only the effects upon the social relations of the individual with other individuals that constitute the social function." To which Malinowski had commented in the margin, "To me the distinction is not relevant."

The relevance of the distinction was not, however, so easily denied. Each man returned to it in print during the following year. In an article on "The Group and the Individual in Functional Analysis" published while he was on sabbatical leave in the United States, Malinowski made a point of distinguishing "plain and pure" from "hyphenated" functionalism, insisting at some length on the priority of the biological individual "both in social theory and in the reality of cultural life" (1939:243). And in his Frazer Lecture on "Taboo," Radcliffe-Brown attacked Malinowski's derivation of magic from individual psychological need, arguing that ritual could as well cause as alleviate anxiety, and insisting at some length on the social function (as opposed to the psychological effects) of ritual activity (R-B 1939). Although the argument was similar in its essentials to that advanced in *The Andaman Islanders*, it is worth noting that there was no longer any reference to "sentiments." In a sense, Radcliffe-Brown's article the following year "On Joking Relationships" carried the argument one step further, by showing that what seemed manifestly to be individual "psychological" phenomena were in fact expressions of structural relationship (1940b).

Apparently, this exchange marks the last direct expression of their own joking relationship. Caught in the United States by the outbreak of European war, Malinowski died there in 1942, leaving Radcliffe-Brown alone as the surviving resident elder of British social anthropology.

The Transition in Personal, Institutional, and Disciplinary Perspective

As Audrey Richards was to note, the reaction against Malinowski was "partly a personal one" (1957:27)—and even an outsider's limited personal contact with the anthropologists trained between the wars offers plenty of confirming anecdote. Without reducing issues of method and theory to epiphenomenal status, one can scarcely turn from the richly personal materials of the present account without some comment on this aspect of the transition.

In modes appropriate to their intellectual temperaments, Malinowski and Radcliffe-Brown were both individuals who inspired strong feelings of attraction and repulsion. Although he jokingly spoke of himself as a Polish nobleman, and enjoyed occasional weekends at the country homes of friends among the upper classes, Malinowski was an earthy man, who enveloped students in the penumbra of an ardent ego. Although his style may have changed somewhat as he came to feel his position under attack in the 1930s, he seems to have been provocatively permissive in intellectual interaction. Hortense Powdermaker felt that what he demanded was loyalty, not reverence; it was all right to argue with him so long as you were clearly "on his side" (1966: 42–43). This was perhaps less problematic in the 1920s when the "other side" was post-Riversian diffusionism, and perhaps also generally in the case of women, for whom contemporary social standards sustained a more dependent interaction. Ironically, however, the critic of the universal oedipus complex seems to have elicited rejection on the part of a number of his male students. The problem became more serious as he came to feel his position threatened from within the lineage of social anthropology, and in the middle 1930s he became involved in rather bitter controversy with three male students over the authorship of ideas that had been discussed in his seminars. Several informants later spoke of the "break" with Malinowski as if it were a regular developmental phase (Fortes 1969b; Gluckman 1969; Schapera 1969).

Although he was known to entertain parties with Andaman dances, and adopted a more democratic style in the United States (where he soon gave up his monocle and cape), Radcliffe-Brown seems normally to have maintained a certain emotional distance and detachment. But as his early experiments with mesmerism suggest, he could cast a spell on those who were susceptible (Firth 1956). Galvanizing small groups by the direct verbal force of authoritative intellect, he elicited if he did not demand discipleship. What was important for him was not the source of particular ideas—about which he could be quite casual—but rather commitment to a systematic analytic viewpoint. In contrast to Malinowski, who attracted students of both sexes, his appeal seems to have been predominantly to men; and in his case the forces of repulsion seem to have been those of exclusion rather than expulsion. Those who did not enter his charmed intellectual circle, or who were pushed outside of it, found much to criticize in Radcliffe-Brown's somewhat mannered and condescending Edwardian style; but with one notable exception, those who entered it did not find it necessary to make a "break" with him (Evans-Pritchard 1973).

Their failure to do so, however, may reflect not only differences in the dynamics of personal interaction, but also the way these articulated with the evolving institutional structure of British anthropology. By the time Radcliffe-Brown returned to England in 1937, these "breaks" with Malinowski had already taken place; and even if interpersonal dynamics had made repetition more likely, the external institutional context made it less necessary. The exasperating dependence enforced by the career-market of the depression was beginning to come to an end. With the phasing out of Rockefeller anthropology in 1937, Malinowski's patronage was curtailed, and already in 1938 anthropological work outside his institutional orbit had begun to open up slightly, with the founding of the Rhodes-Livingstone Institute and a small expansion of anthropological work in British and colonial universities (Brown 1973). With the coming of the war, the younger anthropologists were off to war-related work, and within a year of its conclusion, Radcliffe-Brown had reached retirement age. While Evans-Pritchard as his immediate successor felt perhaps a special need to assert his own individual genius, the rest of that generation, riding on a wave of university expansion, required no intellectual confrontation to establish themselves institutionally. Although by the early 1950s the Radcliffe-Browninan moment was already waning, it was not until after his death that a more general theoretical reaction began.

That the relations of individuals in small groups should play a decisive role in the diffusion and institutionalization of intellectual innovations is scarcely surprising, in view of the literature in the sociology of science on "invisible colleges" and "solidarity groups" (Mulkay 1977). Insofar as the diffusion of intellectual innovations depends on the activities of charismatic individuals focussing the energies of small groups of disciples to exploit restricted institutional resources, one may anticipate departures from the norm of collegiality implicit in the idea of "invisible college." This is especially likely insofar as the relations of charismatic innovator to disciple are inherently asymmetrical, and likely to be charged with the psychological overtones accompanying other types of authority relations. In the early stages of the development of a discipline or area of inquiry, as well as in the intimate process of the later reproduction of personnel, it seems likely that such interactive groups might evidence the psychodynamics of kinship groups—not simply in the Radcliffe-Brownian style of intellectual lineages, but in the more Malinowskian style of intellectual families (cf. Campbell 1979).

But if the earlier transition from "pure" to "hyphenated" functionalism may

be illuminated by placing it in a context of personal interaction within evolving institutional structures, one may also view the change in terms of an "internal" disciplinary dynamic. The succession of dominance in British social
anthropology was also a movement from an inquiry defined primarily in terms
of its observational methodology to one defined equally in terms of its theoretical presuppositions. As many observers have noted, Malinowskian anthropology alternated between two poles: one of detailed empirical observation,
another in which Trobriand "savages" were used to invalidate the grand theories of late nineteenth and early twentieth century social science, or to vali-
date his own later functionalist metatheory (Leach 1957:119; cf. Panoff 1972:
55). This was appropriate, perhaps, to an early phase of "the revolution in
anthropology," when what was required was the discrediting of the old and
the popularization of the new point of view. But when Malinowski's work
was later subjected to general reevaluation by the succeeding generation of
British anthropologists (Firth, ed. 1957), several commented directly or indirectly on the impasse that Malinowskian functionalism had reached in the
middle 1930s. His contribution to the development of ethnographic method
was not then at issue, and there is ample indication in his correspondence
with students in the field that Malinowskian functionalism "worked" in the
sense that it facilitated the collection of large amounts of data (cf. Stocking
1983a). But in some cases problems seem to have arisen when it came to syn-
thesizing the material. As Firth later posed the matter: "If everything is related to everything else, where does the description stop?" (Kuper 1973:94).

Malinowski's own grand synthetic effort, which was discussed as work-in-
progress in the seminars of the early 1930s, provided in some ways a model.
But although *Coral Gardens and their Magic* carried "institutional study" to
the "furthest limit" by means of "correlating one set of activities" with "the
whole," it was not a model easily imitated. As Audrey Richards suggested,
"it was a *tour de force*, but it was not practical politics to repeat such an experiment" (1957:27-28).

Others would not have repeated the experiment even if it were expedient.
Writing to Malinowski in the fall of 1935, Gregory Bateson announced a general dissatisfaction with his approach: "Where you emphasize the need for
complete delineation of all the factors relevant to a total cultural situation,
I emphasize the need to consider these factors one at a time, comparing the
action of the same factor in a whole series of separate situations." Although
granting that the two approaches might each be valid "within their respective
limitations," Bateson nevertheless felt that Malinowski's was "a hopeless mud-
dle out of which simple scientific generalizations can never come" (BMPL:
GB/BM n.d. [October 1935]). Reading *Coral Gardens* in this context, Bateson
had looked for the word "logic" as applied to Trobriand culture and found

not a single instance (BMPL: GB/BM 1/16/36). What he wanted was to dissect the monograph, and rearrange its rich materials to show "not the whole of the mechanism but rather the working of each isolable sociological and psychological law" (BMPL: GB/BM 11/5/35; cf. Bateson 1936).

Although Bateson's case—and Firth's in *We, the Tikopia* (1936)—suggests that it was not simply a matter of a viable Oceanic functionalism running aground in Africa, this shift in ethnographic focus was perhaps a factor in the theoretical transition. If the problem of abstraction was felt even by students of small and bounded Oceanic societies, it was likely to be more strongly felt by those dealing with the larger, more complex, and loosely margined societies of Africa—particularly when the focus was on problems of culture contact. At the conclusion of the African Institute's five-year plan for the study of culture change, Malinowski himself seems to have been less than fully satisfied with the results of studies carried on where the "main presuppositions of functionalism in its simple form break down" (1938:xxxvi).

As several writers have suggested, what Radcliffe-Brown offered intellectually at this point was a theoretical orientation that made it easier to distinguish between generalized empirical connection and specific analytical relevance (Kuper 1973:94). By focussing on particular types of social relations that could be abstracted from a given body of ethnographic data, it not only provided a framework for ordering otherwise less tractable material, but seemed to hold forth the promise of systematic comparative study. It represented a further narrowing of anthropological attention, which for Malinowski as for Radcliffe-Brown had already excluded the concern with material culture and racial type—somewhat to the consternation of ethnological traditionalists like Seligman and Haddon. But it was an approach that must have seemed especially attractive to students who had suffered the frustrations of "contact" studies carried on in the looser Malinowskian functional mode—and had then been criticized by the master in his volume preface (BM 1938).

In this context, Radcliffe-Brown's thinking clearly had an impact beyond the small group to whom he explicated the notions of "system" and "structure" in his rooms in All Souls during the last months before the outbreak of the Second World War (Gluckman 1969). Reiterated at their request in the first of two successive presidential addresses to the Royal Anthropological Institute (R-B 1940a; 1941), it provided the essential analytic underpinning for the two major cooperative efforts of the Radcliffe-Brownian mode: *African Political Systems* (Fortes & Evans-Pritchard, eds. 1940)—four of whose contributors had been included in Malinowski's culture contact volume— and *African Systems of Kinship and Marriage* (Radcliffe-Brown & Forde, eds. 1950). Although both were published by the International African Institute, neither contained a single reference to Malinowski.

Institute of Social Anthropology, University of Oxford. Prof. A. R. Radcliffe-Brown's class 1945–46. *Left to right, front row*: K. T. Hadjioannou, Phyllis Puckle (secretary and librarian), A. R. Radcliffe-Brown, Meyer Fortes (Reader, 1947–50), K. A. Busia; *back row*: L. F. Henriques, W. Newell, J. W. Brailsford, A. A. Issa, M. N. Srinivas (courtesy of the Institute of Social Anthropology).

The Radcliffe-Brownian Moment
in Broader Historical Perspective

A decade and a half after Radcliffe-Brown's death, it seemed to one member of the postwar generation looking back that changes had taken place in British anthropology "such that for practical purposes textbooks which looked useful, no longer are; monographs which used to appear exhaustive now seem selective; interpretations which once looked full of insight now seem mechanical and lifeless." Such images call up once again the metaphor of paradigm, and indeed the "new anthropology"—still hyphenated in authorship, but now a "structuralism" *tout court*—was seen as standing on the other side of an "epistemological break" (Ardener 1971:449). But despite the influence of Lévi-Strauss, no new paradigm swept the field: a decade later, the same writer saw the 1970s as a time when grand theoretical dinosaurs (with "structuralism" leading the parade) had died off "suddenly together," leaving only "small furry mammals" scurrying over the anthropological ground (Ardener 1983). One might view the 1970s as a decade of "institutional stagnation, intellectual torpor, and parochialism" (Kuper 1983:192), or as an "intellectual cocktail" from which something "highly combustible" might yet distill. What, from "one temporal vantage point," seemed "a decline from a golden age" could in the long run be "interpreted as transition to a new one" (Ellen 1983). But if theoretical coherence might be regained at some future point, there was clearly a sense of paradigm lost; from either perspective, the Radcliffe-Brownian moment seemed a thing of the past.

It is worth noting that its distancing was reflected in the heightened relevance of many of the issues in the Murdock/Firth exchange. By 1980, African ethnography had significantly declined in importance, particularly among younger anthropologists, for whom problems of ritual, symbolism, and classification were more salient than those of social organization. If anthropology and psychology remained somewhat distanced, there had been a definite "shift toward a more 'cultural' anthropology"—though the term itself still for some required quotational marking (Kuper 1983:190). There had also been a noticeable rapprochement with history, and there was a significant interest in problems of cultural change and development (Ellen 1983). The problem of the generalizability of "African models" had been a concern throughout the period (Barnes 1962; Cohn 1977), which can be seen also as unified by a concern with the problems of "reification" and "variation." While there was still talk of "parochialism," and the impact of Marxist influences was a matter of debate, the variety of those dying dinosaurs and scurrying mammals could be seen as evidence for broadening anthropological vistas as well as for theoretical disarray.

But if even from this unstable vantage point, the Radcliffe-Brownian moment seemed still to stand on the other side of a divide, the transition of the 1930s seemed now much less sharply marked. From the perspective of many postrupture critics, Malinowskian fieldwork and Radcliffe-Brownian typologizing were simply two phases of the same empiricist butterfly collection (Ardener 1971:450; cf. Leach 1961:2); both represented the same, now-discredited "positivist" point of view.

Indeed, there are many today (especially, perhaps, in the United States) for whom the real problem for historical understanding would seem now to be: how could so many intelligent anthropologists have been so long infected by such a sterile and/or derivative viewpoint? Without accepting the characterization, the question demands serious consideration, as an instantiation of a fundamental problem of intellectual history—one which, in cross-cultural rather than trans-temporal situations, is quite familiar to anthropologists: explaining how it is that people can believe what seems from another perspective manifestly "foolish." Savoring the wonderful irony of its propagation by an expatriate Pole and a self-exiled Francophile—not to mention the diverse origins of many of their disciples—it is tempting to refer the matter to British

intellectual character. Given Malinowski's rather self-conscious intellectual an-
glicization after World War I, and what some would call Radcliffe-Brown's peculiarly English reading of Durkheim, there may be more to this suggestion than
irony would allow. Certainly, the intellectual character of British anthropology has been recurrently affected by the appropriation of French rationalist
models and their domestication to a deeply rooted empirical tradition. In the
end, the historian of "the modern British school" concludes that "anthropology has little to do with grand theory," and comes down four square for a
"regional structural comparison" based upon the "functionalist field studies"
that have been "the distinctive feature of modern British anthropology" (Kuper
1983:204–5)–a program in some respects similar to the one that Radcliffe-
Brown offered in the 1930s. Quite aside from national character, or–as my
colleague Marshall Sahlins would have it, an entrenched cultural bias toward
utilitarian assumption–this essay has perhaps suggested other approaches to
the problem. And despite the attention given to such factors as personal charisma, or career considerations within a particular institutional framework,
it should be clear that my own interpretation gives substantial weight to specifically cognitive factors. Without arguing that this viewpoint is in some time-
less theoretical sense "correct," it seems nonetheless understandable that, in
the context of the alternative viewpoints effectively available at the time,
Radcliffe-Brownian structural-functionalism seemed to many an intellectual
tool of considerable power.

There can be no question now of reentering the period that (allowing for
a large input of Malinowskian romanticism) might be called the "classical era"
in British social anthropology. From across an irreversible historical divide
marked more by decolonization than by the rejection of "positivism"–which,
in the guise of "methodological pragmatism" still has its attractions (Kuper
1983:204)–the best we can do is try to appreciate its distinctive historical
character.

The problem is complicated by the multiple perspectives suggested by the
easily mixable metaphors of lineage and paradigm, and by the difference between what one perceptive historian of British anthropology has called a man's
"theories" and his "views" (Burrow 1966:32). Retrospectively, it is possible to
find in The Natural Science of Society the grounding for a study of cultural
symbols (cf. Singer 1973). Similarly, looking back to legitimate the present
rehistoricizing impulse, one can find an historical interest running throughout British social anthropology (Lewis 1984). If we attend to all the methodological caveats, it is quite possible to show that Radcliffe-Brown regarded
the privileging of synchronic analysis as simply a methodological strategy, and
that what he opposed was not "real" but "conjectural" history. This should
not blind us, however, to what was going on in the first decades of the twentieth century–which is when the very real disjuncture of 1922 was being
prepared (cf. Kuper 1973).

British anthropology in the late nineteenth century may be regarded as a pre-Freudian science of the irrational—the polar complement of political economy, which was the science of the characteristic rational behavior of civilized men. A critical role in this science of the irrational was played by the doctrine of survivals, which (aside from the enveloping assumptional framework of biological evolutionism) is perhaps the specific assumption most sharply differentiating nineteenth-century progressive developmentalism from earlier manifestations of the same viewpoint (Hodgen 1936). If the comparative method was the major ordering principle of cultural evolutionism, then the doctrine of survivals was its key interpretive principle. Presented with an array of inexplicable, irrational beliefs and customs in the recorded accounts of present-day "savages," the armchair anthropologist—archetypically, Frazer—could give them rational meaning through the built-in rationalistic utilitarianism of the doctrine of survivals: what made no rational sense in the present was perfectly understandable as the sheer inertial persistence of the imperfectly rational pursuit of utility in an earlier stage.

The present essay casts only incidental light on why, in the decade after 1900, this approach should have begun to seem unsatisfactory to some anthropologists, why there should have been such a widespread sense of the inadequacy of theoretical categories to empirical data (cf. Stocking 1983a). One is inclined to suggest that the question, "Why do they do this crazy thing?" seemed more obviously presumptuous when carried to the field than when asked from the armchair. But the new functionalism was equally if not more privileging of the position of the anthropologist, since it assumed that he could find reason even where it had never in fact presented itself to the individual savage consciousness. And in the case of Radcliffe-Brown, we are rather led back to particular intellectual influences felt in the moment of paradigm crisis, influences that link anthropology to the more general context of European thought about "consciousness and society" (Hughes 1958). But in this case, the examination of surviving correspondence leads us also to an appreciation of the paradigmatic centrality of the doctrine of survivals—not only for Radcliffe-Brown in 1914, but also for the historian looking back from the present.

More generally, perhaps it may heighten our appreciation of what was indeed a major theoretical transition in the history of anthropology: the break in the cycle of alternating diachronic paradigms that had characterized anthropology up until the early twentieth century. The dehistoricization of anthropological speculation was doubtless a complex phenomenon. It was also happening at about the same time in Malinowski, in a way that was at least superficially even more thoroughgoing: the major point of theoretical difference evident in his marginal notes to Radcliffe-Brown's paper of 1923 was an unwillingness to grant separate but equal status to the methods of ethnology (BMSC, R-B 1923:127, 130)—which, we may note again in passing, in the United

States also underwent dehistoricization during the interwar period (Stocking 1976a). Even so, when Radcliffe-Brown realizes in 1914 that he and Rivers are talking past one another—that fundamental differences in methodological assumption make a continuation of their dispute fruitless—we feel ourselves present at the very moment of a rupture in the history of anthropology. If we now seek to recapture an historical perspective within as well as upon the discipline, it is from the other side of this major historical intellectual disjuncture.

Acknowledgments

This essay is a much-belated (and still partial) fruit of manuscript research carried out during two six-month visits to England: in 1969, when I was invited to Kings College, Cambridge, by Robert M. Young, who had organized a seminar on the social study of the history of science, and again in 1973, when I was a visitor to the Department of Anthropology of the London School of Economics. I would like to thank my hosts on both occasions, the repositories and the archivists of the various manuscript materials consulted, and the several agencies that funded that research: the Wenner-Gren Foundation for Anthropological Research, the National Endowment for the Humanities, and the National Science Foundation. Versions of the first half of the essay, on Radcliffe-Brown and Rivers, were presented at the University of Sussex in 1973 and to several subsequent seminars on Radcliffe-Brown in the Department of Anthropology of the University of Chicago. The second half, on Radcliffe-Brown and Malinowski, was drafted at the Center for Advanced Study in the Behavioral Sciences during the academic year 1976–77 (where my stay was supported by the National Endowment for the Humanities), and has been presented since then to several different groups. Helpful comments on all or part of the argument have been offered by Bernard Cohn, Ronald Cohen, John Comaroff, Fred Eggan, Raymond Firth, Raymond Fogelson, Meyer Fortes, Marshall Sahlins, David Schneider, Milton Singer, Marilyn Strathern, Stanley Tambiah, and others who have been present at one or another presentation. Although I have not cited all of them specifically, this essay has benefitted from the extended reminiscences of a number of living and recently deceased British social anthropologists who knew Radcliffe-Brown and Malinowski (including E. E. Evans-Pritchard, Raymond Firth, Meyer Fortes, C. von Fürer Heimendorf, Max Gluckman, Phyllis Kabery, Edmund Leach, Lucy Mair, Audrey Richards, Isaac Schapera, and M. N. Srinivas), as well as from occasional conversational reminiscences from many others. I have profitted also from seminar papers by my students, including Allen Berger, Lisa Brusewicz, Tom Marett, Ed Martinek, Philip Stafford, and Bill Stamets. I am grateful to Peter Lloyd for access to early minutes of the Association of Social Anthropologists, and to Richard Randolph for access to Malinowski reprints in his personal possession. I would like to express my special appreciation to the daughters of Radcliffe-Brown and Malinowski, Mrs. Cynthia Pike and Mrs. Helena Wayne Malinowska, for their continuing cooperation and encouragement. Secretarial assistance has been provided at various points with the help of the Adolph and Marian Lichtstern Fund for Anthropological Research of the Department of Anthropology and the Morris Fishbein Center for the Study of the History of Science and Medicine of the University of Chicago.

References Cited

ACHP. See under Manuscript Sources.
Ardener, E. 1971. The new anthropology and its critics. Man 6:449–67.
———. 1983. The ASA and its critics. RAIN 56:11–12.
Asad, T., ed. 1973. Anthropology and the colonial encounter. London.
ASAM. See under Manuscript Sources.
Barnes, J. 1962. African models in the New Guinea highlands, Man 2:5–9.
Bateson, G. 1936. Naven. 2d ed. Stanford (1958).
Beattie, J. 1964. Other cultures: Aims, methods and achievements in social anthropology. New York.
BLUA. See under Manuscript Sources.
BM. See under Malinowski.
BMPL. See under Manuscript Sources.
BMPY. See under Manuscript Sources.
BMSC. See under Manuscript Sources.
Brown, R. 1973. Anthropology and colonial rule: Godfrey Wilson and the Rhodes-Livingstone Institute. In Asad, ed. 1973:173–98.
Burrow, J. W. 1966. Evolution and society: A study in Victorian social theory. Cambridge.
CUPA. See under Manuscript Sources.
Campbell, D. 1979. A tribal model of the social system vehicle carrying knowledge. Knowledge: Creation, Utilization 1:181–201.
Carneiro, R. 1973. Classical evolution. In Main currents in cultural anthropology, ed. R. Naroll & F. Naroll, 57–122. Englewood Cliffs, N.J.
Cohn, B. 1977. African models and Indian histories. In Realm and region in traditional India., ed. R. G. Fox, 90–113. Durham, N.C.
Durkheim, E. 1895. The rules of the sociological method. Trans. S. Solovay & J. Mueller. Reprint ed. New York (1964).
———. 1912. The elementary forms of the religious life. Trans. J. Swain. Reprint ed. New York (1965).
Eggan, F. 1956. Alfred Reginald Radcliffe-Brown, 1881–1955. Am. Anth. 58:544–47.
———. 1971. Seminar discussion, May 6.
Elkin, A. P. 1956. A. R. Radcliffe-Brown, 1880 [sic]–1955. Oceania 24:239–51.
Ellen, R. F. 1983. The British school: A premature postscript. RAIN 57:2.

Evans-Pritchard, E. E. 1929. The study of kinship in primitive societies. *Man* 148: 190–91.

———. 1933. The intellectualist (English) interpretation of magic. *Bul. Fac. Arts, Cairo* 1:1–21.

———. 1973. Interview, June 21.

Firth, R. 1936. *We, the Tikopia: A sociological study of kinship in primitive Polynesia.* London.

———. 1951. Contemporary British social anthropology. *Am. Anth.* 53:474–89.

———. 1956. Alfred Reginald Radcliffe-Brown: 1881–1955. *Proc. Brit. Acad.* 42:286–302.

———. 1957. Malinowski as scientist and man. In Firth, ed. 1957:1–14.

———. 1971. Bronislaw Malinowski. In *Totems and teachers: Perspectives on the history of anthropology,* ed. S. Silverman, 103–37. Paperback ed. New York.

———. 1969. Interview, July 9.

Firth, R., ed. 1957. *Man and culture: An evaluation of the work of Bronislaw Malinowski.* Paperback ed. New York.

Fison, L., & A. W. Howitt 1880. *Kamilaroi and Kurnai: Group-marriage and relationship . . .* Reprint ed. Osterhout N.B., Netherlands (1967).

Fortes, M. 1953. The structure of unilineal descent groups. *Am. Anth.* 55:17–41.

———. 1955. Radcliffe-Brown's contributions to the study of social organization. *Brit. J. Soc.* 6:16–30.

———. 1956. Alfred Reginald Radcliffe-Brown, F.B.A., 1881–1955, a memoir. *Man* 172:149–53.

———. 1957. Malinowski and the study of kinship. In Firth, ed. 1957:157–88.

———. 1969a. *Kinship and the social order: The legacy of Lewis Henry Morgan.* Chicago.

———. 1969b. Interview, September 6.

———. 1978. An anthropologist's apprenticeship. *Ann. Rev. Anth.* 7:1–30.

Fortes, M., ed. 1949. *Social structure: Studies presented to Radcliffe-Brown.* Oxford.

Fortes, M., & E. E. Evans-Pritchard, eds. 1940. *African political systems.* London.

Frazer, J. G. 1900. *The golden bough: A study in magic and religion.* 2d ed., 3 vols. London.

———. 1910. *Totemism and exogamy.* Reprint ed., 4 vols. London (1968).

Gathercole, P. n.d. Cambridge and the Torres Straits, 1888–1902. *Camb. Anth.* 3 (3): 22–31.

Gluckman, M. 1969. Interview, September 6.

Harris, M. 1968. *The rise of anthropological theory: A history of theories of culture.* New York.

Hatch, E. 1973. *Theories of man and culture.* New York.

Hodgen, M. T. 1936. *The doctrine of survivals: A chapter in the history of scientific method in the study of man.* London.

Homans, G. C. 1941. Anxiety and ritual: The theories of Malinowski and Radcliffe-Brown. *Am. Anth.* 43:164–72.

Hughes, H. S. 1958. *Consciousness and society: The reorientation of European social thought, 1890–1930.* New York.

ISAL. See under Manuscript Sources

Jarvie, I. 1964. *The revolution in anthropology.* London.

———. 1966. In defense of Frazer. *Cur. Anth.* 7:568–70.

JSBL. See under Manuscript Sources.

Kelly, L. P. 1983. Structure, function, and anarchy in Radcliffe-Brown. Paper, Central States Anthropological Society, April 8.

Kochar, V. K. 1968. Function as social physiology or social paleontology. Typescript.

Kuhn, T. 1962. *The structure of scientific revolutions*. Chicago.

——. 1974. Second thoughts on paradigms. In *The structure of scientific theories*, ed. F. Suppes, 459–82. Urbana, Ill.

Kuklick, H. 1978. 'The sins of the fathers': British anthropology and colonial administration. *Res. Soc. Knowl., Scis. Art* 1:93–119.

Kuper, A. 1973. *Anthropologists and anthropology: The British school, 1922–1972*. London.

——. 1983. *Anthropology and anthropologists: The modern British school*. London.

Lang, A. 1901. *Magic and religion*. London.

——. 1907. Australian problems. In *Anthropological essays presented to E. B. Tylor*, ed. E. Balfour et al., 203–18. Oxford.

Langham, Ian. 1981. *The building of British social anthropology: W. H. R. Rivers and his Cambridge disciples in the development of kinship studies, 1898–1931*. Dordrecht, Holland.

Larcom, J. 1983. Following Deacon: The problem of ethnographic reanalysis, 1926–1981. HOA 1:175–95.

Leach, E. 1957. The epistemological background to Malinowski's empiricism. In Firth, ed. 1957:119–39.

——. 1961. *Rethinking anthropology*. London.

——. 1966. Frazer and Malinowski: On the 'Founding Fathers.' *Cur. Anth.* 7:560-76.

——. 1976. Social anthropology: A natural science of society? *Proc. Brit. Acad.* 62: 1–26.

Leary, D. E. 1982. The fate and influence of John Stuart Mill's proposed science of ethology. *J. Hist. Ideas* 43:153–62.

Lewis, I. M. 1984. The future of the past in British social anthropology. *Vienna J. Anth.* (In press.)

Lombard, J. 1972. *L'Anthropologie britannique contemporaine*. Paris.

McAllister, J. 1978. Personal communication, March 15.

McDougall, W. 1905. *Physiological psychology*. London.

——. 1908. *Social psychology*. London.

McLennan, J. F. 1865. *Primitive marriage*. Reprint ed. Chicago (1970).

——. 1869. The worship of animals and plants. *Fort. Rev.* 6:407-27, 562–82; 7:194–216.

——. 1876. The classificatory system of relationships. In *Studies in ancient history*, 329–407. London.

Malinowski, B. 1913. *The family among the Australian aborigines*. Paperback ed. New York (1963).

——. 1922. *Argonauts of the western Pacific*. Paperback ed. New York (1961).

——. 1923. The problem of meaning in primitive languages. In C. K. Ogden & I. A. Richards, *The meaning of meaning*, 451–510. London.

——. 1926a. Anthropology. *Ency. Brit.* 1:131–40.

——. 1926b. *Crime and custom in savage society*. Paperback ed. Patterson, N.J. (1964).

——. 1927. *Sex and repression in savage society*. Cleveland (1965).

——. 1930. Kinship. *Man* 30:19–29.

——. 1931. Culture. *Ency. Soc. Scis.* 4:621–45.

———. 1934. Introduction. In H. I. Hogben, *Law and order in Polynesia*, xvii–lxxii. London.

———. 1935a. Primitive law. *Man* 35:55–56.

———. 1935b. *Coral gardens and their magic*. 2 vols. Bloomington, Ind. (1965).

———. 1938. Introductory essay on the anthropology of changing African cultures. In *Methods of study of culture contact in Africa*, vii–xxxviii. London.

———. 1939. The group and the individual in functional analysis. In 1962:233–45.

———. 1944. *A scientific theory of culture and other essays*. Reprint ed. New York (1960).

———. 1962. *Sex, culture and myth*. New York.

Mandelbaum, D. R. 1980. The Todas in time perspective. *Revs. Anth.* 7:279–301.

Marett, R. R. 1900. Preanimistic religion. *Folk-Lore* 11:162–82.

Maybury-Lewis, D. 1965. Durkheim on relationship systems. *J. Sci. Study Relig.* 4:253–60.

Morgan, L. H. 1870. *Systems of consanguinity and affinity of the human family*. Reprint ed. Osterhout N.B., Netherlands (1970).

Mulkay, M. J. 1977. Sociology of the scientific research community. In *Science, technology, and society*, ed. I. Spiegel-Rosing & D. Price, 93–148. London.

Murdock, G. P. 1951. British social anthropology. *Am. Anth.* 53:465–73.

Needham, R. 1962. *Structure and sentiment: A test case in social anthropology*. Chicago.

———. 1974. *Remarks and inventions: Skeptical essays about kinship*. London.

Panoff, M. 1972. *Bronislaw Malinowski*. Paris.

Parsons, T. 1957. Malinowski and the theory of social systems. In Firth, ed. 1957:53–70.

Paul, B. 1934. Lecture notes on R-B's "Comparative science of culture," October 8 (courtesy of Ben Paul).

Perry, R. J. 1975. Radcliffe-Brown and Kropotkin: The heritage of anarchism in British social anthropology. *Kroeber Anth. Soc. Papers* 51/52:61–65.

Powdermaker, H. 1966. *Stranger and friend: The way of an anthropologist*. New York.

Radcliffe-Brown, A. R. 1909. The religion of the Andaman islanders. *Folk-Lore* 20: 257–71.

———. 1910a. Peluga: A reply to Father Schmidt. *Man* 10:33–37.

———. 1910b. "Study of native races" [interview with R-B]. *The West Australian*, September 10.

———. 1913a. Three tribes of Western Australia. *J. Roy. Anth. Inst.* 43:143–94.

———. 1913b. An unpublished paper by A. R. Radcliffe-Brown on *The study of social institutions*, with a letter in reply by W. H. R. Rivers and an introduction by Meyer Fortes. *Camb. Anth.* 3(3):32–48.

———. 1914a. The definition of totemism. *Anthropos* 9:622–30.

———. 1914b. Review of BM 1913. *Man* 14:31–32.

———. 1922. *The Andaman islanders*. Cambridge.

———. 1923. The methods of ethnology and social anthropology. In 1958:3–38.

———. 1924. The mother's brother in South Africa. In 1958:15–31.

———. 1926. The regulation of marriage in Ambrym. *J. Roy. Anth. Inst.* 57:343–48.

———. 1929a. A further note on Ambrym. *Man* 29:50–53.

———. 1929b. Bilateral descent. *Man* 29:199–200.

———. 1930. Applied anthropology. *Report of the 20th Meeting*, Aust. & N.Z. Assn. Adv. Sci., 267–80. Brisbane.

———. 1931a. The present position of anthropological studies." In 1958:42–95.

————. 1931b. The social organisation of Australian tribes. *Oceania Monographs*, no. 1.

————. 1932. *The Andaman islanders*. 2d ed. Chicago.

————. 1933. Law, primitive. *Ency. Soc. Scis.* 9:202–6.

————. 1935a. Primitive law. *Man* 35:47–48.

————. 1935b. Patrilineal and matrilineal succession. In 1952:32–48.

————. 1935c. On the concept of function in social science. *Am. Anth.* 37:394–404.

————. 1937. *A natural science of society*. Chicago (1956).

————. 1938. Motherhood in Australia. *Man* 38:14–15.

————. 1939. Taboo. In 1952:133–52.

————. 1940a. On social structure. In 1952:188–204.

————. 1940b. On joking relationships. In 1952:90–104.

————. 1941. The study of kinship systems. In 1952:49–89.

————. 1946. Note on functional anthropology. *Man* 46:38–41.

————. 1949. Functionalism: A protest. *Am. Anth.* 51:320–23.

————. 1952. *Structure and function in primitive society*. New York (1965).

————. 1958. *Method in social anthropology*, ed. M. N. Srinivas. Chicago.

Radcliffe-Brown, A. R., & D. Forde, eds. 1950. *African systems of kinship and marriage*. London.

R-B. See under Radcliffe-Brown.

RFA. See under Manuscript Sources.

Richards, A. 1957. The concept of culture in Malinowski's work. In Firth, ed. 1957: 15–31.

Rivers, W. H. R. 1900. A genealogical method of collecting social and vital statistics. *J. Roy. Anth. Inst.* 30:74–82.

————. 1906. *The Todas*. London.

————. 1907. On the origin of the classificatory system of relationships. In *Anthropological essays presented to E. B. Tylor*, ed. N. Balfour et al., 309–23. Oxford.

————. 1908. Genealogies. In *Reports of the Cambridge Expedition to Torres Straits*, ed. A. C. Haddon, 6:64–91. Cambridge.

————. 1911. The ethnological analysis of culture. In 1926:120–40.

————. 1912a. The disappearance of useful arts. In 1926:190–210.

————. 1912b. The sociological significance of myth. *Folk-Lore* 23:307–31.

————. 1913. Survival in sociology. *Soc. Rev.* 6:293–305.

————. 1914a. *Kinship and social organisation*. Reprint ed. London (1968).

————. 1914b. *The history of Melanesian society*. Reprint ed., 2 vols. Osterhout N.B., Netherlands (1968).

————. 1914c. The terminology of totemism. *Anthropos* 9:640–46.

————. 1916. Sociology and psychology. In 1926:3–20.

————. 1917. Freud's psychology of the unconscious. *Lancet* 95:912–14.

————. 1924. *Social organization*, ed. W. J. Perry. London.

————. 1926. *Psychology and ethnology*, ed. G. E. Smith. London.

Rooksby, R. L. 1971. W. H. R. Rivers and the Todas. *South Asia* 1:109–21.

Rosenfels, E. 1932. Lecture notes on R-B's "Comparative science of culture." Fall (courtesy of Edith Rosenfels Nash).

Salter, E. 1972. *Daisy Bates*. Sydney.

Schapera, I. 1969. Interview, August 9.

———. n.d. Social anthropology [Notes on R-B's lectures at Cape Town University, 1924?] ISAL.

Shand, A. F. 1914. *The foundations of character: Being a study of the tendencies of the emotions and sentiments.* London.

Singer, M. 1973. A neglected source of structuralism: Radcliffe-Brown, Russell, and Whitehead. Paper, Association of Social Anthropologists, Oxford, July 4–11.

Slobodin, R. 1978. *W. H. R. Rivers.* New York.

Spencer, W. B., & F. Gillen. 1899. *The native tribes of Central Australia.* Paperback ed. New York (1968).

Stanner, W. E. 1956. A. R. Radcliffe-Brown. *Kroeber Anth. Soc. Papers* 13:116–25.

———. 1967. Reflections on Durkheim and aboriginal religion. In *Social organisation: Essays presented to Raymond Firth,* ed. M. Freedman, 217–40. Chicago.

———. 1968. Radcliffe-Brown, A. R. *Int. Ency. Soc. Scis.* 13:285–90.

Stocking, G. W., Jr. 1973. From chronology to ethnology: James Cowles Prichard and British anthropology, 1800–1850. In J. C. Prichard, *Researches into the physical history of man,* ix–cx. Reprint ed. Chicago.

———. 1976a. Ideas and institutions in American anthropology: Thoughts toward a history of the interwar years. In *Selected papers from the American Anthropologist,* 1–53. Washington, D.C.

———. 1976b. Radcliffe-Brown, Lowie and *The history of ethnological theory. Hist. Anth. Newsl.* 3(2):5–8.

———. 1977. Anarchy Brown's school days: Cambridge anthropology in 1904. *Hist. Anth. Newsl.* 4(1):11–12.

———. 1978a. Die Geschichtlichkeit der Wilden und die Geschichte der Ethnologie. *Geschichte und Gesellschaft* 4:520–35 [trans. W. Lepennies].

———. 1978b. The problems of translating between paradigms: The 1933 debate between Ralph Linton and Radcliffe-Brown. *Hist. Anth. Newsl.* 5(1):7–9.

———. 1978c. Philanthropoids and vanishing cultures: Rockefeller anthropology between the wars. Typescript.

———. 1979. *Anthropology at Chicago: Tradition, discipline, department* [library exhibit brochure]. Chicago.

———. 1981a. Apes, grandfathers and Rubicons: Some thoughts on an enduring tension in anthropology. Symposium on anthropological implications of evolutionary theory, Chapel Hill, North Carolina, March 2.

———. 1981b. Books unfinished, turning points unmarked: Notes for an anti-history of anthropology. Morris Fishbein Lecture for 1981, Chicago, May 18.

———. 1982. Gatekeeper to the field: E. W. P. Chinnery and the ethnography of the New Guinea Mandate. *Hist. Anth. Newsl.* 9(2):3–12.

———. 1983a. The ethnographer's magic: Fieldwork in British anthropology from Tylor to Malinowski. *HOA* 1:50–120.

———. 1983b. The 'Genesis' of anthropology: The discipline's first paradigm. Distinguished lecture, Central States Anthropological Society, Cleveland, April 8.

———. 1984. Anthropology and the science of the irrational: Malinowski's encounter with Freud. Paper, Association of Social Anthropologists, London, April 10.

Tax, S. 1978. Seminar discussion, February 2.

Tax, S., et al., eds. 1953. *An appraisal of anthropology today.* Chicago.

Thomas, N. W. 1906. *Kinship organisations and group marriage in Australia.* London.

Tylor, E. B. 1888. On a method of investigating the development of institutions applied to laws of marriage and descent. *J. Anth. Inst.* 18:245–72.

Urry, J. 1982. From zoology to ethnology: A. C. Haddon's conversion to anthropology. *Canberra Anth.* 5(2):58–85.

Watson, E. G. 1946. *But to what purpose?* London.

———. 1968. *Journey under southern stars.* London.

White, Isobel. 1981. Mrs. Bates and Mr. Brown: An examination of Rodney Needham's allegations. *Oceania* 51:193–210.

WHRP. See under Manuscript Sources.

Manuscript Sources

In writing this essay I have drawn on research materials collected since 1969 from various archival sources, which are cited by the following abbreviations:

ACHP. A. C. Haddon Papers, University Library, Cambridge, England.

ASAM. Association of Social Anthropologists, Minutes. In the possession of Peter Lloyd, University of Sussex, when consulted in 1969.

BLUA. University Archives, Bancroft Library, University of California, Berkeley.

BMPL. Bronislaw Malinowski Papers, British Library of Political and Economic Science, London School of Economics.

BMPY. Bronislaw Malinowski Papers, Yale University Library, New Haven, Conn.

BMSC. Bronislaw Malinowski books and offprints, University of California, Santa Cruz—in the rare book room, and in the personal collection of Richard Randolph.

CUPA. Archives, Cambridge University Press.

ISAL. Library, Institute of Social Anthropology, Oxford.

JSBL. John S. Battye Library, Perth, Western Australia.

RFA. Rockefeller Foundation Archives, Tarryton, N.Y.

WHRP. W. H. R. Rivers Papers, in the A. C. Haddon Papers, University Library, Cambridge, England.

FUNCTION, HISTORY, BIOGRAPHY

Reflections on Fifty Years in the British Anthropological Tradition

HILDA KUPER

South African Anthropological Beginnings: 1911–1932

What led me to anthropology is a complex question.[1] No doubt it was partly fortuitous events over which I had no personal control: the fact that I was born in the little town of Bulawayo, in the then-British colony of Rhodesia (Zimbabwe), where the white settler population held very privileged positions. My parents, however, were first generation immigrants from continental Europe—my father from Eastern Europe, my mother from Vienna—and very early in life I was made aware of certain political conflicts. I was only three when World War I broke out, and my father was loyal to the British side, while my mother's brothers fought for the "enemy." This was part and parcel

---

1. This account derives from two sessions (May 5 and 14, 1981) of a seminar on "Themes and Experience in the History of Anthropology"—suggested by Lisabeth Ryder and organized by John Kennedy—to which several senior members of the Department of Anthropology of the University of California at Los Angeles offered reminiscences of their anthropological careers. It was originally presented informally from a few notes on cards, and the present text derives from transcribed tapes of the seminar (including portions of the discussion). It has not been systematically reworked as an essay, and the style remains rather more conversational than literary. In this spirit of informality, only minimal documentation has been provided. I would like to thank Professor Kennedy for his efforts in organizing the seminar and having the tapes transcribed, as well as Gelya Frank for her assistance in the editing process.

Hilda Kuper is Professor Emeritus of Anthropology at the University of California, Los Angeles. She has published numerous works on the Swazi, and is currently bringing up to date *The Swazi: A South African Kingdom*, which was first published in 1965.

of a home that was friendly and loving, but which in the external world had to confront these conflicting influences.

I was only one of a group of anthropologists who came from South Africa— Meyer Fortes, Isaac Schapera, Max Gluckman, Monica Wilson, Eileen Krige, Ellen Hellman, Jack Simons. Our social context was one that stressed historical cleavages, not only in terms of "race" or color, but also between the British and the Afrikaner, who were at loggerheads at the end of the world war. As I grew up, the old battle between Briton and Boer was being repeated in all sorts of ways: conflict over language, contrasts of religion, and differences in schools. But if such conflicts helped to generate anthropologists, it is also true that only a few South Africans became anthropologists, and those who did are very different people. So despite all the common experiences that we recall when we talk to each other, each of us came to anthropology as the result of particular personal experiences.

Often, these reflect our interaction with particular people at particular times. My own "conversion" to anthropology was the result of a particular event, a particular relationship. I went to Witwatersrand University in Johannesburg in 1927 with absolutely no idea that I was going to be an anthropologist. The majors I selected were English and French, with history as a minor of special interest. But there were lots of things that I wanted to be. When I had not been allowed to go to study acting in England, I decided to be a criminal lawyer and defend innocent victims, and when I chose my subjects it was with these sorts of dreams in mind.

In the South African university system, each course lasted an academic year, so that you really came to know your lecturer. In the second year, I had a spare course, and while I was talking to a friend about possible subjects, she suggested an interesting course that she had taken, taught by a very interesting woman. To my query, "What was it?" she answered, "Anthropology." And I decided to take it, and so did Max Gluckman, my friend from school days, who thought that it might fit well with his interest in law.

Our lecturer was Mrs. Winifred Hoernlé (née Tucker), who came from an English-speaking South African family of very liberal outlook, and who before the war had studied some anthropology at Cambridge under Alfred Cort Haddon. She had married a professor of philosophy of German extraction, who had written a book on liberalism in South Africa, which although it seems now dated and deterministic, at the time pushed things further than most people would accept. When Witwatersrand decided to follow in the footsteps of Cape Town to establish a Department of Bantu Studies in 1926, Mrs. Hoernlé was chosen to give courses in social anthropology. She had done some fieldwork among the Nama Hottentots before the war, and from 1922 on had been working closely with A. R. Radcliffe-Brown at Cape-Town while she was research fellow at Witwatersrand.

As majors in anthropology, the four of us in the first-year class also took courses in physical anthropology with Raymond Dart, who was very challenging, and in archeology, where our regular teacher was Van Riet Lowe, who was very particular about the methodology of digging. He was quite a contrast to L'Abbé Breuil, who was in Johannesburg that year and took some of us on an expedition. Breuil didn't measure, he just jumped in; but he made some extraordinary finds, and had an incredibly stimulating approach to time.

Mrs. Hoernlé's approach was that we should know all the different schools of anthropology, not just her own. Her lectures began with evolutionism, and she made us read selected pages in the original languages, and set them in a broader historical framework. She gave us the feeling that anthropology was a discipline with many facets, but that at the core were people in relation to culture. One very difficult exercise that Mrs. Hoernlé gave us was to take passages from classical evolutionary writers and reformulate them in our own terms—emphasizing that we must not ridicule and find fault with them, but dissect and interpret what they were trying to say.

Looking back I realize that it was still a time of optimism, in which we expected that "evolution" would bring "progress." Several of us were nonorthodox Jews struggling to achieve a nonethnocentric ethical perspective. We tended to assume that certain ways of living were better than others, and were still very much influenced by ideas of Western progress. We interpreted evolution as an adaptive mechanism, and recognized that there could be a considerable variety of culture and increasing institutional complexity in this process of adaptation; without accepting unilineal development, we retained emotionally, idealistically, an optimistic approach.

After the evolutionists we were grounded in the German *Kulturkreis* school of Ratzel, Schmidt, Graebner, and Ankermann. There was a certain magnificence in looking at the world in terms of great cultural circles, speculating on how cultural "things" that had come together in one part of the earth would reappear in another. While I was there, Frobenius came to Africa to look at the Zimbabwe ruins—some of which were on my uncle's farm—and to be shown around the little museum at Bulawayo. In the beginning I was fascinated, but afterward I grew bored with what seemed a static museum approach—although I still remain stimulated by the relation of culture to different geographical zones. Mrs. Hoernlé fitted the American diffusionist school into the *Kulturkreis* framework, and tried to apply their findings to South African data. The approach was based on collections for museums, building up a major theory of civilization through the pieces you collected. We had a wonderful little museum in our department, and we had Herskovits come out and apply the culture-area approach, dividing Africa into eight culture-areas, tracing the cattle complex, etc. It was interesting, but the boundaries seemed forced and overlapping, without any fixed rationale. After considering a particular trait, like the plough, in all its varied associations and effects, we began to raise questions of social relationships: who introduced it, what power is attached to the person who brought in the thing, and what other person was that person trying to influence? In the end we decided: "No, this is not what we want to do as anthropologists in a society where there are so many living differences."

In this context, Mrs. Hoernlé introduced us to Radcliffe-Brown's approach. Social anthropologists do not look at "things" in isolation, but at relationships that are sometimes mediated by things—i.e., the social values that people have attached to things in relation to other people. These social relationships are not haphazard, but are integral parts of a system. Radcliffe-Brown derived his ideas largely from Durkheim, and with her usual thoroughness, Mrs. Hoernlé introduced us first to the great French school of sociology. It opened up a new world. She had insisted that anthropology was a factual discipline based on observable behavior, and we had read such ethnographies as Boas' Eskimo, Lowie's Crow, and Junod's *Life of a South African Tribe*. I had also read Spencer and Gillen, and when I read Durkheim's interpretation of Arunta rituals in the *Elementary Forms of the Religious Life*, a thousand ideas, connections, meanings, and new insights flooded my mind. I had a particularly heavy dose of Durkheim, because in allotting our reading, Mrs. Hoernlé gave me specific responsibility for Durkheim (Max Gluckman was allotted Maine, Morgan, and Robertson Smith; Ellen Hellman had Bachofen and Frobenius). Partly to satisfy the non-English European language requirement, I read *The Rules of Sociological Method* in French and translated it into English. It made an indelible impression on me—indeed, the idea that social facts should be regarded as "things" seemed powerfully convincing. I subsequently saturated myself in Durkheim's writings. His conceptualization of society, social facts, equilibrium, types of solidarity (organic and mechanical), dominated my thinking for many years. Mrs. Hoernlé rejected the organic analogy, but introduced us to the idea of "function" as it was developed by Radcliffe-Brown and Malinowski. We were all fascinated by Durkheim's analysis of suicide, which we had always thought of as the act of a suffering individual, but which he interpreted in terms of the relationship of the individual to society, his integration within it or his isolation from social relationships.

Although Mrs. Hoernlé did not lecture on applied anthropology (which was on the curriculum at Cape Town), she was active in the Institute of Race Relations and other welfare organizations. When she became chair of the Indian Joint Council, I became secretary. My first research was on housing and recreation of Indians in slum areas of Johannesburg; my next job, as Research Assistant of the Institute of Race Relations, was to investigate the liquor laws and their social effects. Although Africans were prohibited from buying Western liquor or brewing their own beer, illicit brewing was one of the few ways in which women could make money. They made drinks with wonderful names like "Kill Me Quick" from pineapple and potato skins hidden in tins, which the police would come and dig up, throwing into jail any unlucky women who did not know how to bribe them. My research involved finding out what happened to the children of mothers rushed off to prison. There were hours spent in the jail with these women, getting information so that I could go back to their homes, find out how their children were, and come back to report—partly as researcher, partly as someone who could help them. The prison was so soul-destroying and dehumanizing, but what astonished me was the courage of the women, their resilience, their willingness to start brewing again as soon as they returned home. Many children got their school fees and clothing from the work of mothers as illicit brewers.

In 1931, Mrs. Hoernlé took a year's leave, and her place was taken by Isaac Schapera; he had studied first at Cape Town with Radcliffe-Brown, who had suggested that Schapera pursue doctoral work overseas with either Lowie or Malinowski. Schapera chose the London School of Economics but did not get on with Malinowski, so he transferred to Seligman, who trained him in his own more descriptive, less interpretive ethnography. Schapera was not an inspiring lecturer, but he had wonderful material—you had to tell yourself, "Don't go to sleep, what he is saying is good." You could not let your attention wander, because in the middle of droning on for some time, he might direct a question at you. He really taught me very much. What I remember best were his lectures on law, which contrasted Radcliffe-Brown's emphasis on the different systems of law and the different types of sanctions with Malinowski's *Crime and Custom*, with its binding rules of reciprocity. I found Malinowski's approach less "scientific," but more open to understanding of reciprocity and social relations. For me, his perspective linked with Mauss' work on *The Gift*, which I had read for Mrs. Hoernlé; it stimulated my understanding of the interaction of different levels of social relationships through the exchange of objects and duties.

Schapera took a group of us—including Ellen Hellman, Max Gluckman, Camilla Wedgwood, and myself—to Mochudi in Bechuanaland (Botswana). For those of us who had already read Malinowski's *Argonauts*, with its stress on observation as well as recording, it was a strange experience. Staying usually in a trader's home, Schapera would sit on a chair in the sunshine, working at a table with his main informant, whom he would get to collect others, and they would discuss and debate. He was very good at asking demanding questions, and he also went to the courts to listen to cases, but it was an approach very different from Malinowski's. Schapera told us to write down what we saw and heard, but asked us to stay away from his best informant. Gluckman and Schapera stayed with the trader, and all the women at a Dutch Reformed mission station, which created problems because the fieldwork trip coincided with the Jewish Day of Atonement. My mother did not want me to go, but the Chief Rabbi—a great friend of ours—said that it would be all right if I fasted. So I fasted while my Jewish colleagues ate; they thought it funny, but the missionary concluded that I was the only one worth "saving." Such was my introduction to fieldwork.

Though Schapera did not identify with the people as Malinowski did, he collected invaluable texts, histories, and a wide range of other data. He raised also the question of the validity of cross-cultural comparisons, cautioning us against generalizations from one society to the rest of the world, and applying Radcliffe-Brown's comparative method of examining changes in specific systems over limited geographical areas. Echoing Durkheim, he cautioned us, "Don't compare things that are not comparable."

Malinowski and the Mandarins, 1932–1934

Despite Schapera's criticism of Malinowski, it was largely through him that I decided at the age of twenty-one to escape to the London School of Economics. I resigned my job as Research Assistant for the Institute of Race Relations, left the material for Reinhalt Jones to write up, and arrived in London. I had applied for admission to the Ph.D. program and had been told that I was to have an interview to decide the matter. I arrived at Malinowski's study, a tiny little office. A young man was waiting outside, and we introduced ourselves. He was Godfrey Wilson, the son of a famous Shakespearian scholar and the holder of a first class degree from Oxford—a most intelligent, delightful, philosophical, sensitive person, whose outstanding contributions were cut short by his early death during World War II.

We talked on the steps, waiting and waiting, and finally—I had come all the way from South Africa—I said, "Ooooh, I must see him," and rapped on the door. Malinowski came out, and after we introduced ourselves, he said, "I can't see you today, I have a migraine." But he said he would save a place for us in class the next day, and see about our registration.

That period in England was immensely exciting. I had never been to London before. There were many people from the colonies attending British universities, and Malinowski was at the height of his creative teaching career. A number of older students who already had Ph.D.'s were there when I arrived, including Raymond Firth, Meyer Fortes, Schoerd Hofstra, Lucy Mair, and Sigfried Nadel—as well as Audrey Richards and Evans-Pritchard, who left shortly afterwards. Evans-Pritchard was brilliant, really brilliant—as was Malinowski; they sparked each other off, and the sparks flew. Fortes, Nadel, and Hofstra, who all came with Ph.D.'s from other disciplines, were mature and confident. They sat close together, and Malinowski labelled them "the Mandarins"—and treated them abominably. He provoked and insulted them;

it was at times quite extraordinary, but it was stimulating, and he did it deliberately. He was a master swordsman, and could make his thrusts danger-
ously sharp. There were some people he really tried to destroy; but he was
also a builder, and if he saw someone struggling not to challenge him but
to develop an argument—Max Gluckman for example—he would build up
the argument so that it made sense. But if he was challenged and felt that
it was a personal challenge, contrary to the master's line, he could be quite
cruel. Everyone made contributions and there was always someone to record
the session—Lucy Mair was the best at that.

Malinowski did not prepare for the seminars. He would write a few notes
on a specific "institution" or theme under such general headings as law, kinship, economics, and land tenure. And in all his classes he worked out field
methods and techniques and developed charts—something terribly important.
And he always related his seminars to *his* concepts of "function" and "culture"—
which were derived from the individual's "primary needs" for sex, shelter, and
food. In satisfying these primary needs, culture intervened, and he developed
the concepts of "derivative needs" (art, music, etc.) and "institutions" as equally
essential to the well-being of mankind. It was all illuminating, and I think
it was the best possible education for a potential fieldworker—though we were
critical of the idea of "needs" and sought for a better basis for comparison.
I still suggest that students read his article on culture in the *Encyclopedia of
the Social Sciences,* in which he crystallized many years of working through
his ethnographic data toward his scientific theory of culture. Although ultimately tautologous, his ideas seemed brilliant. The seminar was fascinating;
everyone was seeing things, making associations.

He would say: "Look. Let's go into the field and see what the people are
doing. We know why they are doing it. It's because they have to have food,
and therefore they are going to work. But they work at a particular time and
a particular place. Let's see what rhythm they have in their work. Is there
an organizer? Who is this organizer? Is it a magician? An elder? How does
the person get appointed?" He put these questions to you and then he would
say, "You carry on." It was challenging to be able to carry on, trying to get
at the ways in which one could look at an institution in all its manifestations
—its personnel, its place, its purpose—with the ultimate aim of getting to the
values of the people—why certain things have to be done, why certain things
could not be done, the values that were set on the activity or its reward, and
how things fitted into the larger context. The "institution" was his unit of
analysis, and an institution had a time, place, personnel, activities, and so
on that could be charted. On the other side of the chart were headings for
the different aspects or dimensions: legal, economic, political, ritual, social—
always set in a context of time and place. It was like working a jigsaw, or like
a detective story—you finally produced a solution, there was no missing part,

and no part could be eliminated. What he really suggested were lines of development, and only afterward did one realize the tautologies. And there were always the contributions of his core of committed opposition—the Mandarins. We came to realize that for some things we could say, "This is irrelevant, it is not important." But what survived Malinowski were his methods of fieldwork, his brilliant field notes, and his writing.

I was fortunate enough to be his research assistant on the two volumes of *Coral Gardens and their Magic*. He would write, and we would discuss what he had written. I would ask questions: "What are you saying, what is the point? Does it push things further?" I looked up references, and rewrote some passages. He encouraged me to make suggestions and he took some of them. He picked at people who were just passive.

The main residue of his teaching was an awareness of the care and the skill that were required in doing fieldwork. His charts remain an excellent model and guide. Audrey Richards said that she always visualized them, and I find myself doing this almost automatically when I go into a new situation. You can use his analysis of an institution as a unit, and compare his unit with Durkheim's unit (the group) or Radcliffe-Brown's (the dyadic relationship).

Apart from directly anthropological interests at this time, there were two others which affected my development. One of these was psychology, partly because Fortes and Nadel, who were very friendly, were trained psychologists, and Malinowski himself was interested in Freud. In addition to my reading, experience was also important. Godfrey Wilson had been going to an analyst for some time, and he suggested that I might also learn from the experience. So for six months I went twice a week. The analyst was eclectic, and put questions to me that I tried to answer; it was very interesting, but also very expensive, and I had very little money. Finally, I said, "I think you have helped me, but I think music and the theatre would help me more." He was very understanding, and we left on good terms. I never went again; I would rather live a full life even if things are not so right with me. But it did help me realize that there was this other dimension that was not being developed in British anthropology.

The second influence was more relevant to my own interests. That was Marxism, and it was not encouraged by Malinowski. He used to say, "If you are not a Communist before twenty-five you have no heart; but if you are a Communist after that, you have no head." His anthropology was never directed in any Marxist framework. He recognized the importance of economics in a rather simple way; but though he said he had read Marx, we were doubtful. There were a few of us who used to go to Marxist lectures and have our own discussion group, and we were interested in action as well as theory. The London School of Economics was an intellectual center, and there were always debates and challenges. Beatrice and Sydney Webb had been very influential, and were initially among the main Fabian socialists. The Fabians

rejected the idea that the state was a class development destined to be overthrown, and argued that it was a social machine to be captured for the promotion of social welfare. We followed these debates and tried to apply them
to the countries with which we were familiar. Most of my friends were aliens
in the British scene and there was real discrimination against the colonial
student. Fascism and Nazism were on the rise, and later there was the Span-
ish Civil War, in which friends of ours joined up. The protest marches were
very serious, and the police were often very brutal; one had experiences similar to those of young Americans in the 1960s. But we were much more optimistic, and perhaps more idealistic.

Understanding the Conquering Aristocracies of Swaziland, 1934–1940

After two years as a Ph.D. student, I applied to the International African Institute for a grant to do fieldwork in Swaziland. The emphasis of the Institute
was on social change, and I decided to focus on the changing role of the magician in this neglected little British colony, which had a considerable white
population. The Institute simply notified the colonial government each time
one of their fellows—each from a different European country—was coming,
and the local government could not say no. It was taken for granted that the
government would find a place for the student to live.

I was very lucky that Malinowski was going to South Africa at the same
time to give a lecture at Witwatersrand University to the New Education Conference, and to visit some of his students doing fieldwork in Africa; after the
conference he would accompany me to Swaziland. The conference was attended also by Sobhuza, the "Paramount Chief" of the Swazi. I was frightened
that as a novice I would make a hash of the first meeting. It had been arranged by the African Institute that I have my base in Mbabane, the administrative capital, but Malinowski said to Sobhuza, "I don't like my students staying in a government center"; and Sobhuza said, "She can stay with my mother
at Lobamba." The resident commissioner, A. G. Marwick, drove us to Lobamba, which was the ritual capital of the Swazi nation, set in a valley with
high mountains in the background. The Swazi pitched a tent for Malinowski,
and gave me the most Westernized hut in the village. The day before we came
to Lobamba a horse had tramped on Malinowski's toe, and he thought he
might have to have it amputated. But the doctor said the only thing to do
was bathe it in hot water. When he went limping in to meet the Queen Mother,
he found she was immobilized and suffering from a thorn in her foot. Malinowski suggested that they should both be cured together, and the two of them
bathed their feet in adjoining basins of hot water and epsom salts several times

a day. The treatment was marvelously effective, and it made a tremendous difference in her relationship, not only to him, but to me as well. He could provoke people so that they had nothing more to do with him, but he could win over most people if he so wished. He also won Sobhuza's confidence, and they occasionally wrote to each other (cf. Kuper 1978:5–8).

Sobhuza was incredibly helpful, and the success of my fieldwork depended on his patronage and friendship. If I had evoked his hostility, I might never have got any information except from the highly disgruntled. I worked under his protection, but I also tried to get information and opinions from a wide range of informants. I also realized that the patronage and friendship Sobhuza had extended to me made some people suspicious and jealous. One woman later told me, "In the beginning we deceived you like anything because you were White"; and until I learned the language, some of my information was deliberately falsified. Sobhuza "gave" me, as my attendant, informant, and cook, a middle-aged man, who was not of royal stock. I found him intelligent, moody, independent, loyal, and complex, and he drank heavily. It was difficult working with him; I struggled to establish a relationship of mutual trust, part of which was that I trusted him to get drunk.

Malinowski stayed for nearly two weeks. One of the first things he did at Lobamba was to draw a map very quickly of this rather complicated village. He had the children acting as his guides. We went around asking, "Who lives here? Who lives there?"; and then we were ready to begin on the villagers' links—a kinship genealogy. It was rather like learning algebra.

From Lobamba, the ritual capital, I branched out to the villages and to different chiefs, always accompanied by the faithful henchman chosen for me by Sobhuza, who had been told that if anything bad happened to me, it was worth his life to stop it! Early on I spent three months at Sobhuza's suggestion in Namahasha, an area that was very isolated, where the greatest witches were believed to congregate, and where the local chief had recently been killed under strange circumstances. Our car broke down halfway there, and we dragged ourselves to the main village. The acting chief was not at all pleased to see us, but reluctantly agreed that I stay "where a White man has already left his seed"—that is, with a Swazi woman who had been living with a White man. She had a daughter about my age, and she made me welcome, but I will never forget the general atmosphere of fear and suspicion (Kuper 1957).

There are all sorts of difficulties in making rapport, some of them apparently unreasonable; but the rewards are well worth the frustrations—when after being called umlumbi (a being who performs strange things), you suddenly find yourself described as umuntfa wethu ("our person"). At first children were frightened by their mothers: "The umlumbi will take you." It has to be through the language, and through behavior, that the change in perception of identity, in real identity, comes about: to be made a real friend, rather than someone to ask for sugar, or salt, or whatever else you could provide. When you get to the stage where your company is welcomed, you realize that you can be yourself.

I had studied siZulu (a language closely related to siSwati) at Witwatersrand and then at the School of African and Oriental Studies in London, but although I knew the grammar well, I could speak only a few words. At Lobamba I heard no English, and learned to speak siSwati rather quickly; later I began to understand the jokes and even make a few. And then one incredible night I dreamed in siSwati. Unfortunately, when one leaves a place, one tends to change one's language and thought patterns, too. But each time I return I pick it up, and am often pleasantly surprised at how much I remember.

I soon realized that Swaziland was not an isolated or "uncontaminated" little state, and that I would not describe it as such. Although it was on the whole a homogeneous culture, it was not the Trobrianders without the pearl divers and missionaries, but a country wedged between the Union of South Africa and Portugese territory, with pockets of Whites, who owned two-thirds of the land. It was a complex society with miners, missionaries, traders, administrators. I could not just "go Swazi," and I also wanted to learn about and get information from the Whites. But many of them were not eager to respond or to accept me, and after I took part in the *umcwasho*, a ceremony for unmarried girls, I learned that some of the missionaries had preached against me from the pulpit, and sent a request to A. G. Marwick asking for my removal—fortunately he refused.

About four months after I entered the field, I read an article by P. J. Schoeman about the Swazi rain ritual. Although I had witnessed the preparations, and had received some information on the performance, Schoeman's account was so different that I thought, "Good Heavens, am I blind, or are they deceiving me?" I took the article to Sobhuza and said, "What is this?" He asked me to read it to him, and as I did I blushed, it was such a gross, ridiculous distortion, filled with prejudice and contempt—a disrobing, as it were, of another's culture, from the point of view of a Westerner. Sobhuza was so angry he told me he "did not know what to do about anthropologists." I replied that I would write a counter, pointing out things that I had witnessed with my own eyes, and that he must add a paragraph testifying that this was the true version (Beemer 1935). For this, I was very strongly criticized by anthropological colleagues in South Africa.

That first time I stayed in Swaziland for two years, broken into two periods by a six-month break during which I married Leo Kuper, a young Johannesburg lawyer—somewhat to the consternation of the International African Institute, whose fellowship contracts provided extra money for married men, but required women who married to refund every penny they had received! The Institute staff were sure that I was not going to continue; but I told them

I could not repay the money, because I had none, and that I was going on. So they continued to pay, and I continued to work.

I collected a great deal of material, but very early on gave up the idea of focussing on the magician and magic, when I realized the way in which history and clanship and power dominated Swazi life. Much of their conversation with me related to history, to the past, to people of the past, and issues of power and hierarchy were constantly raised. I tried to follow Swazi interests, to understand their approach, and these issues were part and parcel of the culture.

When I finished my fieldwork in 1937, I settled down to write my dissertation, but a five-year bout with malaria delayed things considerably. I had taken into the field a number of what I called "issues," which were juggled around in my head as I was writing. First of all there was the question of "function" —which I decided to avoid as much as possible. I was conscious of at least three levels of "function": the native ("emic") explanation, the Malinowskian cultural-contextual interpretation, and the Radcliffe-Brownian structural system. I decided to emphasize what would later be called the "emic," and not to seek a "purpose" or a logical relationship in everything. Weighting, selection, focus were essential. And there was the question of the use of the terms "structure" and "culture." Both are abstractions based on empirical data, but you could not see structure, and though you could see *things* you could not see the relationship between them which constitutes "a culture." I have always been concerned with people as individuals, but see a particular individual in relation to others. I approached informants as individuals with their own idiosyncratic personalities as well as fixed status and roles. Radcliffe-Brown felt that studies of the individual should be left to the biographer and the historian, that the sociologist must look for general laws and principles. But when you look at the "laws" he developed—the equivalence of siblings, the unity of the lineage, the principle of alternating generations—they do not seem very impressive.

I anguished over the very difficult questions of periods of time and the process of history. I was against playing with history, and accepted Radcliffe-Brown's attack on "conjectural" history. He favored a diachronic approach in which you went back after a period to see what had changed; but it is really difficult to get at the process of history that way, because what you are looking at is not moving in one simple direction, and the process—the tempo as well as the component parts—is uneven.

Political anthropology was beginning to develop at about this time, and in some strange way my interests were drawn away from religion, from magic, and the more exotic. My first major article, published in *Africa* under my maiden name (Beemer 1937), was a structural and functional analysis of the Swazi military organization. In it I showed that although superficially the structure of the regiments remained the same, the content had changed radically, since control of the most important traditional function (warfare) had been usurped by the British. The article showed how a key traditional institution was being incorporated into the modern educational system, with the king trying to get every school child to belong to an age regiment, and the missionaries pushing them into the Pathfinder movement of Black Boy Scouts.

But I had trouble with the dissertation itself. I did not feel committed to functionalism, or structuralism, or any other "ism," and I made a number of false starts. I was looking for a theme rather than a theory, a theme that was sufficiently flexible to accommodate the diversity of facts, and yet to make sense of the interaction as a whole. Suddenly I had an illumination. I realized that the overriding influence—that which had directed me into so many channels, and which was reflected in so much of the evidence I was given—was related to *stratification*: the particular system of rank and discrimination—rank by pedigree in the Swazi society, discrimination by color from Whites to Swazi. I looked at the various institutions—the military organizations and the economic systems—and I saw the way they played into the whole system of stratification, of hegemony, within a total society. There was an overriding hegemony drawn by the British system of colonial government, and in the internal Swazi system there was a traditional hegemony of kingship under a ruling clan. I realized that I had been forced by my material into an essentially political analysis of traditional and modern power.

Finally, I decided to write my thesis in two parts: *An African Aristocracy* (1947a), which deals with rank, power, and bureaucracy in the traditional system; and *The Uniform of Color* (1947b), which was about the situation that developed under colonialism. In all this I had to look at the question of how one could view history beyond the "ethnographic present," in which most of Malinowski's students until this time had written. I was aware that there was a "before" and "after," and a continuity in change. So I struggled with the difficulties, and wrote my introduction to *An African Aristocracy* in two parts, each entitled "Conquering Aristocracies"—one about the Dlamini (the royal clan), the other about the Whites. I showed two techniques of conquest, and the way in which higher-status Blacks in the traditional hierarchy were still subordinate to the lowest of the whites in certain situations. At that time, it was a new sort of political analysis.

I began the introduction to *An African Aristocracy* with an analysis of the status and role of the anthropologist in a field situation—the complex relationships of the anthropologist as a particular type of stranger, within a set of different categories of strangers, who were automatically stereotyped on arrival in terms of color, dress, equipment, spending power, language, sex, education, age, etc. It was all very like the current interest in the relationship of the anthropologist's self and the question of how true is what we think is true. From there I went on to the question of scope or focus, and the need to define key concepts—what did I mean by "rank," "stratification," and "hegemony"—and the relation of individual differences to status groups. The third issue I treated was that of changes set in a social context, or the question of historiography: the details of the past are blurred, distorted, or forgotten, but it is a rationalized and idealized past that provides standards of value in the present—standards that differ, even in relation to the same event, depending on whether you are a member of an absorbed defeated clan or one of the dominant conquering ones. The fourth point of the introduction concerned conflict. It was a culture with uneven, conflicting parts—not as in Malinowski's tripartite scheme, nor as an harmonious whole, but one composed of groups and individuals who were often actively hostile to each other. The final chapter criticized the American school of Benedict and Mead with their emphasis on consistent patterns, showing the inconsistency of Mead's evidence on the "peaceable" Arapesh—whose mothers were a few pages before described as beating their children.

The *Uniform of Color* was a study of Black and White interaction from the angle of structural inequality in a colonial period. It was about questions of race, power, and privilege: who rules whom, and what are the techniques and strategies, and the advantages, etc.? It was also directed at racism and the assumption of White superiority, and some sections were very unpopular with the Whites, especially one in which I suggested that for some administrators retirement imposed no marked mental relaxation.

My first draft was completed in 1939, the year before Fortes and Evans-Pritchard published *African Political Systems*. The Zulu system described there by Max Gluckman had many similarities with the Swazi, which we had discussed during our fieldwork. But the emphasis on hierarchy of rank by pedigree was not a feature of the Zulu system, which had derived from the conquests of Shaka, who had very little family to extend to the whole fabric of the political system. Part of Sobhuza's skill was the way in which polygynous marriage was used to link together clans; in contrast, bravery and individual loyalty to the military leader created men of influence in the Zulu system.

Two South African Liberals at Home and Abroad, 1940–1961

I finished my dissertation as a "camp follower" in a little town in the eastern Transvaal, where Leo was undergoing military training. South Africa was under the relatively liberal leadership of General Smuts, who supported the allies, but his opposition included open supporters of Hitler and racism (united secretly in the Broederbond), who were to move into the government in 1948.

Obviously there could be no conscription in South Africa, but there was a volunteer army, and Leo enlisted. I stayed during one university vacation with an Afrikaner family—who told me how terribly the English had treated their families during the Anglo-Boer war, but whose son had joined the British army and ended the war as a prisoner in Germany. By this time, the war had involved every British anthropologist more or less personally, directly or vicariously. Thus Audrey Richards, who had taken Winifred Hoernlé's place at Witwatersrand, returned to do war work in England. I had been appointed her successor—my first teaching job.

My teaching was directed primarily against racism and prejudice—and with very adequate scholarly evidence, since there were so many books showing the falseness of racial assumption, including those by Cedric Dover, Jacques Barzun, Julian Huxley, Ashley Montagu, and Ruth Benedict. During the five years that I taught at Witwatersrand, Leo was away most of the time, and I worked very hard in order to keep my own balance and sanity. I did urban research in a township with some of my best students, including Ruth First, who was later to be assassinated in Maputo by a letter bomb in August 1982. I learned survey methods, because this urban fieldwork in a complex area required mass sampling. We got questionnaires out which were not at all bad, and we went into the townships to administer them. But I also did writing that was not directly anthropological—articles for political journals and newspapers, research for broadcasts to Africans, stories, poems. Throughout this period, and these diverse modes of expression, ran the common thread that anthropology was a humanist discipline.

Toward the end of the war, Leo got involved in The National War Memorial, designed as a "living memorial" to promote health services for Africans, many of whom had lost their lives in an army in which they were not allowed to carry guns, but only machinery and parts. I did some of the publicity research, writing pamphlets, getting them widely spread, speaking on platforms. Leo was organizing secretary and carried on the work until the organization was established. After that Leo decided to undertake training for what would be his future career: sociology.

So in 1947 we came to Chapel Hill, North Carolina, where there was a good Sociology and Anthropology Department—including John Gillen, Jr. (through whom I had my first direct contact with American psychological anthropology) and Guy Johnson, who had been working with Myrdal on The American Dilemma. In fact, we found that the issues that had concerned us in South Africa were repeated in what had been described to us before we came as an "oasis" in the South. There was an interaction of ideology and action, a questioning of national identity and nationalism. The techniques of discrimination and oppression were somewhat different—in South Africa, the police did what Ku Klux Klan members did in the South, and discrimination was embedded in the law itself. It was also the time of concern with "un-American activities," and Guy Johnson recounted to us his experience before a congressional committee. Paul Robeson, whom I had met in London through his wife, who attended Malinowski's seminar, sang in Wallace's campaign, and we went along to hear him. Wallace was preaching his ideal of One World, the National Association for the Advancement of Colored People was active, and it was a time when one was not certain which way America would go.

Chapel Hill was beautiful, but it seemed a protected environment with an other-worldly aura, and we decided we had to get out. We planned to go to Chicago, where Leo would finish his degree and I would teach, but family illness took us back to South Africa, where we stayed for some months. From there we went to England—not London, but Coventry and Birmingham—where Leo had a university appointment and carried out research with the town planning team on the reconstruction of Coventry, which had been badly bombed during the war. Coventry was very parochial, and although I enjoyed the time with our two children, I suffered from academic isolation. However, our friends from London, Oxford, and Cambridge came to see us now and then. The composition of departments had changed during the war and early postwar periods. Oxford had Radcliffe-Brown and Evans-Pritchard; London had Firth, Schapera, and Leach; Fortes had just been given the chair at Cambridge, and brought Leach in 1953 to help reinvigorate Cambridge after a long period of decline; Gluckman, after spending the war years at the Rhodes-Livingston Institute in Central Africa, and a brief period at Oxford, was appointed to the newly created chair at Manchester. I was offered and accepted a readership at the London School of Economics, but unfortunately had to withdraw on account of illness, so I spent the time in the Midlands doing two monographs for the International African Institute (Kuper 1952, 1955).

This was the period our nephew Adam Kuper described in his book as "From Charisma to Routine." Evans-Pritchard had concluded in his Marett Lecture in 1950 that social anthropology was a kind of historiography; and the argument was going on across the Atlantic as to whether or not it was scientific. I frankly found these debates not very inspiring or stimulating. I had already decided on an historical perspective for my work since I was unsure of the validity of the so-called "general laws" that were being propounded in the name of scientific social anthropology (Kuper 1945). In this atmosphere, I was quite willing to go back to South Africa when Leo was offered the post of head of the Department of Sociology at the University of Natal campus in Durban.

We returned in 1952, at the time of "The Defiance of Unjust Laws" campaign, organized by the Indian National Congress and the African National Congress. That campaign was also the start of the Liberal Party, with which we identified ourselves fairly early. At that time, the Kriges (who had family ties to Smuts) were the anthropologists at the university, and there was no position open for me. But frankly, I was much more interested then in trying to understand the complexities of the heterogeneous Durban population. Dr. Sydney Kark, who had started community health centers in rural areas in Africa, was then director of an Institute of Family and Community Health, and asked me, as an anthropologist, to work with his team of doctors and health educators.

The Institute was engaged in developing promotive health services for different racial groups, and I was to work with Indian immigrants settled in Durban. Less was known about them than about Africans and "Coloureds." There were numerous objective indicators (birth weight, infant mortality, patterns of disease) that one could look at and ask, "Are these differences genetic, or/ and are they cultural?"—but there were many problems of field technique, and I had to see how the traditional anthropological tools of participant observation could be applied. Indians themselves were immensely diversified by religion, area of origin, occupation, language, and class. How far did I have to go into their history, or into the history of the relationship between India and South Africa? There was a tremendous literature on traditional Indian culture, and also material on Indian communities in the diaspora (in Fiji, Mauritius, Trinidad). The sheer contrast with the organization and values of Swazi society was exciting, and the techniques had to be very different. I did not live in Indian villages or Indian homes, but I had many close Indian friends. I had to select my assistants with thought to the groups who would receive them. My closest friend was a Muslim woman, very radical and trained in sociology; and I had two very sophisticated woman assistants, one Tamil, one Hindi-speaking.

All of us were involved more or less in political action, and the government reacted punitively. It was a hard time, a time in which I kept remembering that a person is not divided into a scholar in the daytime and a political person at night. The political situation made us schizophrenic enough. One had to try to keep a balance, not to become too extreme, nor overafraid, nor overrational, and so on. When Max Gluckman arranged that I receive a Simon Research Fellowship to come to Manchester in 1958, at a time when Leo was to have his sabbatical, it seemed too wonderful to be true. Leo's book *Passive Resistance* had come out in 1957—to be banned by the government, along with Dollard's *Caste and Class in a Southern Town*. I took with me the completed draft of my book *Indian People of Natal* (1960), and it had the benefit of criticism from my colleagues at the Manchester School.

Those months at Manchester were most stimulating. Gluckman's seminar technique was very different from that of Malinowski. If you were trying to make a point, he would help you develop it; if he saw something in it, he would make it sound good. He built up his team, and it was a team with a mascot: the Manchester United football team. Every week, Gluckman would pick up members of his department in his big car, and they had to watch the game and give moral support. If you did not come, it was a black mark. The morning after the terrible plane crash in which many United players were killed, there was a mourning ritual in class, in which we all stood, while Max made a speech. There was no doubt that this was a ritual, and not a ceremony—we were a tight-knit clan!

Gluckman built a school. It was nothing like Malinowski's seminars, where there was always friction and you drew blood. Victor Turner, Arnold Epstein, William Watson, Ronald Frankenberg were not easy personalities, but somehow they worked together extremely well. The general approach they developed, a particularly useful one, was an analysis of conflict and of conflict resolution in different structures and different contexts; in *Rituals of Rebellion* Gluckman had reinterpreted my description of the Ncwala ceremony in this framework. About this time Gluckman and his colleagues decided to explore what they called the "extended case study." Instead of using incidents as illustrative examples, they took a single case and carried it through with all its repercussions, bringing out greater depth and detail. This method was first employed, less self-consciously, by Turner in his *Schism and Community* and by Van Velsen in the study of kinship. In all of this, the fieldwork was being refined; Clyde Mitchell was one of those who introduced better statistical methods—but with the constant caveat, "Don't let figures do to you what you can do to figures."

We returned to South Africa in a period of heightening tensions, and there were spies at the university, where I was now appointed lecturer in anthropology. There was one we knew in Leo's department during a period of emergency, when the university was surrounded by police. How absolutely strange it was! Once a suspicious-looking character came to listen when I was lecturing on the Eskimo, and I took great pleasure in dealing with their songs of ridicule! The policy of apartheid was by now implemented with ruthless logic; it moved step by step from prohibition of mixed marriages, through the Group Areas Act, to the final breakdown of the opportunity for shared ideas: separate schools, separate universities, separate curricula. Verwoerd, the Prime Minister, had been trained in sociology, and he used this background to implement the apartheid policy.

The Anthropologist as Royal Historiographer

In October 1961, we left South Africa to come to the University of California at Los Angeles, where Leo had been offered an appointment in what was then a combined Department of Sociology and Anthropology. Because of the university policy on "nepotism," I could not teach in the department, but in 1963, when the department was divided, I was given an appointment in anthropology. My reaction to the university was mixed. The interchange with colleagues was friendly but limited; my most stimulating intellectual companion was M. G. Smith, who had used the ideas of Maine and Weber on corporations to criticize the theory of government proposed in Fortes and Evans-Pritchard's *African Political Systems*; I was sad when he left to take the chair of his old teacher, Darryll Forde, at University College, London.

I particularly enjoyed running seminars, where we could discuss issues and interests outside the ordinary curriculum. In 1963 I introduced my students for the first time to Lévi-Strauss and Leach, and we also dealt with Turner's ideas on rituals, the meaning of independence celebrations as symbolic systems, human rights in non-Western societies, concepts of social space and time, the politics of religion, women in power, and anthropology through literature. These were topics that could not be dealt with in the ordinary departmental courses; they needed the exchange and the dialogue of a seminar to make them meaningful. Most were based on recent publications, but it was interesting to see that these recent publications had many old ideas.

In 1966, National Science Foundation funds enabled me to return to Swaziland, where I lived for nearly a year in the home of one of Sobhuza's daughters, close to the capital. In September 1968, Swaziland became independent, and Leo and I and our two daughters came to the celebrations as Sobhuza's personal guests. Two years after that he gave me Swazi citizenship by *kukhonta*, which means by traditional allegiance—thus waiving the necessity of five years' continuous residence. I had been travelling reluctantly on a South African passport, and I felt a little uneasy about becoming an American citizen, although I had applied for an American passport. I felt very much at home in Swazi culture, and honored at the recognition and acceptance.

In 1972, I was asked to write the official biography of Sobhuza. As a person trained in structural-functional anthropology, I had never contemplated writing biographies, though I had by this time tried many other media, including short stories, a novel (1965), plays (1970), and poems. At first I said no—not out of coyness, but because I felt I could not do it; I knew the man too well. But finally, largely through Leo and out of gratitude to Sobhuza—and because I did not altogether approve of some of the others who wanted to write it—I agreed.

It set me off on an entirely different line of research, a combination of history with traditional interviews. A biography sometimes is described as a combination of career and character, and I found that I had to introduce the whole concept of culture deliberately. And in all of this I had to be very aware that Sobhuza said, "This is an official biography; it is not my story alone, it is the

story of my country, of my people." It was an even more extraordinary assign-
ment because it was a cabinet appointment, and I had to work with an ad-
visory committee composed of the King's Private Secretary, the Minister of
Justice, and the first Swazi Ambassador to the United States.

This was not the first time I had discussed my work with Swazi friends.
Previously I had put the various interpretations of the Ncwala ceremony—
mine, Gluckman's, Beidelman's—to my friends, and we would sit down and
discuss them. They would laugh: "Oh, no, very *clever* man. He might think
it's like that, very interesting, but we don't." And when I presented the same
matter to the committee—without saying which interpretation was mine—
they said, "This is the right one—that one is clever, but it is not the right
one." But now I was writing, as it were, under oath. It was a creation under
oath, and I had to eliminate things under oath as well. Every page had to
be read by the committee; every chapter went back to Swaziland when it was
finished. I felt like a shuttlecock. I would send them the original, they would
go through it and make their comments, and then they would say, "Come,"
and I would fly to Swaziland, sometimes for a week, sometimes for a month.

When I was returning to the United States after a long and agonizing period in 1974, I sent a huge tin trunk, chockablock with notes, via a Lufthansa
travel agent, with caution that it must go through Portugese territory rather
than the Republic of South Africa. Upon inquiry three months later, I received a cable: "Regret everything stolen from car in Johannesburg." The material was never recovered. When I told Sobhuza about it, I said that I had
told the man I could not put any value on it because "it's beyond value; it
is my life." He responded, "It serves you right—do you think a man would
not want to have something that was your life?"

The last chapter was particularly difficult. It dealt with the recent past—
after 1973, when Sobhuza repealed the "Westminster Constitution" of 1968,
and assumed "Supreme Control." The committee kept on saying, "This is true,
but you shouldn't say it; we don't want people to know about this." And always there was a reason: it was "politically sensitive," or the information was
"given to you in confidence." One piece of evidence I still feel really angry
about not publishing was the full royal genealogy. For six months or more,
I had collected details about the whole royal family, the king's many wives,
their parents, their children, whom their children had married. It was a really
rich genealogy, and I had presented it deliberately in such a way that an intelligent person could see who might be the contestants for Sobhuza's position on his death. The committee members said, "No, the choice is going
to be decided by the Council of Princes, in confidence." (Sobhuza died on
August 21, 1982; the period since has been one of bitter conflict between royal
factions.)

But despite all the difficulties, I managed to complete the biography (Kuper

1978). It has received very mixed reviews; many have felt that I concentrated on Sobhuza's positive contributions and glossed over his weaknesses, and there is some justification for this criticism. But as I stated in "An Essential Introduction," an official biography has inherent limitations, and there will undoubtedly be other biographies with *their* inherent limitations. To me, the main character of a biography is never an "object" for dissection, as I argue in "Biography as Interpretation" (1980): every biography reflects, consciously or unconsciously, the bias of the biographer. "Personal histories" seem to have a universal appeal, but the modes in which they are expressed are culturally circumscribed. Autobiographies, biographies, case studies, and life histories are essentially Western genres or constructs, and the complex interaction between an ethnographer and a central character or characters is of relevance to everyone interested in the methods of social research.

Looking back upon my development as an anthropologist, I feel that my early training convinced me that anthropology is a scholarly and well-defined discipline. At the same time, I have become convinced that the interpretation of anthropological data cannot be objective, because of the element of uncertainty in human interaction. I have become increasingly concerned with the need for an historical approach to both individual and social behavior. This historical perspective is not guided by any assumptions of progress or clear direction to human actions. Development is uneven, conflict inevitable but not necessarily predictable, and there is no single synthesis. In the past, I have described my approach as that of a functionalist-structuralist. I would no longer give myself any such limiting label, or refrain from employing other approaches where I thought them useful. I attribute this to what has become a very conscious committment to a world beyond any specific anthropological field—a development, if you like, of a particular moral philosophy. I have moved from the excitement of discovery of other cultures to a recognition of how the values gained through a disciplined study of other cultures can be applied. I think it is really an emphasis on the humanism of anthropology. It is the application of the knowledge that is obtained through the disciplined approach to the complex situations of a tormented and conflict-ridden world.

References Cited

Beemer, H. 1935. The Swazi rainmaking ceremony. *Bantu Studies* 9:273–80.
———. 1937. The development of the military organization in Swaziland. *Africa* 10: 55–74; 176–205.
Kuper, A. 1973. *Anthropologists and anthropology: The British school, 1922–1972*. London.
Kuper, H. 1945. Social anthropology as a study of culture contacts. *South Af. J. Sci.* 41:88–101.

————. 1947a. *An African aristocracy.* Oxford.

————. 1947b. *The uniform of colour.* Johannesburg.

————. 1952. *The Swazi.* London.

————. 1955. *The Shona.* London.

————. 1957. The amazement of Namahasha. *Africa South* 1:102–7.

————. 1960. *Indian people of Natal.* Natal.

————. 1965. *Bite of hunger: A novel of Africa.* New York.

————. 1970. *A witch in my heart.* New York.

————. 1978. *Sobhuza II, Ngwenyama and King of Swaziland.* New York.

————. 1980. Biography as interpretation. Eleventh Annual Hans Wolff Memorial Lecture, Bloomington, Ind., April 21.

Kuper, L. 1957. *Passive resistance in South Africa* New Haven.

FROM PHILOLOGY TO ANTHROPOLOGY IN MID-NINETEENTH-CENTURY GERMANY

JAMES WHITMAN

In 1920, in the wake of military defeat and social revolution, the eighty-eight-year-old Wilhelm Wundt ended his career with a bitter polemic against foreign influences on German science—above all against the English tradition and all its works. He summoned the German nation to its destiny as "the leading power among civilized peoples in the struggle to acquire and secure the riches of civilization," and begged Germans to rally to German forms of thought mortally threatened by the poison of "Benthamite egoistic utilitarianism." Finally, he proclaimed the triumph of a seventy-year-old German science: *Völkerpsychologie* ("folk," "ethnic," or "national psychology"). (1920:16, 3).[1]

With Wundt's last writings, a national scientific tradition had declined into a nationalist one. *Völkerpsychologie* had first appeared as one of several presumptive disciplines labelled "Psychologie" that were called forth in the 1850s by German text-critics—either classical philologists or theologians. The scholarly men who founded *Völkerpsychologie* had read foreign sources calmly and calmly footnoted them. Only with the consuming nationalism of the world war did *Völkerpsychologie* become *völkisch*: a science, as Wundt proclaimed it, founded by Germans, who alone understood, amid the seductions of "Western individualism," that man was morally alive only through participation

---

1. Except where an English translation is listed among the references, all translations are mine. Where a translation is listed, page references are to the translation.

James Whitman is Special Humanities Fellow in the Department of History at the University of Chicago, where he is working toward the Ph.D. His research focusses on the history of German classical philology, and on nineteenth-century social theory.

in the national character (1920:4). By contrast, the philological founders of
the discipline, writing when Germans preferred to think of themselves as poets
and philosophers, had taken as their subject the extraordinary individual:
the artistic genius, the brilliant statesman, the inspired thinker. Philological
Psychologie arose in the mid-nineteenth century when German text-critics felt
compelled to give a new scientific formulation to an old philological fascination: the social conditions of individual genius. Culture as philologists understood it—culture as it had produced Sophocles, Pericles, and Plato—became
the subject of social science. This preoccupation with individual genius ended
when Wundt became the leading representative of the discipline in the 1880s.
But philological *Psychologie*, the congeries of putative disciplines of which
Völkerpsychologie was just one, lived on elsewhere: for in its scientized,
"psychological" form, the traditional philological conception of culture passed
to German scientific anthropology.

Our best testimony, both to the origins of philological *Psychologie* and to
its influence on anthropology, comes from the great early ethnologist Adolf
Bastian—who without being part of the new movement was deeply influenced
by it. Returning to Germany in 1858 after seven years of wandering among
primitive peoples, Bastian found a changed intellectual scene:

> There was a great deal that seemed strange to me . . . what with slow communi-
> cations overseas. . . . I had heard nothing of Moleschott's *Kreislauf des Lebens*
> (1852), nor of Vogt's *Bilder* (1852) and his cutting slogans, [Büchner's] *Kraft und
> Stoff* (1855), [Czolbe's] *Sensualismus* (1855), etc., and hardly even anything of the
> uproar at the Congress of Natural Scientists in 1854, from which had emerged,
> as the dust settled, Noack's *Psyche* among others. All of this had to be absorbed
> within a year, along with the literature I needed in order to publish my own
> book, *Der Mensch in der Geschichte* [1860]. And while I was busy with that, there
> appeared the first volumes of Waitz' *Anthropologie der Naturvölker*, a work in-
> vested with a comprehensive understanding of the needs of the age, as well
> as, at almost exactly the same time, the plan for the *Zeitschrift für Völkerpsy-
> chologie und Sprachwissenschaft*, the ideas for which it was my privilege to hear
> from the mouth of Lazarus himself . . .
>
> (1881:32–33)

In this compact list of names and titles can be found the intellectual conflict
that created philological *Psychologie*, and so made possible the influence of
traditional German philology on nascent German anthropology. Moleschott,
Vogt, Büchner, and Czolbe were the most notorious of the so-called "vulgar
materialists"—men who insisted, to the revulsion of German humanists, on
physiological explanations for human actions (Gregory 1977). Noack, Waitz,
Lazarus, as well as Lazarus' brother-in-law and collaborator Heymann Steinthal and the philosopher Hermann Lotze, were all trained in the text-critical
disciplines. All these trained text-critics attempted to create new disciplines

in response to the vulgar materialist challenge, and all of them called their studies *Psychologie*.

Crisis and Regrouping in German Philology

Materialism had two ugly connotations to German philologists: application of natural scientific method to all fields of knowledge, and reduction of all phenomena to a single material substrate. With the growing prestige of the natural sciences in Germany at the expense of the prestige of the classics since the mid-1820s, classicists had long agitated and organized against "the equally dangerous enemies of growing industrialism and growing materialism" (Paulsen 1921:II, 434; cf. Ringer 1979; 2–3). But the tone of the writings and programmatic lectures classicists produced became noticeably uneasier and more bitter with the appearance of the "vulgar materialists," between about 1848 and 1858. Within this unsettled decade, shifts and reevaluations within the discipline of philology brought to the fore recognizably "anthropological" interests. Historians have long noted that German philological doctrines had a special applicability to the problems of anthropology, because German philologists emphasized national character: "the classical nations" rather than just classical texts (e.g., Bausinger 1971:30 ff.). But it was not simply the case that men interested in creating a science of anthropology looked to philology for methods or concepts. Rather, a spontaneous and crucial new interest in primitive life sprung up among classicists themselves in response to vulgar materialism.

This catalytic new interest in primitives came naturally to philologists. Their deepest conviction was of the superiority of Greek and Roman culture, and their impulse when challenged was to contrast the Greeks and Romans with the barbarians, to hold up the gifted and inspired peoples of the past against the dark background of primitive life. Thus Georg Curtius, the Professor of Classical Philology at Prague, began an 1848 lecture by acknowledging the "powerful upsurge" the natural sciences were enjoying, and apologized for lecturing only on "the small and narrowly limited life of two peoples." But he insisted that the Greeks and Romans were different, for "in a time when the majority of peoples still led a prehistorical, merely vegetative existence . . . the most lively of the Greek tribes, the Ionian, had already created for itself an epic . . ." (1848:9). This propagandistic appeal to prehistory was taken up throughout the philological community. In 1855, August Boeckh, the preeminent classicist of the day, gave a long account of the rise of the natural sciences that began with the same *topos*. Some nations were more talented than others: The Indo-Europeans had not been "entirely rough and wild, like the wild and depraved tribes of America, from whom conclusions have been drawn about the condition of earliest man; rather, nobler races stood out among the rest, and raised themselves by their native inner strength above their animal instincts" (1855:II, 117). Here then was a motive wholly internal to philology for the study of "the condition of earliest man": classicists who had lost their enviable position of supremacy in German intellectual life, responded by proposing invidious comparisons between the Greeks and the primitives. Among some, the appeal to prehistory was paralleled by a shift in terminology, as text-critics began to refer to their work as *Psychologie*. The theologian Franz Delitzsch published a book advertised as the reconciliation of the conflict between naturalists and philosophers, and entitled *System der Biblischen Psychologie* (1855:viii). Ludwig Noack, a lapsed theologian, published the first number of *Psyche*, the volume that caught the eye of Bastian, with the promise that his *Psychologie* would end "the party squabbles of so-called 'materialism'" (1858:I, 1). And in a famous lecture the classicist Ludwig Lange reminded his audience that the Greeks had been the first to rise, in the youth of mankind, to high culture, defended the position of philology as the first of the sciences, and described philological study as providing "a *Psychologie* of the classical nations" (1855:9–10, 14).

In turning to *Psychologie*, text-critics took up with incongruous company. The great German precursors of modern scientific psychology—E. H. Weber, Gustav Fechner, and the young Wundt, not yet a convert to *Völkerpsychologie* —were publishing their works during precisely these years (Boring 1950:275– 347). The work of these men was quite alien to the spirit of aesthetic humanism in which classical philology was practiced. But text-critics had their own history of using the term *Psychologie*. The overlap in vocabulary was important, for it enabled philologists and their partisans to reformulate their old practices in terms more in tune with the new understanding of "scientific": by calling their studies *Psychologie*, they could blend into the new terminological landscape without seeming faithless to their forbears within the tradition. Among a number of scholars who had ceased to practice text-criticism professionally, but who had maintained their personal and intellectual ties with the text-critical world, the attempt was made to combine the old text-critical use of *Psychologie* with the natural scientific use, and make of the two strands in the history of *Psychologie* one social science. The appearance of these new *Psychologe* constituted an important second step in the development of a scientized humanist conception of primitive life that could contribute to the rise of German anthropology. The new *Psychologe* all hewed to the defensive line established by practicing philologists: their *Psychologie* was concerned to contrast primitive and cultured peoples, and so point up the continuing need for scholars who specialized in the study of culture.

These men—Moritz Lazarus, Heymann Steinthal, Theodor Waitz, Hermann Lotze—had the best authorities within the philological tradition for their use of *Psychologie*. To Greek scholars, *Psychologie* literally signified the study of *Geist*, the great iconic concept of German romanticism. In this etymologically self-conscious sense, the term had been used by Wilhelm von Humboldt, the leader of the German neo-humanist revival of classical education. Early in the century, Humboldt had called for the creation of a scholarly study of national *Geist*—a *Völkerpsychologie* (Spranger 1960:60–61). Moreover, the term had its uses within hermeneutics, the elaborate canon of principles for text-criticism that grew rapidly over the first thirty years of the century. As first used by the great theologian Schleiermacher, *Psychologie* was a study of inspiring spirits; to theologians, the study of how the gospel-writers gave individual yet reliable expression to the Holy Spirit; to classicists the study of how ancient authors gave distinctive individual expression to the common national spirit (Wach 1933:I, 95, 209). As we shall see, this hermeneutic conception of *Psychologie* strongly colored their understanding of their own new science.

As important as the authority of great philologists was the authority of Johann Friedrich Herbart, a man uniquely acceptable to the philological community because he represented the traditions of both natural science and idealist philosophy. Herbart was a pivotally important figure in the application of natural scientific method to psychology. He had created a highly mathematicized "statics and dynamics" of mental operations that deeply influenced the evolution of psychology after his death in 1841 (Leary 1977:155–96). Philologists and their partisans could comfortably keep company with this mechanizer of the mind for two reasons: First, Herbart was an avowed Kantian, and so seemed to yield modestly to the high culturalist tradition in Germany; second, and most important, Herbart was a pedagogue. As thoroughly mechanical as it was, Herbart's psychology had been developed for its applications to education (Dunkel 1970:123–50), and education lay at the heart of German humanism.

Indeed, education lay at the heart, not only of the humanist conception of the individual, but of the humanist conception of the nation. A cultured nation was "educated," and the progress of culture was progress in the education of the nation. It is true, the roots of this viewpoint lay ultimately in the cosmopolitan Enlightenment, in Lessing's slogan, "the education of the human race" (1780; cf. Herder 1774; Schiller 1793). But the slogan had taken on new meanings in the three-quarters of a century since Lessing. The nationalization of the slogan dated to the Reform Era in Prussia: the Prussian minister Hardenberg had called reform "die Bildung der Nation"—"the education of the nation" (Jeissmann 1974:282–83). And the concept of culture implied by the slogan was very much of the Reform Era—it included a brilliant military and political national life as well as a brilliant artistic one. The scientization of the slogan was the work of the philological *Psychologe*. All of them attempted to create a new social science with the same single scientific stroke:

the Herbartianization of "the education of nations." This procedure brought with it two great advantages to men determined to secure the prestige and practices of philology. It gave them a fully natural scientific fundamental conception in the "statics and mechanics" of mind. And it aided in the effort to distinguish between cultured and primitive nations. Herbart had emphasized the fact that some children are more talented than others (Weiss 1928: 177–78). The observation needed only to be nationalized: it is Herbart's voice we hear behind the statement of Boeckh cited above, "Some *nations* are more talented than others."

Philological Psychologie: Lazarus, Steinthal, Waitz, Lotze

The first to introduce the new mix of Humboldt and Herbart into the rhetoric of the German intellectual world was Moritz Lazarus. Lazarus was an observant Jew, and a philological student of August Boeckh (Belke 1971:xiv–xlii). It was he who, in 1851, revived Humboldt's half-century-old proposal for a *Völkerpsychologie*. But Lazarus introduced the crucial Herbartian modification as well: his new science was to explore the differences in *Bildungsfähigkeit*, or "educability," between the nations of the world—among whom he gave the Greeks and Romans a special place (Lazarus 1851:122; cf. 1855:I, 6). The formula proved deeply appealing, and by the middle of the decade a new disciplinary community had formed around Lazarus' program.

The new *Psychologe* had all received advanced training in philology and all drifted away from active philological practice. Two of them—Waitz and Lotze—had even strayed so far as to publish rigorously naturally scientific psychologies. But while the methods of natural science had attracted all of them, the vulgar materialism of the 1850s propelled them back into philological concerns. They did not, for the most part, work together or with any single research program. Waitz devoted his energy primarily to primitive life. Steinthal and Lazarus ranged much more widely over human history as well as prehistory, and presented their work in a difficult jargon derived from Hegel and Humboldt. Lotze philosophized without attempting substantial research. But the fundamental strategy underlying all the different psychologies of the movement was remarkably uniform. These men shared, not a scientific approach, but a set of metascientific myths, borrowed from the humanist tradition and designed to demonstrate the continuing value of philology. The *Psychologe* all began by elaborating the distinction between primitive nations and cultured nations, between more and less talented peoples: primitives could be explained by means of natural science alone, but only philology could account for culture. And they proceeded by adopting from traditional humanism the central tenet of philological *Psychologie*: culture appeared and progressed only with the appearance of brilliant individuals, great leaders whose genius natural science could never succeed in dissecting.

The career of Theodor Waitz is exemplary. Waitz was a philological prodigy, publishing a major edition of Aristotle's *Organon* (1844–46) at the age of twenty-three, on the basis of which he received an appointment at the University of Marburg. At Marburg, Waitz fell under the influence of Karl Ludwig, one of the leading materialists of the day, and in 1849, he published his *Lehrbuch der Psychologie als Naturwissenschaft*, a work that seemed to put him securely in the materialist orbit. But in the tense air of the 1850s Waitz turned his attention to pedagogy, becoming involved in violent controversies over school reform (Gerland 1896:631) and publishing a series of theoretical works on education. These Herbartian studies on the education of individual children were of a piece with his *Anthropologie der Naturvölker*, the first volume of which appeared in 1859. Waitz' special interest in his pedagogical studies was in determining the special circumstances, physical and otherwise, that allowed the teacher sometimes to succeed, sometimes to fail in educating his pupil (Weiss 1928:242). With *Anthropologie der Naturvölker*, Waitz simply nationalized the approach: his book was to determine the special circumstances, physical and otherwise, that allowed the nations of mankind to rise up to culture, or held them back in savagery (1859:380–81).

Waitz is often mentioned in histories of anthropology as an opponent of racial explanations for the differential success of various nations in attaining high culture (Lowie 1937:17). It has recently been noted, however, that, although Waitz rejected the belief in "specific differences" among races, he was capable of comments such as "all uncultured nations possess, in comparison with civilized nations, a large mouth and somewhat thick lips" (Harris 1968: 102–3; cf. Waitz 1859:267). The apparent contradiction may be resolved in the context of Waitz' educational theory. One of the prime concerns of his pedagogy was to outline the limits set to a child's educability by its innate physical disabilities. Mental abilities were potentially equal in all children, but in practice blindness, deafness, and a host of lesser disabilities presented the teacher with material obstacles. When Waitz elevated his pedagogy to the national level, he maintained the same approach: mental abilities were potentially equal in all men, but race limited their exercise. However, Waitz saw no reason to believe that disabilities that were permanent in the case of the individual should be permanent in the case of the larger community, where Lamarckian assumption provided an escape from the limitations of race. As he repeatedly said, he believed in "the influence of intellectual culture on physical form" (1859:74); this belief ran through Waitz' work "like a red thread." Waitz did indeed think that men of lower culture had thick lips. But as their community rose to higher culture, the thick lips would be lost (Gebhardt 1906: 128–29). There was an implicit antimaterialism in this national educational

Lamarckianism: Waitz was not simply denying the claim that the physical determined the mental, he was inverting it.

Waitz made it clear that his effort to exalt technical pedagogical theory into a social science was intended as a response to the controversy over materialism. He began his book by drawing a triple distinction between *Physiologie*, *Psychologie*, and *Kulturgeschichte*. Whereas *Physiologie* admitted in practice of natural scientific explanations, *Psychologie* admitted of natural scientific explanation in principle, but had so far escaped successful scientization. In contrast, *Kulturgeschichte* (a term classicists often used for their own studies) (Wach 1933:I, 179n) so far gave no hope of natural scientific explanation. Once man had entered history, he became altogether too complicated for natural scientists to understand. Thus, to develop a sound fundamental understanding of man in his scientifically explicable physiological and psychical aspects, it was necessary to study "uncivilized nations, man in his primitive state" (1859:9). The task of *Anthropologie* was "mediation between the physical and historical portion of our knowledge of man" (1859:8): it was to determine when and how man's *Geist* carried him up and out of the realm explicable by natural science alone, and into the realm in which the services of historians of culture were needed—"to indicate why and wherefore the history of one people has undergone a different process of development from that of another people; why one people has no history at all, and in another the sum of mental performances never exceeds a certain limit . . ." (1859:8). On behalf of his own, threatened, teachers, Waitz thus took upon himself the teacher's task of sorting out the brightest.

Hermann Lotze also returned from the wilderness of materialism to come to the aid of philology in the 1850s. Although Lotze's degree was in medicine, his academic appointment was in the philosophical faculty, and he devoted his career to the philosophy of science. By 1852, an early materialist bent in his thinking had culminated in the publication of *Medicinische Psychologie*, like Waitz' *Lehrbuch* a scrupulously scientific study. But under the pressures of the period, Lotze changed direction just as Waitz did. Becoming involved in a pamphlet war with the vulgar materialist Czolbe, he also made learned contributions to classical scholarship, and published the first volume of his *Mikrokosmus* (1856a), a "psychological" work that embodied a long and careful attack on materialism (Prantl 1884:288–90; Lotze 1855, 1857).

Lotze was not the crucial figure in the development of German anthropology that Waitz was. His most important direct contribution to the anthropological tradition was his German translation of Andersson's *Lake Ngami: Explorations and Discoveries . . . in Southwest Africa* (Lotze, trans. 1857); primitive nations played only a small, although important role in *Mikrokosmus*. Nevertheless Lotze's biography is significant for the light it sheds on the internal crisis in German intellectual life, and on its power to turn Germans to the study of primitive life. Lotze has left us a revealing description of his motives in writing the *Mikrokosmus*. With the exhaustion of the impulse that had produced the classics of German poetry, the study of man in Germany had fallen more and more into the province of natural science, "which alone, of all the elements of our educational curriculum [*Bildung*] had enjoyed a satisfactory development" (1856b:304). Lotze hoped to remedy this cultural crisis by examining "the great products of that *Bildung* which has unfolded itself in the course of history," moving "backwards" through the history of the evolution of *Geist* to show how man had differentiated himself from the animals (1856b: 310–311). To this end, his *Mikrokosmus* began with a two-volume (1856a, 1859) exploration of the mechanics of individual psychology, followed by a final volume (1864) that traced communal life first through the *Naturvölker*, then through the *Kulturvölker*, before completing a review of all human culture. Like other humanists, he had entered the primitive world, but only in order to retrace his steps.

Lazarus and Steinthal were probably the most important figures in the movement, because they founded a journal, the *Zeitschrift für Völkerpsychologie und Sprachwissenschaft*, that could serve as a forum for the whole constituency of *Psychologie*. Waitz' close associate Georg Gerland presented the doctrines of the *Anthropologie der Naturvölker* in the *Zeitschrift*. Bastian contributed articles, as did the classicist Georg Curtius. But despite their connection as editors to all these men, Steinthal and Lazarus have not been placed in the wider context of philological *Psychologie* (cf. Leopold 1980:84–87; Mühlmann 1968: 74; Ribot 1885:57). Although Lazarus was the first to revive the term *Völkerpsychologie*, he generally deferred to Steinthal in making theoretical pronouncements, and it is through Steinthal that we must understand the relevant doctrines of their new discipline—which Steinthal, in an interesting footnote, suggested was the equivalent of John Stuart Mill's proposed "political ethology, or the science of national character" (1863:491). Like Lazarus, Steinthal was an observant Jew and a student of Boeckh. He pursued his philological interests on a high philosophical plane, and is considered a leading figure in nineteenth-century hermeneutic theory (Wach 1933:III, 206–50). Steinthal never had the serious flirtation with exclusively naturalist practices that Waitz and Lotze did. Nevertheless, his attempt to create a natural scientific psychology that would somehow leave play to both philology and to human free will is in many ways the most interesting and significant that the movement produced. Steinthal formulated his Herbartianism in linguistic terms, applying the "statics and mechanics" of the mind to human understanding of language (Bumann 1965:27–30, 58–70). Because all thought was linguistic, the structure of a language could determine the mental capabilities of its speaker. Speakers of the inflected languages, the Indo-European and Semitic, were favored in the course of development (Steinthal 1850:82; cf. Bumann 1965:103–15)—a thesis Steinthal owed to Humboldt (cf. Manchester 1982). This linguistic Herbartianism may have had a direct influence on the young Saussure and so on the course of structuralism (cf. De Mauro 1981:388). At any rate, linguistic Herbartianism was linked closely to Steinthal's understanding of primitive life. The creation of language was a common act of the prehistoric community, and the ground of common human existence (Steinthal 1863:45).

Like the rest of the "psychological" literature I have surveyed, the *Zeitschrift* offered itself as a means for the reconciliation of the natural and cultural sciences (Steinthal & Lazarus 1859:I, 16–17). Point for point, its program was formulated to leave philologists a secure preserve in which to carry on their trade. However, the *Psychologe* took their partisanship a significant step further when they adopted the old philological doctrine of the individual genius in the practice of their new movement. The individual genius appeared in all their work at the pivotal moment in their guiding myth, the moment at which man left the state of nature and entered history.

For this conception of the rise of culture, they had authority as old as Cicero's. Cicero's defense of rhetoric had begun precisely with the contention that civilized society could only have appeared "when some man, obviously great and wise" convinced all the others, "scattered in the wilds and hidden in the tops of trees," to assemble together, and then "led them in some useful and honest project, at first by decrying their worthlessness, then, by more polished speech and oratory, turning these savages and monsters into mild and gentle men" (Friedrich, ed. 1884:118). This myth had become the common property of rhetoricians and humanists, repeated by Alcuin in the Middle Ages and Bartolomeo Ricci in the Renaissance (Garin 1957:51, 117) and far and wide in eighteenth-century Germany (Reill 1975:128). Merely by repeating it, the *Psychologe* were asserting the continuing vitality of the classical tradition. The great genius also had the special advantage that he was, by definition, inexplicable by natural scientists. Thus Lotze could deride the "organic" theory of history, "that events must necessarily have happened as they did." Biological metaphors would not suffice, for "those mighty men who, through inventive genius or obstinacy of will, have had a decided influence upon the course of history, are by no means merely the offspring and outcome of their age" (1856a:II, 188). The individual genius bestrode Waitz' work, too, though he made Waitz uneasy. Exaggerated importance had been given to "the emergence of highly gifted individuals from the mass of the people, who, as its rulers, heroes, lawgivers, transform the position of their people, change its relations with other nations, expand its horizons in science and art, improve its morals, and direct its attention to nobler objects" (1859:475). But despite his qualms, Waitz returned to the individual genius again and again. "The great mass occupies almost everywhere a very inferior position as regards civilization, and . . . it is by individual great teachers of humanity that the progress of the mass is most effected" (1859:475). His Herbartianism and his humanism meshed easily: "The intellectual development of individuals is doubly important for our investigation; partly because the most and least gifted of every people gauge the limits of its intellectual capacity, and thus furnish us with an indication whether we have to do with specific differences; and partly insofar as the most gifted may, under favorable circumstances, elevate the people to which they belong to a higher degree of civilization, and . . . to a higher degree of mental capacity" (1859:267).

Steinthal and Lazarus presented this great individual in more elaborate Hegelian and Humboldtian dress. To Humboldt, culture was marked by its wealth of great individual forms (Leopold 1980:82). Practicing classicists during the period borrowed the assertion and identified the rise of culture in Greece with the rise of the individual (Boeckh 1855:II, 73; Lange 1855:135). Steinthal elaborated this postulate theoretically. There were three kinds of nation: unhistoric peoples, which would never rise to individual existence; prehistoric peoples, which might, under favorable circumstances, rise to individual existence; and historic peoples. "The most certain mark of the historical *Geist* as opposed to nature and unhistorical *Geist* seems to me to lie in the presence of something individual which is itself general, of a man who lays claim to the value of his whole kind and gives himself his own norm." Such a man, Steinthal continued, brought his people to the pitch of "classic" culture (1863:40, 45; cf. Belke 1982).

With this, Steinthal had achieved the scientific formula at which all philological *Psychologie* aimed: he had reinstated traditional hermeneutic *Psychologie* in the new order of German intellectual life. The hybrid social science he and Lazarus founded succeeded in attracting many of the most prominent cultural scholars of the younger generation, not least Hermann Cohen and Wilhelm Dilthey. A safe harbor had been found for philology.

Bastian: The Tradition Goes Awry

This was the movement that excited Bastian when he returned to Germany in 1858. Cultural scholars had in effect created a new academic territory—primitive life—in order to banish their materialist rivals to it (cf. Ryding 1975). It was precisely the territory Bastian himself was determined to open.

But Bastian's background and sympathies were significantly different. He had received the normal secondary classical education, but not the elaborate advanced training that conditioned the loyalties of the philological psychologists. Bastian's training was in law and medicine. And where Steinthal, Lazarus, Waitz, and Lotze were typical members of the "armchair" generation of early anthropologists never leaving Germany, Bastian had had first-hand experience of primitive life all over the world (Fiedermutz-Laun 1970:5–9; cf. Koepping, ed. 1983).

All this did not make Bastian hostile; on the contrary, he sustained a profound influence from philological *Psychologie*. But lacking the strategic interests that had motivated the rise of the discipline, Bastian produced a book— *Der Mensch in der Geschichte* (1860)—that presented the whole range of the philological psychologists' delicate metascientific constructs in the jarring context of absolute, strident materialist rhetoric. When Bastian adopted it, *Psychologie* entered the mainstream of the history of German anthropology, but at the cost of its original meaning.

Der Mensch in der Geschichte retailed all the doctrines of philological *Psychologie*, but in strangely altered forms. Bastian began by declaring his *Psychologie* the incarnation, in a new world, of old practices: "When every secure prop has fallen away, philosophy must become *Psychologie*" (1860:I, x). But he refused to allow that philosophy could retain any of its old character after the forced transformation. "*Geist* belongs alongside all other products of *Natur*; and it will be understood as they are, according to the exact-positive research methods of the natural sciences, when their youngest sister, *Psychologie*, receives the position she deserves" (1860:I, ix). He conceived the rise of culture entirely in terms of the great geniuses of art and thought; but he insisted unwaveringly on explaining them by means of natural science, and indeed by means of the very organic metaphor Lotze had condemned five years earlier. "The blossoms with which [the nations] bloom in inspired poems, the fruits they produce in the teachings of the philosophers, these things we shall value and collect, to employ them as ornament and nourishment; however, in order to investigate the mysterious energies of Becoming within Being, what is required is the dissection and analysis of the great *Stamm* that produced them" (1860:I, xii). At once "tribe" and "trunk" in German, *Stamm* provided Bastian with his governing pun. While the ancient humanist fascination with genius survived in Bastian's work, the careful dichotomy between freedom and determinism that the *Psychologe* had built around it did not.

A new life for philosophy, a culture of which geniuses were the measure— these were philological ideas, if ripped blindly out of context. As unsympathetic as he was, Bastian was thorough in ransacking philological *Psychologie* for ideas. The crucial concept of humanist social Herbartianism was there: the origin and evolution of culture were conceived as stages in humanist *Bildung*. Indeed, Bastian was if anything more thoroughgoing than any of the philological psychologists in building a social theory out of educational psychology: the degree to which a *gebildete* society would continue to evolve depended on the general extent of *Bildung*. Accordingly, education for all was an evolutionary imperative (1860:I, 141–42). Humboldt's early educational theories (cf. Sorkin 1983) were resurrected more faithfully in Bastian's work than in Steinthal's—though Bastian pressed Humboldt into the service of atheism: "Psychological education must be directed toward bringing the feelings of the beautiful and the good to unmediated intuition . . . not through forceful commands of otherworldly and so incomprehensible origin (for all authority is crippling . . .), but rather from within the individual" (1860:I, 251).

But in his *Bildungspsychologie* as elsewhere, the difference in Bastian's background showed through: Bastian's classics had been acquired in *Gymnasium*, in secondary school. Although learned and often illuminating quotations from the Greek and Latin authors filled his book, they sometimes had the pat aphoristic air of Jakobs' elementary readers: "Physici mundum magnum hominem et hominem brevem mundum dixerunt" (1860:I, 24). And as he rose to his greatest height of passion over the triumph of natural scientific *Psychologie*, he quoted the author who stood at the pinnacle of secondary-school *Bildung*: Xenophon—all amid denunciations of the "decayed ruins of Antiquity" (1860:I, 27–28). Cursing and quoting in the same breath, Bastian entered the new world of scientific anthropology still trailing the prejudices his teachers had bred in him fifteen years before.

In one sense, of course, Bastian belonged to the same community as the men whose ideas he borrowed: only an educated German could have lifted the doctrines of philological *Psychologie*. But within the isolated German intellectual world, he represented a hostile party. The communal affiliations that had gone into the creation of philological *Psychologie* counted for little once the new doctrines were published and available to the literate world at large. In this sense, the "ideological origins" of *Psychologie* were irrelevant. From the point of view of the history of anthropology, Bastian's borrowing was an episode in the "history of ideas" and not in the "history of ideologies."

From the point of view of the history of philology, Bastian's depredations were not a bad thing. In the end, they meant a longer lease on life for the "psychological" conception of culture. Within *Völkerpsychologie*, the most lively branch of the movement, the individual genius and the study of *Kulturvölker* were banished by Wilhelm Wundt in the first decades of the Second Reich. Culture, Wundt blandly declared, was inaccessible to scientific psychology because of its individual character: he restricted *Völkerpsychologie* to the natural scientific territory of prehistory (Belke 1982:225). Like Wundt, the philological founders of the discipline would never have considered applying a conception of culture derived from the Greeks to the Hottentots. Only because Bastian lacked their loyalties was he willing to look indiscriminately for genius in jungles and deserts. No philologist could have accomplished the productive introduction of the philological understanding of the rise and nature of culture into the study of primitive man.

From the point of view of the larger history of disciplines, this reconstruction of the events of the 1850s points up both the importance of ideological analysis and of careful national contextualization. It is not new to observe that elements of German romanticism entered the history of German anthropology (e.g., Mühlmann 1968:67–73). If Lotze has been left out of histories of anthropology, Steinthal, Lazarus, and Waitz have not (cf. Leopold 1980: 84–87). But the complex motives and loyalties at work in the early years of the discipline have gone unrecognized. As a result, historians have not done justice to the complexity of influence operating between disciplines. Historians have tended to view the rise of anthropology as the response to new research opportunities—whether the product of expanding scientific horizons within Europe or the product of colonialism. But it was also the product of loyalty to old research practices. For that reason, the history of new disciplines cannot escape the history of old ones.

Acknowledgments

This essay was written under the guidance of Professors John Boyer and Jan Goldstein in their University of Chicago 1982–83 graduate seminar, "Politics and Culture in France and Germany 1871–1914." Earlier versions were presented to the 1982 University of Chicago seminar, "Hermeneutics and Philology in Nineteenth-Century Germany," led by Professors Arnaldo Momigliano and Samuel Jaffe, and to the October 1983 meeting of the Chicago Group in the History of the Social Sciences (sponsored by the Morris Fishbein Center for the History of Science and Medicine). The author is grateful to the participants of all three seminars for their comments and criticisms.

References Cited

Bastian, A. 1860. *Der Mensch in der Geschichte*. 3 vols. Leipzig.
———. 1881. *Die Vorgeschichte der Ethnologie*. Berlin.
Bausinger, H. 1971. *Volkskunde. Von der Altertumsforschung zur Kulturanalyse*. Berlin.
Belke, I. 1971. Einleitung. In *Moritz Lazarus und Heymann Steinthal. Die Begründer der Völkerpsychologie in ihren Briefen*. Tübingen.
———. 1982. Die Begründung der Völkerpsychologie in Deutschland. *Rivista di Filosofia* 22–23:192–233.
Boeckh, A. 1855. Festrede gehalten auf der Universität zu Berlin. In *Kleine Schriften* 2:116–30. Leipzig (1859).
Boring, E. 1950. *A history of experimental psychology*. 2d ed. New York.
Büchner, L. 1855. *Kraft und Stoff*. Frankfurt a. M.
Bumann, W. 1965. *Die Sprachtheorie Heymann Steinthals*. Meisenheim am Glan.
Curtius, G. 1848. *Ueber die Bedeutung des Studiums der Classischen Literatur*. Prague.
Czolbe, H. 1855. *Neue Darstellung des Sensualismus*. Leipzig.

Delitzsch, F. 1855. *System der Biblischen Psychologie*. Leipzig. Trans. Wallis as *A system of biblical psychology*. Edinburgh (1867).

De Mauro, T. 1981. Notes biographiques et critiques sur F. de Saussure. In F. de Saussure, *Cours de linguistique genérale*, 319–94. Reprint ed. Paris.

Dunkel, H. 1970. *Herbart and Herbartianism*. Chicago.

Fiedermutz-Laun, A. 1970. *Der kulturhistorische Gedanke bei Adolf Bastian*. Wiesbaden.

Friedrich, W., ed. 1884. *Ciceronis Rhetoricae libri duo*. Leipzig.

Garin, E. 1957. *L'educazione in Europa*. Bari.

Gebhardt, O. 1906. Theodor Waitzs Pädagogische Grundanschauungen. Ph.D. Dissertation. University of Leipzig.

Gerland, G. 1896. Theodor Waitz. *Allgemeine Deutsche Biographie* 40:629–33.

Gregory, F. 1977. *Scientific materialism in nineteenth-century Germany*. Dordrecht, Holland.

Harris, M. 1968. *The rise of anthropological theory*. New York.

Herder, J. G. 1774. *Auch eine Philosophie der Geschichte zur Bildung der Menschheit*. In *Werke* 3:39–137. Berlin (1982).

Jeissmann, K. 1974. *Das preussische Gymnasium in Staat und Gesellschaft*. Stuttgart.

Koepping, K.-P., ed. 1983. *Adolf Bastian and the psychic unity of mankind: The foundations of anthropology in nineteenth-century Germany*. St. Lucia, Queensland.

Lange, L. 1855. Die classische Philologie in ihrer Stellung zum Gesammtgebiete der Wissenschaften und in ihrer inneren Gliederung. In *Kleine Schriften* 1:1–21. Göttingen (1887).

Lazarus, M. 1851. Begriff und Möglichkeit einer Völkerpsychologie. *Deutsches Museum* 1:112–26.

———. 1855. *Leben der Seele*. 3 vols. Berlin.

Leary, D. 1977. The reconstruction of psychology in Germany, 1780–1850. Ph. D. Dissertation. University of Chicago.

Leopold, J. 1980. *Culture in comparative and evolutionary perspective: E. B. Tylor and the making of* Primitive Culture. Berlin.

Lessing, G. 1780. *Die Erziehung des Menschengeschlechtes*. In *Werke* 8:489–510. Munich (1976).

Lotze, H. 1852. *Medicinische Psychologie*. Leipzig.

———. 1853. Quaestiones Lucretianae. In *Kleine Schriften* 3:100–144. Leipzig (1891).

———. 1855. Review of Czolbe, *Neue Darstellung des Sensualismus*. In *Kleine Schriften* 3:238–50. Leipzig (1891).

———. 1856a–1864. *Mikrokosmus*. 3 vols. Leipzig. Trans. Hamilton & Jones as *Microcosmus*. New York (1886).

———. 1856b. Selbstanzeige des ersten Bandes des *Mikrokosmus*. In *Kleine Schriften* 3:303–14. Leipzig (1891).

———. 1857. Review of Czolbe, *Entstehung des Selbstbewusstseins*. In *Kleine Schriften* 3:315–20. Leipzig (1891).

Lotze, H., trans. 1857. *Antigona, Sophoclis fabula*. Göttingen.

———. 1858. K. Andersson, *Lake Ngami: Or explorations and discoveries during four years' wanderings in the wilds of Southwestern Africa*. New York (1854).

Lowie, R. H. 1937. *The history of ethnological theory*. New York.

Manchester, M. 1982. Philosophical motives in Wilhelm von Humboldt's defense of the inflectional superiority thesis. *Historiog. Linguis.* 9(1/2):107–20.

Moleschott, J. 1852. *Kreislauf des Lebens.* Mainz.

Mühlmann, W. 1968. *Geschichte der Anthropologie.* 2d ed. Frankfurt a. M.

Noack, L. 1858. *Psyche.* Vol. 1. Leipzig.

Paulsen, F. 1921. *Geschichte des gelehrten Unterrichts in Deutschland.* Vol. 2. 3d ed. Berlin.

Prantl, C. 1884. Lotze, Rudolf Hermann. *Allgemeine Deutsche Biographie* 19:288–90.

Reill, P. 1975. *The German enlightenment.* Berkeley.

Ribot, T. 1885. *La psychologie allemande contemporaine.* Paris.

Ringer, F. 1979. *Education and society in modern Europe.* Bloomington.

Ryding, J. 1975. Alternatives in nineteenth-century German ethnology. *Sociologus* 25: 1–28.

Schiller, F. 1793. *Ueber die ästhetische Erziehung des Menschen.* In *Werke* 5:560–679. Munich (1967).

Sorkin, D. 1983. Von Humboldt on self-formation. *J. Hist. Ideas* 44:55–73.

Spranger, E. 1960. *Wilhelm von Humboldt und die Bildungsreform.* 2d ed. Tübingen.

Steinthal, H. 1850. *Die Classification der Sprachen.* Berlin.

———. 1863. *Philologie, Geschichte und Psychologie in ihren gegenseitigen Beziehungen.* In *Kleine Sprachtheoretische Schriften,* 436–511. Hildesheim (1970).

Steinthal, H., & M. Lazarus. 1859. Einleitende Gedanken. *Zeitschrift für Völkerpsychologie und Sprachwissenschaft* 1:1–73.

Vogt, K. 1852. *Bilder aus dem Thierleben.* Frankfurt a. M.

Wach, J. 1933. *Das Verstehen.* 3 vols. Tübingen.

Waitz, T. 1849. *Lehrbuch der Psychologie als Naturwissenschaft.* Braunschweig.

———. 1859. *Anthropologie der Naturvölker.* Vol. 1. Leipzig. Trans. Collingwood as *Introduction to Anthropology.* London (1863).

Waitz, T., ed. 1844–46. *Aristotelis Organon Graece.* 2 vols. Leipzig.

Weiss, G. 1928. *Herbart und seine Schule.* Munich.

Wundt, W. 1920. *Die Weltkatastrophe und die Deutsche Philosophie.* Erfurt.

INFORMATION FOR CONTRIBUTORS

Future Volume Themes

Normally, every volume of HOA will be organized around a particular theme of historical and contemporary anthropological significance, although each volume may also contain one or more "miscellaneous studies." Topics and tentative titles of future volumes include the following:

HOA 3: *Displaying Humankind: Essays on Museums and Anthropology* (in press).

HOA 4: *Anthropology Between Two World Wars: 1914–1945.*

For this volume we welcome articles on any subdisciplinary field of anthropology (including archeological, applied, biological, linguistic, and sociocultural anthropology), as well as articles of general anthropological interest. Topics may have a focus that is biographical, institutional, conceptual, or methodological, within one national anthropological tradition, or bridging between them. Authors are encouraged to consider topics in relation to specific bodies of documentary material, as well as in relation to general historical and cultural trends (intellectual, aesthetic, political, economic, etc.), including the impact of the wars that mark the beginning and end of the period. The deadline for completed manuscripts is August 31, 1985; potential contributors are encouraged to communicate with the editor about their work before submitting drafts.

HOA 5: *Anthropology and the Romantic Sensibility*

Like much of Western intellectual life, anthropology has always been impelled by two contrasting motives: the rationalistic and the romantic (polarities which correlate, perhaps, with others that are the staples of intellectual history: progressivism/primitivism, natural science/humanism, materialism/idealism, etc.). While anthropology is often spoken of as the child of the Enlightenment, reborn with Darwinism, the romantic current has run very strong, and the tension between the two continues to the present (strongly to be manifested, for instance, in the recent controversy about the work of Margaret Mead). Volume 5 will be devoted to the history of this tension, with special emphasis, as the title suggests, on the romantic current.

Themes of subsequent volumes will be chosen in the light of the responses of potential contributors. Among topics actively under consideration are:

"Anthropology and the Expropriation of Native Land"
"Anthropology as a Field of Political Contest: Sex, Class, and Race"
"Anthropology Within and Without the Academy"

"Biological Perspectives in Anthropological Inquiry"

"Diachronic Perspectives in Anthropological Inquiry"

Researchers interested in one or another of these topics are encouraged to communicate with the editor about their work, either completed or in progress.

Manuscript Preparation

Manuscripts submitted for consideration to HOA should be typed 26 lines to a page with 1¼-inch margins. All material should be double spaced, including indented quoted passages in the text, as well as footnotes, which should be grouped together at the end, beginning on a separate sheet. Documentation should be in the anthropological style, with parenthetical author/date/page references (Boas 1911:120) in the text and a list of "References Cited" at the end of the article (begun on a separate sheet). For exemplification of stylistic details, consult previously published volumes. Note especially that primary published historical sources should be cited by the date of the original or historically significant edition, with the date of the edition actually consulted at the end of the reference list entry. Note also the abbreviated form for citing "Manuscript Sources" (FBP: FB/F. Putnam 1/20/96), which should be listed separately under that heading, with abbreviations cross-referenced under "References Cited." Please do not abbreviate journal or series titles, which will be shortened as necessary by the copy editor. Manuscripts should be submitted in two copies (original typescript and photographic copy). Photographic illustrations (single copies) should be on glossy paper, 5 × 7 or 8 × 10 inches. Unsolicited manuscripts will not be returned unless accompanied by adequate postage. All communications on editorial matters should be directed to the editor:

George W. Stocking, Jr. (HOA)
Department of Anthropology
University of Chicago
1126 E. 59th St.
Chicago, Illinois 60637 U.S.A.

INDEX

Aberdeen, 45
Academic anthropology: in Britain, 59–60, 63, 87, 99, 100, 131, 143, 158, 170, 177, 207; in Australia, 160; in South Africa, 197; in Germany, 224
Ackerman, R., 38
Acosta, José de, 6
Adam, 21
Adler, Mortimer, 172
Africa, 59, 70–71, 118, 166. See also International Institute of African Languages and Cultures; South Africa; and particular African peoples
African Institute. See International Institute of African Languages and Cultures
African National Congress, 207
African Political Systems, 71, 179, 205, 210
African Systems of Kinship and Marriage, 131, 179
Afrikaners, 193, 206
Alcuin, 223
Amateurs, 90, 97, 136, 146
Ambrym, 164
America: Locke on, 6; "Wastes" compared to England, 27; wild tribes of, 216–17
American Anthropologist, 131
American anthropology: as hegemonic, 5; and Radcliffe-Brown, 134, 168, 172; dehistoricization, 136, 183; diffusionist, 158, 194; psychological, 171, 206; mentioned, 76, 172, 205. See also Boasian anthropology
American Indians. See Native Americans
Ancient Monuments Protection Act, 87
Andaman Islands, 72, 107, 110, 118, 120, 123, 124–28, 140, 144, 149, 150, 151, 157, 158, 160, 175
Angles, 61
Anglo-American anthropological tradition, 4
Anglo-Saxonism, 84
Animism. See Frazer, J. G.; Tylor, E. B.
Ankermann, B., 194
Anthropological Institute of Great Britain and Ireland, 87, 88, 95, 98, 131, 179
Anthropological Society of London, 85

Anthropology: national traditions of, 3, 5, 76, 135; as science, 3, 36, 77, 216, 221; unity of subdisciplines, 3, 68, 86, 99, 132; as holistic study of man, 3, 88, 97, 98, 101; as study of "savages," 3–4, 137, 221; antinomies in western anthropological tradition, 4; sequence of paradigms in, 4–5, 135–38; as child of Enlightenment, 11; as cultural criticism, 78; as diachronic inquiry, 136; as humanist discipline, 206, 212. See also American anthropology; British anthropology; French anthropology; German anthropology
Anthropometric Laboratory, Dublin, 88, 89, 90, 95
Anthropometric Laboratory, London, 86
Anthropometry, 85, 88, 90, 94, 95, 96
Anthropos, 153, 155
Applied anthropology, 165, 166, 167, 195
Arabs, 32, 37, 45, 48
Aran Island, 88
Archaeological Museum, Cambridge, 113
Archeology: as component of anthropology, 4, 68; and British racial history, 84, 86, 87, 101; three age system, 85, 86; local, 93, 94; professionalization of, 100, 101; influence on ritualist classicists, 108; mentioned, 143, 194. See also Prehistory; and individual local archeological societies
Aristotle, 172
Arunta, 122, 123, 137, 148, 195
Aryans, 35, 36, 37, 51, 52, 84, 101
Asad, T., 135*n*
Association of Social Anthropologists, 59, 131
Australian Aboriginals: *intichiuma* ceremonies, 37, 46, 49, 50; totemism, 46, 47, 146, 148, 154, 160; ethnography of, 108, 109, 144; of Western Australia, 109, 146, 147, 148; languages, 118; as homogeneous primitive society, 142, 146, 147, 149; social organization, 147, 148, 149, 160, 170; mentioned, 115, 119, 126, 171. See also Arunta; Diëri

Balliol College, 51
Barth, Karl, 54

DESIGNED BY IRVING PERKINS ASSOCIATES, INC.
COMPOSED BY METRICOMP, GRUNDY CENTER, IOWA
MANUFACTURED BY THOMSON-SHORE, INC., DEXTER, MICHIGAN
TEXT IS SET IN GOUDY OLD STYLE
DISPLAY LINES ARE SET IN BERNARD ROMAN AND GOUDY OLD STYLE

Library of Congress Cataloging in Publication Data
Main entry under title:
Functionalism historicized.

(History of anthropology ; v. 2)
Bibliography: p.
Includes index.
1. Functionalism (Social sciences) – History – Addresses,
essays, lectures. 2. Ethnology – Great Britain – History –
Addresses, essays, lectures. I. Stocking, George W.,
1928– . II. Series.
GN363.F86 1984   306'.0941   84-40160
ISBN 0-299-09900-8